"For most of the four decades I have known Lamin Sanneh, I have urged him to write a memoir of his personal pilgrimage. At last my prayer has been answered! I treasure this marvelous addition to the history of Christian and African autobiography that reaches back to Saint Augustine."

— PATRICK J. RYAN
Fordham University

"Lamin Sanneh's autobiography is moving, humble, and very thought-provoking. A convert to Christianity from Islam and now a leading missiologist at Yale, Sanneh speaks simply from a rich and sensitive Christian faith. . . . He has the rare quality of a top academic as well as a humane and spiritually discerning communicator."

— GAVIN D'COSTA
University of Bristol

"This moving narrative vividly portrays the many stages of Lamin Sanneh's religious journey, connecting his personal experiences on four continents with major cultural shifts in the last fifty years. . . . Sanneh offers a sobering critique of Western Protestantism and explains his confidence in the progress of African Christianity, expressed in the mother tongue. His painful memories of multiple rejections should sharpen our reflection on our Christian past and present."

— JOHN B. CARMAN
Harvard Divinity School

All this goes on inside me, in the vast cloisters of my memory. In it are the sky, the earth, and the sea, ready at my summons, together with everything that I have ever perceived in them. . . . In it I meet myself as well. I remember myself and what I have done, when and where I did it, and the state of my mind at the time. In my memory, too, are all the events that I remember, whether they are things that have happened to me or things that I have heard from others. From the same source [of memory] I can picture to myself all kinds of different images based either upon my own experience or upon what I find credible because it tallies with my own experience. . . . The power of the memory is great . . . it is awe-inspiring in its profound and incalculable complexity. Yet it is my mind; it is myself. What, then, am I, my God? What is my nature?

ST. AUGUSTINE

Summoned from the Margin

HOMECOMING OF AN AFRICAN

Lamin Sanneh

William B. Eerdmans Publishing Company

Grand Rapids, Michigan / Cambridge, U.K.

Published 2012 by

Wm. B. Eerdmans Publishing Co.

2140 Oak Industrial Drive N.E., Grand Rapids, Michigan 49505 /

P.O. Box 163, Cambridge CB3 9PU U.K.

Printed in the United States of America

17 16 15 14 13   7 6 5 4 3 2

Library of Congress Cataloging-in-Publication Data

Sanneh, Lamin O.

Summoned from the margin: homecoming of an African / Lamin Sanneh.

p.   cm.

Includes bibliographical references (p.   ) and index.

ISBN 978-0-8028-6742-1 (pbk.: alk. paper)

1. Sanneh, Lamin O. 2. Christian converts from Islam — Biography.   I. Title.

BV4935.S34A3   2012

270.8′2092 — dc23

[B]

2012018930

www.eerdmans.com

To K and Sia Manta:

I have tried; you will do better.
Of that I cannot be more certain.
It's my greatest consolation.

Contents

❋   ❋   ❋

Contents

PART III

Foreword

✦　　✦　　✦

If my father had grown up in more comfortable, less precarious circumstances — in a hardscrabble American small town, say, raised in a harried but happy working-class family — then perhaps he would have been able to use the run-of-the-mill deprivations of his boyhood as an effectual rhetorical tool. My sister and I might have nodded (or, more likely, sighed) while he told us about the chores he had had to do, the vacations he had foregone, or the months and years it had taken him to save up for the bicycle he wanted. We might have been urged to compare our charmed lives to his, and to reflect upon our good fortune.

Instead we learned, in stray sentences and anecdotes, about a childhood that was entirely incomparable to our own. Dad came from a country that none of our friends had ever heard of: *Zambia,* they usually thought we said, and some couldn't believe there was another African country, even more obscure, with almost the same name. No, we told them: *Gambia.* His mother was a member of a small, complicated team of wives — a social arrangement that sounded, to a pretty-much American boy and his all-American friends, like a dirty joke come to life. Even my father's journey, as a teenager, from a tiny town on a tiny island to the biggest city in one of the smallest countries on earth, seemed to belong more to myth than to the world of station wagons and trolley buses that I knew. He made his way, somehow, to Europe and to America, then back to Europe, back to Africa, and then, finally, to Scotland (where my memories begin), and then to America — for good, it turned out.

I always wanted him to put his life into a book, not least because I wanted to read it. This is, as my father puts it, the story of his "unlikely beginnings," although of course they only seem unlikely in retrospect, because of his stubborn and in some ways mysterious determination to live a life radically different from the one that his circumstances predicted. I have heard a few of these stories before, often at the table after dinner, as dessert (apple pie and vanilla ice cream, ideally) arrived and, nearly as quickly, disappeared. My sister and my mother and I would try to keep up as my father explained why he and his friends feared hippopotamuses more than crocodiles, or how his impoverished undergraduate years permanently ruined his appetite for Dunkin' Donuts. But most of these stories are new to me, and, taken together, they capture clearly and movingly something I had only dimly perceived: the curiosity and restlessness that propelled my father out of the Gambia, and have propelled him ever since.

This book is also, perhaps mainly, a conversion narrative, though not a straightforward one. "It felt like being awakened," my father writes about his growing awareness of the faith that has shaped his life and career. But he soon realized that waking up was hard work: "The consternation that met me on my way to joining the church was a measure of the symbolic distance I had to travel from the Axis Mundi of my Muslim culture and history to the Christian faith — which turned out to have its own margins to offer." In Banjul, Gambia's capital, he found churches staffed by expatriates who felt uneasy about converting a local boy. Maybe they didn't realize that my father was already, in a sense, converted; in Banjul, he was merely searching for a community of believers who lived up to the faith that had already captured him. He had no way of knowing, then, how long that search would be, or where it would lead him. He had no way of knowing, either, that as Christianity became ever more truly a world religion, it would be at the so-called margin where the faith would thrive.

"I believe it is difficult for those who publish their own memoirs to escape the imputation of vanity." This was Olaudah Equiano's verdict, more than two centuries ago; the first sentence of the story of his own journey from the margin. I know my father has, similarly, long been hesitant to write a book like this. As a scholar, he'd prefer to be the reliable narrator of other people's histories, instead of the inevitably unreliable narrator of his own. And he's wary of turning his own testimony into a product, exhibited for the delectation of paying customers. (With any luck — though luck may be unnecessary — the success of this book will give him plenty of reason to ponder, anew, the relationship between faith and commerce.) I suspect this book was harder for him to write than any of the ones that came before, and so I imagine that he will be gratified, though perhaps slightly surprised, to hear a wide range of readers — and maybe even a few family members — telling him this is the best and most important book he has ever written.

KELEFA SANNEH
New York City
2012

Acknowledgments

I am grateful to Kelefa and Sia who together have nudged me to write an account of my life. Their filial challenge ultimately overcame many decades of procrastination, hesitancy, and indecision. When finally it came to putting pen to paper, so to speak, long-suppressed reasons for my procrastination began to surface and to threaten my decision. In the end, my promise to K and Sia prevailed over my tentativeness. Writing about myself after a lifetime of writing about others is poor practice for the art. Finally the habit kicked in. Or maybe it would be better to say that practice at it helped to give that feeling, and to ease me into doing it. Even there, I took the precaution of combining facets of the personal and the professional in order to achieve my end.

Over the years several people have expressed interest in the turning points of my life, and, because of our closeness, Muslim friends have been among the most solicitous. I remember once receiving a call from a woman in Monterey, California, who heard that I would be teaching summer school in Marin County. She had converted to Islam and was keen to meet me because she said I could help her understand her new faith precisely because I had also made the faith journey, though it was the other way. She urged me to write my story after our meeting, saying, "Your understanding of religion is good for Islam, and is a corrective to popular misconceptions." It shows that, as fellow pilgrims, Muslims do long for interfaith company, the politics of the culture wars notwithstanding. I have learned to cultivate that company rather than to reduce it to a word game on dialogue that is tantamount to nothing more than a monologue. Only talking to myself when there is rich company seems pointless.

About the same time I was introduced to a young blonde woman, Susan, who had heard about me from a mutual friend. One late afternoon over pizza in the company of the friend who introduced us, she described a little of her life, and I remember being moved beyond words. She had been sexually abused at home, and, at her wits' end, sought refuge in a Protestant church where, sadly, the pastor who offered refuge as her confidant in turn abused her, leaving her emotionally devastated and bewildered. Susan wasn't asking me about converting to Islam, which in her situation would not be too far-fetched. Rather, in spite of her troubled past, she wanted confirmation of her hunch that experience of the love of God in Christ could still be life-changing. That in itself, I thought, was extraordinary enough. Still, on first take, I expressed distress and sadness at what happened to her, but she interrupted me and asked to hear about my journey of faith. I parried and ducked and veered, but she wouldn't let up. I was feeling down about the way people close to her had hurt her, so eventually I threw out a few fragments of testimony as a concession, which she grabbed and mulled over for a while before resuming her interrogation. By the end of the meeting she had extracted the main outline of my story. "Please, promise me that you will write your story and share it as the gift of God it is," she pleaded. Her generosity of spirit totally disarmed me. She was a spirit wounded many times over, for whom grace still meant everything, and I crumbled in apologetic agreement. The memory of that meeting has continued to haunt me all these many years, and I could not banish the thought of wolves coming among us in sheep's clothing. It made me extremely cautious about claims of altruism in God's work of salvation. I made mental apologies to her for not being able to find it in me to do promptly what I promised. Now I can finally tell Susan, wherever she is, that her patience has borne this tardy fruit.

Back at Harvard where I was teaching at the time, a visitor turned up in my class introducing himself as a Muslim exchange student from Izmir, Turkey. I welcomed him. At the conclusion of the course he divulged the information that his professors at Izmir had asked him to check me out to see if, as a convert, I harbored any ill will toward Islam. In turn disconcerted that he had insinuated himself into the class to track me, and at the same time relieved that his confession was a tacit endorsement of his experience in the course, I asked about how he rated the teaching of Islam at Izmir. I was totally unprepared for his candid answer: he wished his professors who were suspicious of me had the same understanding and sensitivity to Islam I did. "Otherwise, Islam wouldn't be in the defensive rut it is now in," he said despairingly. He had come to smoke me out; he stayed to defend me. The student's attitude is of a piece with the importunity of so many Muslim acquaintances to give an account of how I came to embrace Jesus. After the fact, the reason was very simple: the claims of Jesus demand a clear-cut response. You would have to have very good reasons to reject those claims, but even there you could not escape the implications of such a decision. I think the continuing solicitude of Muslim friends shows how high the stakes are. I am deeply grateful for their solicitude.

Space does not permit recounting more of such anecdotes; suffice it to say that they converge in the direction of this memoir. Christian friends and acquaintances have never stopped asking what the political motivation was for my conversion in the face of Muslim opposition, while Muslim friends wondered whether what they perceived as the deep spirituality of my experience would find welcome place in a humanistic Christianity. "Would Christians really understand and respect your reverence for God?" my Muslim friends inquired with a note of incredulity. "Christians have no confidence in God as Revealer. How would you fare in the church unless you compromise your faith?" It is important to recognize that sometimes Muslims distrust Christians not because they think Christians are religious, but because they are afraid that Christians are not religious enough. I hope these Muslims will find in this book a sincere attempt at answering their concern for Christian faithfulness, such as it is. It behooves us on each side to spare no effort in love and trust to believe the best in the other.

I am grateful to K for reading an earlier draft of the book and for firmly pointing me in the direction I should take. Only at this stage has he seen the book in its present form, but I hope he will recognize my attempt to take to heart his entreaties. After all, I owe this account to my family more than to anyone else. Patrick J. Ryan, S.J., of Fordham University, performed a yeoman service by reading through the entire manuscript, drawing my attention to matters of fact, detail, sequence, style, interpretation, and clarification. He saved me in numerous ways from the embarrassment of carelessness, and I cannot thank him enough for that and for the many other ways he has generously rescued me from my inadequacies. Huge thanks are also due to John Leinenweber, who read through the manuscript with due diligence, and offered corrections and helpful suggestions. As a supporter and personal friend, Phil Lundman very kindly read an early draft of the book and called my attention to matters of detail. I am thankful for Phil and Nancy's friendship and encouragement over the years. Edward Cleary, O.P., of Providence College, and Fr. Peter Phan, of Georgetown University, read through a draft of one of the chapters, and I am grateful to them both for their comments and observations. All this help has been indispensable to me, but I move without hesitation to absolve all these people from responsibility for any surviving faults, blemishes, shortcomings, and peculiarities of the book. For those I curry the reader's favor, as I take full responsibility.

Up to this point I had put off coming out with a book on this subject while I toyed with the idea of doing short accounts as an alternative. Mainline Christianity's prickly scruples on conversion provided a handy excuse for postponing the project. At the time I would have had to contend with too many suspicions and reservations to be able to speak openly and confidently. Yet there were indications that the religious atmosphere was changing quietly and becoming more propitious. At Harvard I recall the encouragement of the late Wilfred Cantwell Smith, specifically his support for my wish to offer a religious account that pays full regard to interfaith questions of truth and commitment. We both lived in Arlington, Massachusetts, at the time, and since Wilfred didn't drive, I ended up often becoming his traveling companion. It gave opportunity for conversation going back and forth between Cambridge and Arlington, with the slow traffic sometimes extending our conversations quite a bit. Wilfred generously shared with me not only matters of common scholarly interest, but reflections on many personal issues, helping me to know him as a person. I felt a genuine bond of friendship with him as he took me under his wing.

In a similar fashion John B. Carman, Wilfred's successor as director of the Center for the Study of World Religions, was equally encouraging in his sensitive, scrupulous attention to the intercultural connections of my personal journey. John's has been a memorable collegiality and friendship, and it is a bonus to have been able to maintain contact since those Harvard years.

Many other colleagues at Harvard were a source of much valued encouragement: at the Divinity School, Dean George Rupp, Paul Hanson, Harvey Cox, H. Richard Niebuhr, Gordon Kaufman, Diana Eck, and William R. Hutchison, and at the School of Education, Robert LeVine, Merry White, Leonie Gordon, and Howard Gardner, among others. Cambridge was a particularly stimulating environment in which many ideas came to fruition, and for that I am very grateful.

I acknowledge the help of other colleagues, particularly at the University of Aberdeen, where Andrew Walls was an important influence in my life. As my colleague in the Department of Religious Studies of which he was chair, Andrew challenged me to diversify my academic responsibilities by teaching the course on African Christianity. After the initial shock of being presented with the suggestion, and after overcoming my reluctance to go beyond the terms of my official appointment in Islamic Studies, I accepted with trepidation Andrew's invitation. It came to be a turning point in my academic career, and so great was the surprise for me that I remained in deep intellectual recovery for many years afterward. It was not how I planned my professional career. Andrew was also responsible for recruiting me for preaching rotation, and thus for introducing me to the parishes of the Methodist church north of Aberdeen. It offered me the chance of a rare and unique experience, which, combined with my academic responsibilities at the University of Aberdeen, expanded my horizons in fresh and rewarding ways.

The Yale phase of my career has turned out to be the longest, and I am enormously grateful to the president of Yale, Richard Levin, who generously supported my travel and research activities, and to colleagues at the Macmillan Center for International and Area Studies for their help and encouragement. I record my thanks, too, to the Whitney Humanities Center where, under Peter Brooks's directorship, I shared in the Fellows Program for many wonderful years. At the Yale Law School I am grateful for the friendship of Owen Fiss and Tony Kronman, who invited me to participate in the Middle East Legal Studies Seminar. At the Yale Divinity School I am grateful for the support of Dean Harry Attridge. I recall with a full heart the friendship of George Lindbeck, Lee Keck, Harry Adams,

Acknowledgments

Chris Seitz, Nicholas Wolterstorff, David Bartlett, all now retired, and Gaylord Noyce and Jim Dittes, both deceased. I am also thankful for the support and encouragement of Dean Thomas Ogletree, since retired. He followed my work with close attention and interest. I do not know if Tom realized what an inspiration he was to me and how much I have missed him as a colleague and friend.

Given the nature of this book as an exploration of religious and intercultural themes, it stands to reason that many people across the world are entitled to my thanks and gratitude. I cannot possibly list them all, but I hope that they will recognize their influence in the values I have tried to represent and to convey in the following pages. I entered the church in one bound, as it were, and my transition might have been uncomfortably rocky and episodic but for the friendship and kindness of so many on both sides of the interfaith corridor, among them Terry Iles, Colin and Joan Eastwood, Jim and Muriel McNeir, John B. Taylor, Humphrey Fisher, John Hick, Elham Eid, Carl Smith, Darwin Kirby, Ted Lockwood, Lewis Rambo, Dr. Jack Faal, Kenneth Cragg, Albrecht Hauser, John Crossley, and the following who have since died: Tom Beetham, Eleanor Smith, Richard Gray, Imam Abdoulie Jobe, Lesslie Newbigin, Bryan Green, Cecilia Moore, and Stanley Samartha. I am very grateful to Jon Pott for his genial forbearance over the many decades it has taken to bring this writing project to completion. My repeated stumbling attempts did little to shake his confidence. I owe a special debt to David Bratt for the care, detail, and thoughtfulness he devoted to the manuscript, and for the encouragement all of that has meant.

Most importantly, I owe an inestimable debt of thanks to Sandra, who as wife and mother lived through most of the experiences described here. At first uncertainly and uncomprehendingly, and then with growing confidence I set out on the professional and vocational paths of my life in her company and with her support and encouragement. The scale of this debt is all too obvious in retrospect, but it was clear even at the time when in nearly every move we made we were involved in a transcontinental change of address, with all the stress and disruption that entailed. In those and other situations she helped put together the scattered pieces of my Humpty-Dumpty to hand me a fresh start. She provided shelter for my personal and professional life, and was a tower of

Acknowledgments

strength in many critical situations. This story of my life is framed by our memorable companionship and is as much a tribute to her as it is to my parents. She and everyone who played a role in this adventure "deserve to be had of us and of posterity in everlasting remembrance. . . . Therefore blessed be they, and most honored be their name."

Part I

I will instruct you and teach you

the way you should go;

I will counsel you with my eye upon you.

PSALM 32:8

CHAPTER 1

What God Wills

When in January 2008 my wife and I, and, for the first time, our children, visited Georgetown in the middle reaches of the River Gambia and saw the shabby compound where I was raised, littered with tumbledown houses merging unobtrusively with the disheveled backyard, a flabbergasted Kelefa, my son, and Sia, my daughter, asked how I made it "from here to there. No, really, Dad!" To my children it must have felt like coming back from the dead. Also called Janjangbureh, Georgetown is situated on MacCarthy Island about 350 kilometers from the river's discharge point in Bathurst, later Banjul. The town has fallen on hard times, becoming a forlorn, scrappy abode that sits forgotten in the middle of the great river that was once the main artery of the region's trade. As Kelefa said, the island could easily make the grade as the site of the reality television show "Survivor."

Before we were married I had taken Sandra to meet my relatives so they could give her the traditional going over. There was no hesitation: they gave her a rousing warm welcome. One relative, an elderly woman, said she must first examine Sandra's hands to see if they had any callous marks on them, for that would be a sign that she was fit to grow rice, the staple crop farmed by women. The relative decided in the end that her test was unnecessary, and, amid much hearty laughter, she signaled that Sandra passed the scrutiny with flying colors. I made her a gift for her approval. My sister renamed her Jarai after herself to express heartfelt acceptance. Children lined up proudly proclaiming or inventing their place on the Sanneh family tree and reminding Sandra that she would have to include them in the list of her own household. The thrill was palpable that *tubab musu*, the white woman, would bear titles of wife, and many times mother and aunt, and be an adornment in the *nyancho* royal house. The sentiment runs strong in the repertoire of the Manding musical tradition. I let relatives have their own private time with Sandra while I attended to some family business. Word spread quickly about our visit, and by the time I emerged the crowd, part curious and part dutiful, had filled the compound and spilled out on to the street. We hadn't organized a celebration for our coming, but you wouldn't know it from the crowd, the excitemnt, and smiles all around us. We raised quite a stir then, and I wondered this time, with our children in tow, what awaited us.

There was a hint on the ferry crossing when we were hustled by two teenage boys who ride the ferry all day long. Getting an early start on their daily errand to nowhere, they gave the impression of induced lightheadedness, such being the fate of unemployed school dropouts. Their imperviousness to orders and their impetuous loquaciousness for their age suggest they were in suspended reality. They were too far adrift to respond to any gentle nudge, aptly reflecting the island's washed-out, limpid mood.

Georgetown was important in colonial times as the headquarters of the resident chief and the expatriate district commissioner, along with his lean staff of civil servants who came on rotation from Bathurst, the capital. Being a practical man, the commissioner tackled boredom by hunting hippos at night, and followed other not-so-licit nocturnal pursuits to lighten the burden of empire. The power station was a diesel generator capable of supplying power, and a disproportionate amount of air pollution, for a couple of hours every day. The attendant I used to know there was a stubby, genial fellow who spent most of his time reclining on a mat he spread out beside the outside wall of the power station. His work involved using metal buckets to draw diesel oil from the mounted barrels and filling the tank from time to time. There was also a glass-housed barometric gauge, wishfully called the weather station, manned by a meteorological officer. The police station was the hinterland outpost of law and order, its existence a token show of the authority needed to keep the pacified natives in line — and in the process to cultivate liaisons with demure, impressionable local women.

The Gambia (as both the river and the nation around it are known) came under colonial rule in the first decades of the nineteenth century, although the river had come under the control of one or another European power beginning with the Duke of Courland in the Baltic region in the seventeenth century. A month after the outbreak of the American War of Independence in July 1776, the British authorities began exploring the establishment of a convict settlement on the Gambia. A survey of the river in 1784 came up with the suggestion of Lemaine (later MacCarthy) Island as a site. Richard Bradley was detailed to arrange for purchase of it from the chief. The idea of a penal settlement even in remote MacCarthy Island in the Gambia attracted the interest of British humanitarians, with John Wesley in particular inveighing against the inhuman treatment of convicted offenders. When a committee of the House of Commons took evidence on the proposal, witnesses familiar with conditions in the Gambia observed poignantly that the convict scheme fell little short of one of murder. The Commons committee in the end abandoned the idea — not for humanitarian reasons, but because "the outcasts of an old society cannot form the foundation of a new one; therefore it is impossible to form a colony solely of convicts."[1] Colonization bypassed the Gambia for the time being.

While British official interest in the Gambia lapsed with the abandonment of the penal settlement idea, private interest in charting a route to Timbuktu maintained British attention on the river. The Peace Treaty of Versailles of 1783, which ended the American War for Independence, formally recognized the River Gambia as a British possession. MacCarthy Island, on which the town of Janjanbure was situated, appeared to offer security to merchants and traders worried about the unrest of wars and the slave trade in the hinterlands. Others joined them in Janjanbure,

1. J. M. Gray, *A History of The Gambia* (Cambridge: Cambridge University Press, 1940, repr. London: Frank Cass, 1966), 280.

which as the name signifies was a refuge for fugitives, the most prominent of which were dislocated Muslim elements fleeing persecution by Soninke pagan rulers. The Muslim quarter, known as Morikunda, "holy city," showed the devout hopes of those who came to settle there.

The feuding chiefs of the mainland were engaged with the chief of Janjanbure in a war of massacres, abductions, and frequent raids, without a conclusive battle to decide the issue. In 1823, in exchange for an annual payment, Kolli as chief agreed to cede the island to Major Alexander Grant, acting for the British government. Grant was accompanied by the Wesleyan missionary John Morgan, who arrived in the Gambia in 1821 and was considered the architect of the small settlement on St. Mary's Island that came to be known as Bathurst. That settlement proved to be crucial when, some years later, Britain considered abandoning the Gambia altogether; the fact that Britain had a foothold on the upper reaches of the river tipped the scales in favor of its continued presence. "To Grant therefore belongs the credit of founding not only the Colony but also the Protectorate of the Gambia," as one historian later declared.[2]

The resettlement of the island was undertaken at the direction of Sir Charles MacCarthy, who was governor of Sierra Leone and also responsible for the Gambia. The original mud fort was eventually replaced by Fort George, and as a result the name "Georgetown" began to gain currency. The establishment of the Methodist mission on the island facilitated the settlement there of "recaptives," as the liberated Africans were called, and soon the population grew to a respectable size. Morikunda, the Muslim quarter, thrived, enabling the commandant to remit the administration of Muslim affairs to the community leaders. The arrangement meant that Muslims remained a self-contained group without interference from the mission.

In all this time Georgetown continued to receive an influx of recaptives from Freetown, such that by the end of the 1830s over 250 of these recaptives were settled there. The houses built for them were distinctive for their architectural style: single-story houses built on a brick foundation, with framed windows, floors and walls made of wood, and corrugated tinned roofs. The houses were furnished in European styles.

2. Gray, *A History of The Gambia,* 336.

The town was a center of missionary work on the upper reaches of the river, which led in 1842 to the convening there of the Methodist District Meeting. Church membership at the time was 266, compared to 286 in Bathurst, though the Georgetown school population was only one-third the size of Bathurst's.

African leadership was considered crucial to the running of the Georgetown school. While it has a checkered history, the Georgetown school represents a significant initiative by a young church undaunted in exercising its missionary warrant: raising the quality of life of future leaders of church and society and transmitting the gospel in partnership with local agency. After the passage of the first Education Ordinance in 1882, the government became a partner in the education enterprise; after all, it needed the students of the schools to man the offices of the state. With the commencement of regular steamer service up river in 1897 with the *m.v. Mansa Kilah,* the church renewed efforts to revive the now-dilapidated school at Georgetown. But Muslim resistance proved impossible to overcome, and the decline of the liberated African population resulted in the collapse of the school. A hundred years later a revived version of the school became the foundation of the government's attempt to establish primary education in the area.

As a foothold, if also as an improbable outpost of empire, Georgetown in time grew to become a link in the chain of authority devised to rule the Protectorate of the Gambia. At the time of our family visit, the line of *seyfos* (chiefs) and district commissioners who administered the town had long been reduced to random anecdotes about colorful characters and their eccentricities. As twentieth-century inheritors of the town's colonial history, Farimang Singhateh (who was later knighted as the first — and last — governor-general of the Gambia), Musa Sanyang, Junkung Jobarte, Kebba Sidibe, Balla Jatta (a veteran of World War II), Sulayman Haidara and his brother Sidi Haidara, along with the Diab and the Musa Lebanese families, among others, were eyewitnesses to the momentous changes in Georgetown in the twentieth century. They have all long since left the scene, and with them went a rich storehouse of memories and reminiscences.

In the twentieth century a few loose threads remained by way of scattered, incidental recollections. There was the *seyfo's* staff bearer suited up in a khaki gown, waistband, crimson fez and a bronze medal proudly pinned to his chest; he beat the dusty trails in his role as chief's attendant and go-between. The town crier, Nano Galloga, was a one-woman information service who relayed messages for the government while serving at the same time as chief landlady to the town. Visitors reported to her, giving her an unrivaled role as cultural broker. She it was who toured the town announcing names of the newly born before any naming ceremony could take place. She also received and relayed marriage proposals. Good humored and with a hearty voice, she lived a charmed life as head of her own household. She was a dominant social force in the decades stretching from the 1940s to the early 1960s. The men deferred to her, while children adored her.

To the scandal of his Muslim family recently established on the north bank, my father, Ousman, more commonly known as Suti, accepted employment in the transport office of the infidel colonial administration. The family never forgave him for leaving them and working for the white man. To assure them that working for the white man was not the same as handing over his whole family, Father refrained from sending his children to the Western school, which was resented as a promoter of unbelief. But even that way of putting the children out to pasture as paternal scapegoats failed to restore Father's reputation with his people entirely.

The idea that we as children had to take the hit to avenge the offense to Father's family for working for the white man was deep-seated in the tradition, but my mother, whom we called Nunu, egged on by my grandmother, Hawa, broke with my father and conspired to have me enrolled in the Western school while my father was away. (Grandmother was never reconciled to my mother's marriage, resenting my father as a mere arriviste from the hinterlands.) By the time he returned, the deed was done. But he refused to pay my school fees, or to buy me clothes or school supplies. He thought Western education was nothing but atheistic propaganda, and that it would claim me as a prize. So to pay my fees, I washed plates, cleaned floors, and fetched water for a Catholic family on a civil-service rotation from Bathurst. For her pains and her solidarity, I thought my mother was due the small leftover change from my wages. She was absorbed in her own chores, in the trivial round and common task, with room only to deny herself. I wished her better. I was no more than nine, but it was clear to me early on that education was my passport to a better future. I made the mental journey out of my world long before I made the physical journey. Just imagining the possibility of life beyond the island was a turning point.

My son came to appreciate the precarious nature of local educational opportunities when we visited Armitage High School, where I had eventually gained admission on a government scholarship, to Mother's great relief. Armitage was a government Islamic boarding school run as something of a boot camp. There village boys had their wild impulses broken as they were counted, registered, and put in laundered uniforms. Intended as a magnet to overcome the resistance of chiefs to infidel colonial rule, Armitage succeeded in attracting the sons of chiefs, which was why my father allowed me to enroll there, instead of sending me to the Methodist Boys High School in Bathurst, where he was certain they would take me moral captive. When we saw it on our family visit, the school was an old dump of a place, the unfenced grounds strewn with the remains of animal carcasses, discarded plastic bottles, and pieces of broken glass blending into the surrounding bush. The teachers we surprised with our visit seemed content just lounging around and whiling away time with spacey camaraderie. Boarding facilities had disappeared, classrooms lay deserted, and what remained of the assembly hall was now a hangout of unoccupied workers and casual visitors. Armitage had a cachet under colonial rule as a subsidized concession to Muslim scruples, and thrived on account of that. But that distinction quickly faded in the post-independence era, when Islam no longer was under infidel siege. The mosque now existed only as a memory, and the school bell no longer summoned students to meals and prayers. Visitors and the few teachers we met accounted for a high proportion of the visible school population. We met no groups of students on our visit. The school had been languishing in a persistent drought of resources and morale in its own version of the rain cycle.

Georgetown was still an easygoing place when we visited it, and people seemed accustomed to leading a life of good-natured rambling by following the genial monotony of daily life. The bare demands of the daily cycle induce a state of general resignation that the collective imagination attributes to the will of God: accordingly, all time is God's time, and whatever happens is the will of God. School is the will of God, or, in this case, is not the will of God. Getting a wife and having children is the will of God, and being able to feed them is also the will of God. Being unemployed is the will of God. Life on a small island in a small country scales down your expectations: you need little clue beyond seeing the sun rise and following it to its setting, which is the will of God, too. The grinding daily regularity spins in an unvarying rhythm to ease and knead the mind. The men shuffle up to the *bantaba,* the all-male rendezvous and stakeout, where they while away the time talking themselves silly all day long and wearing themselves out "with shapeless idleness." The women, for their part, are absorbed all day long in domestic and household chores. All that is God's will, too.

The years are measured by the annual rain cycle: so many rains make so many years. People inquire about how old you are by asking how many rains you have. The proper answer is "a lot of rains," never "not many rains," for that means, not that you are young, but that you do not wish longevity for yourself. The idiom here is the clue to the right answer. A person had so many rains at death, and a town is so many rains old. When someone dies people say he or she has run out of rains. Life ends when we run dry. Prayers for newborns go something like, "may the new baby see many, many rains," followed by looking up to the sky, spitting into the cupped hands, and rubbing the face, as if the cupped hands are a vessel that catch the rain to drench the face, which is the symbol of earth.

When people thank you they say, "May it rain on you a lot," or, with a pious flourish, "May God let you see many more rains." Not to see many rains is a misfortune not to be wished on anyone. In this case, where rain is age, it can only be like good health from heaven. A drought throws a complication into the computation, and in that case you talk about it like a family secret, with a hand over the mouth to signify anguish. During droughts, even the river seems to whine as it sweeps along in its meandering sluggish drop into the sea. To amend T. S. Eliot's remarks on the great Mississippi, in the drought the river is no longer a strong brown god — sullen, untamed, and intractable. Rather it is desultory, flabby, and sad in defeat, flowing along neither honored nor propitiated. In scattered flocks, pelicans and kingfishers wade and peck for fish on the muddy banks of the river instead of doing their regular soaring dives. Droughts fall from the sky to become castigation on earth.

In this environment that requires so much interconnectedness for survival, relationships make identity. Everyone is everyone else's cousin, niece, uncle, aunt, in-law, spouse, or the relative of a relative. Others cannot touch you except by touching something of themselves in you. "Do you remember me? Have you forgotten me?" are standard questions you will be asked constantly and persistently, even though in my case I couldn't possibly know since I had never seen them before. "You wouldn't know me, would you?" they will say, expecting me to say, "Yes, you are the relative of So-and-So." They would beam with pride and thrust their hand before you for money — always the right hand, the auspicious hand.

Although people value relationships, they are not much curious about personal details and experiences. In fact, their interest seems to be motivated by hope of reward. Someone will greet you or offer you a gift only to turn round and ask you to do them a favor. Even a friendly smile will be followed by a demand for a favor. I recall running into an old boyhood acquaintance who was scarcely done greeting me when he stretched out his hand for money. I barely recognized him, but it made little difference. Would I help him build a house on a piece of property he recently acquired, he asked expectantly? Otherwise, he showed no interest in what I had been up to. I was waiting once to board my flight at the Dakar airport when a man, a complete stranger, fished out what seemed a simple scheme of self-enterprise from his luggage and laid it out before me, saying I should send him funds when I returned to America. He said he knew my family, and I gathered he thought that entitled him to my help. One is in the circle of people by virtue of someone else, and so, consequently, the incidents of one's life and experience are discounted a priori. Rules of social etiquette discount individual merit. "Doesn't he know where he comes from? Don't we know his father and mother?" is one typical attitude. (The attitude is reminiscent of that described in Mark 6:3.)

It is as if knowing your parents gives people the right to discount you on your own merit, especially when money is at stake in that bit of social knowledge — and usually money is at stake. The profit motive drives the kinship business.

The statement "This is the accustomed way of doing things among us" is the law of collective immunity; it is also exculpatory of the individual. If people can say that, then they can stand above blame or culpability. The rule can be employed to put you off your stride, in fact to put you at a disadvantage. People will take shelter behind group or family loyalty, and that means you cannot hold them to account because of collective immunity. Yet the same people will insist that what you have is for sharing, because that "is the accustomed way of doing things among us." That is, it is the will of God.

There is no word in the language for thank you, or for acknowledgment. The usual terms, *inimbara* and *a-baraka,* are only approximations, only polite substitutes. Meaning "you are at work," for instance, *inimbara* occurs in a variety of settings: hailing workers in the field, greeting women at the well, or complimenting people on errands. Similarly, *a-baraka,* derived from the Arabic, means "may you be favored," in the sense of "may you do me more favors." Separately and together the terms are fundamentally terms of self-interest. A combination of the idea of fortune *(harjê)* and entitlement *(n'tâ)* scrubs out the notion of personal gratitude. "I will pray for you," or "With abundance may God replenish you," as a standard response to gifts received, suggests that the act of giving places you the giver rather than the beneficiary under obligation. The beneficiary is center stage, while the giver is only a link in the system of relaying good fortune, like a goodwill messenger — what the people call *sábó* (Arabic *sabab,* cause). The expression "You have been my bar of soap" *(sâfuno,* by way of the French *savon),* that is, "You have been the means of my looking my best," conveys the idea simply. This attitude is far from how the West understands economic aid to developing nations, and it might explain why international development aid has been fated to such mixed results. Aid received is a stroke of good fortune. Waiting does pay, and God will reward patience *(sabr).* Such is God's will.

All this has given me a newfound appreciation for Émile Durkheim. Society here is not just the sublimation of sacred, binding customs, but the commissary of God. Here the idea of God is the fiction of relationship crystallized in concrete notions of bargain, exchange, and social obligation. This is religion as a charm of good fortune, the sacred text a tablet of manners, customs, and duties, and blessing is material benefit, what people call *nafaa.* You have children so they may be an answer to prayer as *nafaa* to you, as "a bar of soap" to you, not so that they may fulfill themselves in their own right.

Such religion means people will invoke faith for its perceived benefit. The begging bowl is piety's community depository. Social obligation fills the begging bowl with the fruits of good fortune, and you draw from it with the goodwill of custom. When someone begs from you, you may refuse only at risk to your social standing — in other words, at risk to your religious advantage. "Please forgive me," is the proper way to decline. It is a moral deficiency not to give when asked; you are thereby put in the position of needing exoneration. In giving, your feelings are irrelevant, while your deference to custom is not. The curse *(danka)* is when religion as social offense deals with a dark hand. In both cases we encounter religion in its material benefits and effects, in religion as gain or punishment. In a popular prayer manual used by pilgrims, *Manasik al-Hajj,* one prayer declares: "Whatever blessing I have called down it has been upon him whom You bless; whatever curse I have cursed with it has been upon him whom You curse." I once heard a prominent Gambian family elder with a base in Michigan denounce the widow of his recently deceased brother for abandoning the sick brother's bedside to undertake the once-in-a-lifetime pilgrimage, saying for that reason he would not observe the levirate and inherit her as his wife. He added: "I will refuse her admission to paradise." The man's attitude is evidence that society determines religious conduct, for good and ill, so that belief is an element of social observance. People speak for God when in fact they are speaking for and with society.

Greetings fill a similar social role. The greeting "How are you?" demands a response there and then. It cannot be ignored or delayed. A greeting delayed is an offense incurred. I have seen the greeting used to break into a meeting, to quiet a hubbub, to interrupt and insert oneself into an ongoing conversation, to satisfy a curiosity, to accost a stranger, to poke an inquisitive nose into the business at hand, or to make a demand. A greeting will end invariably with demanding *(dáne)* a personal favor.

Experience will teach you to use the greeting yourself as an asset *(tóo diya)* while still conforming to custom and usage. It requires great social skill, and does not come easily for visitors. People know that, and so they pile in when opportunity, including clumsiness on your part, allows. "How are you? How are the people over there? How is it with your associates? Hope everyone is fine back in your neighborhood." (Again) "How is it with you? Hope your journey went without a hassle. How were your fellow passengers?" And then the *coup de grâce:* "What did you bring for me?" followed by a smile and an outstretched hand. The logic here is that a gift is due because people greeted you and so placed you under obligation of rewarding them. But if you are experienced enough, as I said, you can use the rules of greeting to your advantage by repeating the words in turn, thus equalizing the relationship. Word would spread: "Do you know, he has not forgotten us. He still has respect for us *(a moya ta)*." That is guaranteed to win you favors here, there, and beyond, thanks to the multiplying power of word-of-mouth transmission.

Family reunions are striking for the rapidity with which conversation gravitates to talk about money. You would be disappointed if you expect people to take an interest in the experiences of individual family members. In our case, the expectation of financial gifts from America created something of a feeding frenzy. All stories had the mercenary ambition of establishing relationship, however tenuous or fictitious, and demanding cash payment, regardless of degree or veracity of relationship. The more quickly one can make, or be perceived to make, the family connection, the sooner can one demand a gift of money and then more quickly move out of the way so others can have their turn at the till. As a boy, that was how I would approach visitors in town, thrusting out my hand — the favored right hand — for gifts of cash or in kind. I would jump for joy and run all the way home to show my mother. My father frowned on that as something beggars do.

On its own, gift-making commits you to more gift-making: you give so you may give more. People feel that this also is God's will. People who make a gift to you will not hesitate to trumpet the news to their neighbors, and to demand praise for it — exactly the sort of behavior Jesus warns against in the Sermon on the Mount (Matt. 6:2-4).

All these and other ideas have been stamped on society by repeated and unified practice and observance, allowing individuals to invoke them as a way of representing to themselves the society they belong to, and their relations with it. Unless, as E. E. Evans-Pritchard objects,[3] this is a piece of crowd psychology, with the herd instinct driving consciousness rather than consciousness shaping behavior, it comes pretty close to what I understand Durkheim to be saying. It bears thinking about.

One cannot help but reflect on how this attitude encourages a thoroughgoing instrumental political culture with few qualms and scruples about invention, manipulation, and social blackmail (something we are all too familiar with in the United States at election time). In politics as in custom, people are fair game. Stories and rumors are minted and bandied about for effect. One can see how such hustling can play havoc with people's lives. People swear that they are telling the truth when in fact they are tilting at windmills. Why should truth-telling require such strenuous oath-taking every time, as it seems to? Why can't it be direct and straightforward? How otherwise to tell the boundary between true reports and devout wishful thinking?

Reports were circulated that as principal of Armitage Secondary School a brother of mine, Musa, harbored secret sympathies for the political opposition, and he was fired on the basis of self-propelling rumors in spite of his publicly acknowledged accomplishments for the school. There was no outcry over this; instead, people chalked up the incident to God's will. Whatever happens is simply the will of God, people say, in effect giving human problems over to non-human solutions.

Yet life is not so simple, and what may appear as a good answer turns out to have a serious drawback. People waver between resignation to God's will and anxiety about the future, with not much trust in either. Events seem out of people's control, and that makes resignation natural, though still not satisfactory. Similarly, the sparse, rickety structures people call home are standing reminders of how fleeting life is and how quickly material conditions can deteriorate; they give little sense of permanence. Together, these two factors produce a take-what-you-can get-now attitude. An early death from malaria, say, or a fire, or a road acci-

---

3. E. E. Evans-Pritchard, *Theories of Primitive Religion* (Oxford: Oxford University Press, 1965), 53-73.

dent can wipe out in a flash the modest but precious assets of a short life. Besides, the bush climate does not favor the accumulation and preservation of riches. Things rust and crumble easily and quickly. The people, therefore, give in to the attitude they have reduced to a rhyme: *soto je, domo je, bang je* ("get it there, consume it there, and exhaust it there"). This self-indulgent philosophy is pretty close to the Epicurean ideal of "eat, drink, and be merry, for tomorrow we die." There is little sense in either view of time bearing any discernible moral purpose.

If you take this background into account, you can see that people are just being rational when, with felt sincerity, they say something is the will of God: there is so much over which people have so little power or choice. Better to dress that in wishful thinking than to give in to paralyzing disillusionment. Yet saying it is the will of God is only half right. It can also be the will of God that you do something about it. People will have children and say it is the will of God, only to turn around and ask you to help support them, leaving you wondering what happened to the will of God now. The real point of saying that it is the will of God seems to be to hope that things will turn out well. When the chips are down and responsibility stares you in the face, hope alone is not enough. Someone else should take the flak for not stepping in. The closer the relationship with a would-be helper, the higher the sense of entitlement, and the more readily aroused the spirit of resentment. At this point trust in the will of God turns suddenly personal, revealing how people understand religion as what is useful. Several words in the language point to that: *barakah, duwa jaabi, nafaa, harije* — all these words have the sense of gain and benefit, showing how materialistic terms define religion, and vice versa.

Kelefa's and Sia's question about how I made it from there to here is the reason for attempting this account of my education and my intellectual journey from the margin of remote Africa to the center of the world. In contrast to the rules of my professional training, this requires me to be personal. The account attempts to weave into a coherent narrative the miscellaneous details of my life without prejudice to anyone. Indeed, without the help and support of people impossible to list here, my journey would not be as it turned out. The path I chose to pursue a better life would be inconceivable but for the generosity and intervention of others.

I started out falteringly. Before I began school I learned on my own the letters of the alphabet by parking myself in convenience stores amidst the pile of empty sacks and cardboard boxes. There, I would laboriously spell out words on packages, boxes, and sacks. Items like candles, milk of the "Peak" brand, sugar, tomato, oil, sardines, salt, onions, and matches formed my vocabulary, with the pictures helping me to match letters to things. I tried to cram in as many words as I could in the few hours the store was open.

I was often stumped by a word whose meaning was elusive because of the accompanying picture. One of the most notorious in this regard was the safety match carrying the brand name "The Palmtree." I recognized the palm trees, all right, including a palm-wine tapper proudly bearing on his right shoulder a pole sagging at both ends with palm-wine-filled gourds. My difficulty arose with the description at the base of the matchbox, "Impregnated Safety Match," which was followed by "Manufactured in Sweden." The word "impregnated" threw me for a loop, and when I learned its dictionary meaning I was more confused than enlightened. I thought the fact that the matches were made in Sweden might be a clue, except that I hadn't the foggiest idea where Sweden was, or why it sent us matches. Once I could say the word "impregnated" confidently, I took pleasure in the way it sounded, even though I could not use it in any other context. The words "impregnated" and "pregnancy" I later learned are related etymologically, deepening the enigma of the connection with matches. I was frustrated that the clever people who manufactured impregnated safety matches left no help on the match box itself. How inconsiderate of them!

By what can only be regarded as a miraculous coincidence, a chance encounter with the writings of Helen Keller (1880-1968) burst the chains of my intellectual confinement. When I was around eight years old, I was walking down a dirt road and I kicked up a pile of papers strewn at a garbage dump. What looked like the remnants of a book caught my attention. After I rummaged in the pile and stood up, I was holding torn leaves from Helen Keller's autobiography, *The Story of My Life* (1902). I had recently learned to read, and with the thrill of a beginner stumbling on a godsend, I devoured Helen Keller's words, entranced by her description of how she herself learned to read. She described how she acquired literacy by Braille, and how she moved from silence and darkness to a life of vision and triumph over adversity. She insisted that although the world is full of suffering, the world is also full of the overcoming of suffering. I was enchanted, and could barely contain myself. I was not blind in the physical sense, true, but I was trapped by my adverse circumstances. The world felt strange and impenetrable, and this was God's will, I thought. In stepped Helen Keller with a new message: *"nil desperandum,"* never despair. The true adventure of life, Helen Keller taught me, lies not in destinations but in having new eyes to see the world.

Helen Keller taught me that education is the key to overcoming physical and personal handicaps, and although she knew nothing of life in the Gambia, her experience could not have been more inspiring and relevant. Her moving, indomitable courage catapulted me into regions I never dreamed existed. I resolved early that nothing would stand in my way, no sacrifice would be too great, to experience the free and bountiful life of the mind. Father had forfeited his patrimony for his compromise with infidel rule; heaven knew what greater scandal I risked by wishing to follow the infidel example of a blind Helen Keller. Churchill once called Helen Keller "the greatest woman of our age." For me, however, Helen Keller was simply hope and courage transfigured. Mother would be proud to know that, and the thought would bring a smile to my face every time I recalled Helen Keller. Her spirit must be the anonymous guardian spirit of every child everywhere struggling to overcome overwhelming odds.

Religion suffused my world; it filled my thoughts and guided my actions; it was the register of consciousness and experience, the reflex of my moral will, the path and goal of striving, and the inner ear of my secret thoughts. I knew my parents only by that way. With religion I knew myself in the midst of others. Religion was structure and order before it was any kind of mood. In *The Idea of the Holy* (1934), the Lutheran theologian Rudolf Otto wrote otherwise, saying that emotion has religious merit, and that our concept of God cannot be reduced to a set of moral and rational constructs. But this was not the standard by which I was raised. We learned as children that subjective emotions were acceptable in children, but not in adults, for whom they were the devil's dominion.

The Qur'an teaches us to shun Satan, who "whispers into the heart of mankind" (Q 114). In that sense, religion was a rite of passage from childhood to adulthood, Otto notwithstanding.

I was never able to tell my parents before they died whether I succeeded in my ambition of doing well in my studies in Europe and the United States, so I am left to turn now to living family members to render this account of my intellectual journey. The kinship sentiments I imbibed from Mother still murmur in me long after I have been initiated into the solitary, individual ways of the West. Thanks to kinship roots, sentiments of family, friendship, and community still resonate with me. I do not know myself except in and through relationship. Other people have a part in who I am.

This book is about my spiritual and intellectual journey, and tracks the path of my career from its unlikely beginnings in a traditional African Muslim society to its eventual culmination in the world of academia. Thus the title of the book, *Summoned from the Margin: An African Homecoming. Summoned* in this context refers to the sense I had after stumbling on a religion I had never given much thought to. Only in hindsight could I see a purpose in coming to embrace it. The summons turned out to be real, even though it had been only a faint awareness at the time. It felt like being awakened. *Margin* refers to the fact that Christianity lay far out on the dim borders of the world of Islam that was the center of my universe. There was no church in town when I was growing up; I had never seen a Bible in my life; I had never heard anyone teach or preach about Christianity; there was no mention of Christianity in the books we read at school. There was not a single missionary in my town that I knew of. The known history of the Mandinka, my people, is for the most part the history of Islam among them. In their far-flung dispersions following the fall of the Mandinka Mali Empire in the sixteenth century, the Mandinka have remained marginal to areas of Christian impact elsewhere in Africa. More than a thousand years of Islamization had contributed to making Christianity virtually invisible to us. The consternation that met me on my way to joining the church was a measure of the symbolic distance I had to travel from the Axis Mundi of my Muslim culture and history to the Christian faith — which turned out to have its own margins to offer. As for *homecoming*, I use it here as a metaphor for pilgrimage in the sense of "coming home" to faith in God in the way that has subsequently shaped my life and work, both personal and professional. The narrative of that experience is the substance of this memoir.

Literature of any kind was scarce in my childhood, which reinforced the position of the Qur'an as the paradigmatic book, its holy character proof that books were oracles of the enlightened spirit. I remember seeing the pages of the Qur'an gathered in a skin cover, tied with a red ribbon, and carried with reverence. A small crowd would gather when someone opened the book to read it. That was how I thought books in general were treated. Olaudah Equiano tells the story of how, arriving as a slave in America, he once came upon his master reading the Bible. Entranced, he stopped to marvel at the spectacle: how could someone be so engrossed in a book unless the book was secretly speaking to such a person, Equiano puzzled. After his master put down the Bible and was out of the room, Equiano approached circumspectly and gently knocked on the Bible, held his breath, and put his ears close to the book. Filled with anticipation, he waited for the book to speak. The sense of awe and wonder Equiano describes is reminiscent of my own earliest encounter with the Muslim Scripture, and the feeling extended to other books. I would listen in rapt attention when I saw someone reading from a book, not even waiting for a translation. Just the mere fact that an arrangement of silent words on a page contained meaningful sounds that someone could recognize and pronounce was enough of a marvel to keep me riveted in sheer amazement. At the time my parents applauded my attentiveness, little realizing the depth of the impact it had on me. In retrospect it seems to fit into a pattern. My life of study, teaching, and writing placed me in the world of books, and religion persisted through much of it. Only now have I begun fully to appreciate that fact. When I heard news of banning or burning books of any kind it would trigger in me feelings of sadness, and I felt myself fortunate that the scarcity of books made book-burning a virtually unknown event in much of my childhood. Only later did I learn it was commonplace in some parts of the world. The thought of it made me shudder.

As I traveled and read, I felt myself increasingly drawn into accounting for the religious contribution to a humane engagement with the world. It is perhaps no accident that the study of Scripture and of translation came to occupy so much of my academic life, even though I did not set out on that path initially or consciously. It should also not be surprising that my career has involved a great deal of travel and trying to communicate across language barriers. By necessity, we have to decipher other cultures, either on the basis of a common humanity, or on the basis of difference. Yet deciphering assumes a capacity for mutual recognition, just as the words on the page leap to life as they are mediated through attentive understanding. We find our way by such mutual deciphering. It is the answer to alienation.

It has been an extraordinary privilege to have worked in some of the world's greatest universities, with unprecedented access to colleagues, students, contacts, materials, and resources that few dream of. Such opportunities have afforded me an unusual vantage point. I cannot claim any entitlement to such good fortune, nor to have made the most of it. Being educated on four continents has deepened my appreciation for what has been an adventure in encounter with people, places, and ideas. It was my choice that I took the spiritual and intellectual directions I will indicate in this book, yet unforeseen circumstances have added their incalculable share to the particular design of my life. In so many situations I have felt the imperative of a still small voice demanding that I respond: what purpose am I here to serve? That question is the narrative cord that has helped to bind my life and work into some sort of reasonable coherence and to make sense of the contexts and events of my personal circumstances. To amend Coleridge, the light that experience sheds on our lives is like a lantern on the stern that shines particularly bright on the waves behind us, making hindsight an occasion for gratitude and for looking ahead. We recall the goodness of others to understand ourselves better, and as an encouragement. Whatever our individual achievement, others have helped us more than we realize.

There are so many people to thank for my life, so many memories of the goodwill and support of family and friends without whom little of what I have learned would be possible or of much value. My implicit gratitude knows no bounds, and I beseech the reader to join me in acknowledgement of the intimate solicitude of my guardian angel and of the One source of all truth and wisdom:

> For each achievement human toil can reach;
> For all that patriots win, and poets teach;
> For the old light that gleams on history's page
> For new hope that shines on each new age.
>
> May we to these our lights be ever true,
> Find hope and strength and joy for ever new,
> To heavenly visions still obedient prove,
> The Eternal Law, writ by the Almighty Love!

CHAPTER 2

Negotiating Childhood

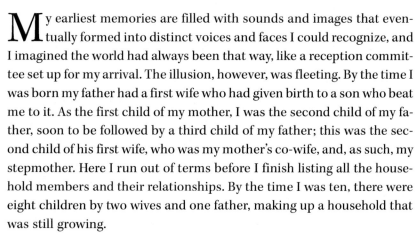

My earliest memories are filled with sounds and images that eventually formed into distinct voices and faces I could recognize, and I imagined the world had always been that way, like a reception committee set up for my arrival. The illusion, however, was fleeting. By the time I was born my father had a first wife who had given birth to a son who beat me to it. As the first child of my mother, I was the second child of my father, soon to be followed by a third child of my father; this was the second child of his first wife, who was my mother's co-wife, and, as such, my stepmother. Here I run out of terms before I finish listing all the household members and their relationships. By the time I was ten, there were eight children by two wives and one father, making up a household that was still growing.

You need to dig deeper than the mere number of people in a household to appreciate the true nature of the criss-crossing, multiplying impact of polygamy's effects. Simple computation gives an idea of a bustling household, but not the teasing complexity of relationships and alliances that a plural home spawns. In a household of many mothers and siblings, and with one man as the lone multiplier, there are as many combinations and permutations as there are co-wives, children, and other appendages. I learned to count, not with numbers, but with people. I added by listing names, each name trailing a story that numbers alone cannot measure.

In traditional Gambia, the social code allows a man up to four wives at any one time, and if they are of early childbearing age, as is often the case, these wives can produce among them several dozen children, united in a common father and divided by having different mothers. The very ideas of unity and difference take on the peculiar complexity of polygamy. Sibling rivalry is rife among children of the same father, whereas children of the same mother observe a uterine pact that prescribes collaboration and mutual bonding. The word for sibling rivalry on the paternal side is *faden-ya,* and is used always in the unmitigated sense of homebred jealousy and distrust. In contrast, its opposite, *baden-ya,* means mutual support and trust on the maternal side. Children by the same paternity are born to strife and to abiding distrust, while, to make for a viable household, children on the maternal side are like peas in a pod. Rivalry has a built-in safeguard against the extreme of domestic meltdown, especially when aunts and uncles and in-laws wade in to mine cracks and antipathies. Polygamy's complex norms incite factionalism, admittedly, but also provide safeguards against the household self-destructing.

As I was Mother's oldest child and Father's second oldest, the women of my mother's age-set staged a double naming ceremony; the name they gave me, Malamin, eclipsed the name my father gave me, Karamo. People called me by my maternal name, and tagged on my father's house name as an identifier, thus "Malamin-Suti." On the road to obtaining an education, "Malamin-Suti" faded into the remnant that is the name by which I am known today, but the earlier designation shows the advantage women enjoyed in their bid for domestic honors. Feminism of the local variety held uncontested claim to sovereign nature's prerogative to make us male and female, whatever society's masculine pretensions. The fact that my grandmother had a bone to pick with my father kept my father ever on the defensive, and made me aware of a sensitive, watchful tension between the maternal and the paternal sides of my family. Mother lugged a complex baggage of sensibilities into her married home, and the same was true for her senior co-wife. This left me wondering where all that put my father — what was his secret, coded portion of this ticking time-bomb?

By the time I was able to count I knew that the number one by itself was unreal. Children came in bunches and went out as confederates. In a crowded home with competing factions, life was a high-contact sport, and so it paid to forge alliances of the preemptive kind, with built-in checks and balances. We formed opportunistic coalitions to fill the gap between, say, age advantage and uterine preponderance; in a street fight the size of a bigger boy could in theory be overcome by lots of smaller kids banding together. (I say "in theory" because the imposing psychological advantage of size would beset the mind of any would-be diminutive challenger.) In tree climbing, to take another example, size was not an advantage, for in the branches nimble limbs were an asset, and mass and bulk a liability, so survival was not a function of stamina, but of nimble footwork. Yet even here we were careful not to cross someone older than us, and so we did not boast of the advantage of our size in the trees.

We certainly were careful about not incurring the displeasure of an older paternal sibling. Conceived in kinship, and constrained by calculations of payback, relationships and alliances were made for social advantage. Keeping scores made relationships highly quantifiable: you would count on your fingers those who owed you a favor and hold it up for general approbation. People were around day and night, but not necessarily with you. We children shared one bed, as many as the bed could take. Grievances of the day followed us to bed like thorn pricks, expressed as sharp elbows in our chests, or pummeling knees in our backs. Older siblings had the choice of sleeping on the wall side, which gave them the advantage of using the wall to push you out of bed. After picking ourselves off the floor in the middle of the night, and fending off mosquitoes while adults were asleep, we learned that submission was the smarter choice and our best ally.

✸   ✸   ✸

An African childhood such as mine was not littered with the kind of stimuli we associate with age-specific gadgets, including toys of every description and sophistication. An African child learns pretty quickly that playmates are not the same as playthings, and that having friends is altogether different from possessing things. A childhood landscape in Africa is a pretty stripped-down scene, with not even the barest of things made for children. But what a child lacks in mechanical toys is more than made up for in the organic richness of human contact and relationship. Society was designed that way.

What to a Western eye looks like childhood of deprivation, then, is to the African a stage of life brimming with assets of childhood enrichment. The African child lives in a close, crowded world, a world teeming with faces and sounds and movements that the child learns to decipher eventually into recognition and affirmation, each smiling face a lighted clue in the growing shape of knowing and belonging. In the workaday world a mother carries her infant on her back, tied with a strip of cloth. She talks to the infant, rocking and humming to reassure it, pointing out things, singing lullabies, and in general letting the infant in on greetings and exchanges with friends and passers-by. The education of the child begins on the mother's back, with the mother's daily chores and physical exertions the setting of real-life experience. The child is nurtured with the mother's milk and trained on the mother's back, always within reach, never forgotten or out of mind, and everywhere attended and surrounded by people. It provides a strong sense of company and society, reinforced with the steady hand of familiarity, support, and encouragement. Isolation and loneliness are considered extreme forms of child abuse, a form of social strangling. Women in the Gambia would weep if they saw a child alone, even if not their own.

Such sentiments drew few bounds, as an incident recounted by the eighteenth-century Scottish traveler Mungo Park illustrates. He describes how, feeling lonely and abandoned, he found himself surrounded by women in a village in present-day Mali. It was evening, and he was approaching bedtime with considerable apprehension when, there and then, the women, led by a young woman singer, composed a comforting song for him, which went as follows: "The winds roared, and the rains fell. The poor white man, faint and weary, came and sat under our tree. He has no mother to bring him milk; no wife to grind his corn." The women appended a chorus line: "Let us pity the white man, no mother has he." Park responded, "I was oppressed by such unexpected kindness; and sleep fled from my eyes."[1] For Mungo Park, a hardened, lone-wolf European traveler in "Darkest Africa," the world of human contact was un-

1. Mungo Park, *Travels in Africa* (1954; reprinted London: Everyman's Library, 1969), 152. Park's travels occurred 1795 to 1797. He had previously visited Sumatra in 1792.

forgettable — how much more for those whose entire childhood was formed by human companionship?

Mealtimes offered a chance to negotiate the minefield of intrasibling rivalry. The key was to acknowledge the pecking order by making calculated concessions of self-interest: giving up the piece of meat or fish on your side of the bowl; holding back from taking too generous a portion of the gravy and rice as a conciliatory gesture; yielding your vantage point around the food bowl; and forgoing your turn at the water jar. You would top it off by running errands and carrying messages for older paternal siblings, and for their mothers. All that did not necessarily spare you strife, but it could earn you important leverage in the jockeying and jostling. The stakes were high, and for survival you took such measures to ensure your well-being. Occasionally things got out of hand as an irate co-wife muscled in to defend her child in a fight to inflict injury on the other child. The shock of this, not to say the scars, set feelings aflame, and it sent co-wives and their offspring to resentful aunts and nieces and nephews to incite an extended family arms race.

In such situations my father would step in to break the tension with an order to cease and desist; that would douse the fires, and the feuding would abate with the household drawing back from war. Yet the toxic memories would fester. The only thing that might stop a co-wife from poisoning the meat or the water supply to harm the children of the other women is that her own ate and drank from the same source. Polygamy extinguishes the nuclear option, as it were, but not the embers of domestic malice, whose ashes discharge easily into bad blood and witchcraft accusations. That explains why the witch is seldom a stranger or an outsider. As Ogden Nash notes,

> One would be in less danger
> From the wiles of a stranger
> If one's own kin and kith
> Were more fun to be with.

Under siege on an island without bridges to relieve social congestion, people fed on accumulated grievances, and it did not take much for a rash of quarrels to break out and fester from rumors and innuendos.

In traditional society, where the will of God reigns supreme, witch-craft poses something of a moral puzzle: people do not say, as they appear to say of everything else, that witchcraft is the will of God. What does this amount to? A convenient bit of hairsplitting allows both sides to be affirmed: witchcraft is the work of malicious relatives or neighbors, even though people will still insist that what happens to a victim happens because it is God's will. The chain of cause and effect in events and experience is expanded to make room for the theory of divine agency, and that allows religion to be invoked without giving in to fatalistic resignation, or to fear of the unknown. It allows people to say that something is God's will without that requiring them to attach blame to God.

A husband of many wives may pretend to be above the fray, but in truth the male ego is no match for the jealousy of women unsheathed for battle. Nature itself wills it so. The jealousy of co-wives is impregnable to the thunder of a husband intent on exercising his authority. The male temper is a mere tempest in the household teacup; in short order, it subsides into nothing more than a tepid fuss. The man wishes strife away, and when he meets it in his wives he flails in this and that direction, unsure of which way to turn. He demands attention but cannot command it. It is easy enough to appreciate the husband's weakened influence; individually or in concert, the co-wives are the prime movers in the domestic sphere, with the man bobbing in and out of his wives' lives on a rotation dictated by the women's natural cycles. At any given point in the week or month, the man is on a time ration in the house of one wife or another, and in that sense he has no permanent resting place.

If, as can happen, the women live in different compounds, the man rides the shuttlecock back and forth across the fence in a ceaseless round of wife-pleasing. The system commits him to a gypsy conjugal life. He will be fence-hopping or bed-swapping in the next nocturnal round, and will be out of sight of most of his children at any time. It is the women who insure that the man attains the indispensable status of fatherhood. It is rare that a father would know the birthdays of his children, let alone be at home to celebrate them — which home, exactly? With the maternal cue, the children hail the man as father, and the man hears that as filial deference to him, not as evidence of his paternal proximity. Only mothers fill that role. That is why the *jelis*, traditional musicians, as custom's defenders, speak about worthy children as the reward of good mothers: *ina-le sonta aye kanda wulu* ("an honorable mother will beget a worthy child").

We do not generally realize the extent of the secondary social margins to which the system of plural wives confines men, with the children showing up as standard issue of masculine virility. With a polite nod in the direction of the women, the verb "to father" enhances the subject, the father, but not the object, the child. Children elevate fathers on the ladder of social prestige. A man might say to a challenger, "Don't you know I fathered so many more children than you?" That is supposed to count favorably with respect to status and seniority. But fatherhood merely launches children as live specimens, and detaches to leave them to the safe care of the maternal embrace, and otherwise to life's vagaries. That is God's will, and He will provide, is the stock attitude.

The ineffectual intervention of the man shows the drawbacks of being a husband by turns, and a father only for its competitive bragging value. Children make their way in that world by weaving and dodging among complex patterns of maternal assurance; cultivating paternal respect, where respect functions as avoidance, concession, polite distance, and submission; ingratiating with the co-wives; negotiating a system of give-and-take with siblings; deferring to in-laws, and to aunts and uncles; and observing the rules of seniority toward elders. At first the child learns to curry favor and to appease, but in the end the child learns primary rules of attachment and allegiance in a system fashioned to pay handsome dividends just to be and to belong.

It does not take more than common sense — and a twinge of self-preservation — to calculate that if you forgo your portion of the meat and rice you will win the favor of a restful night's sleep, and that is worth the price of going hungry. Similarly, a co-wife's goodwill is worth seeking in spite of the smudging of the lines of domestic truce and earning the displeasure of a maternal brother or sister. You can make it up to a maternal sibling eventually, whereas you can't risk provoking the ill-will of a paternal sibling. It is even worth pleading with your mother or with a disgruntled aunt to concede a dispute for the sake of domestic peace. I learned that in a crowded household, what counted was not the frequency of quarrels and disputes as much as the frequency of letting go, of letting sleeping dogs lie. A short memory never fails you. Otherwise, relationships could be a catalogue only of bad memories stoking the motive for getting even, which in turn piles up more bad memories, and so on. It is a recipe for inter-generational cold war.

Of course, the relationships of my childhood were more than just a series of uneasy truces. Celebration, enjoyment, humor, games, music, and dancing all featured prominently in community life. Playmates excelled in all sorts of ways, whether it was carving, building simple bamboo toys, making frescoes, playing the fiddle, building a telephone line with two cups and a connecting wire, sewing rags together into a ball for tennis, tying the four corners of a handkerchief to make a cap, or making drums with the skins of animals killed in religious and communal festivals. Women fashioned woven fabrics with patterned colors made with local vegetable dyes. Songs were composed to celebrate special occasions.

My first taste of marshmallows (heaven forgive my excitement) was a highlight of my childhood. The soft wool-like texture fascinated me, and when I tried to squeeze it the fluffy sweetness coated my fingers all over, which I licked before munching on the marshmallow itself. Marshmallows were a scarce commodity in my day, and their scarcity made them the object of street fights. Chocolates were also a contested sweet, but I enjoyed them less because they made me queasy. My favorite fruits included mangoes, custard apples, guavas, oranges, and bananas. I loved roasted peanuts and fried bean cakes. Garlic, sorrel *(kucha),* and okra *(kanjo)* I detested. Garlic simply smothered all other flavors with its own pungent power; fortunately, it was too expensive for everyday liberal use — onions were a handy alternative. The sour sorrel set my teeth on edge, while the runny okra gave me the equivalent of gastronomic goose bumps. When Mother cooked them, I would look for an excuse to go and eat at Grandmother's. I remember protesting loudly when I had to eat either — the words themselves made me recoil. Except that it is sour, sorrel is like spinach, and is reputed to have the same value. It was the favorite food of my royal forebears, though they never passed the gene to me. With Grandmother echoing her, Mother insisted on the health value of eating vegetables, and here garlic, sorrel, and okra erased the boundary between eating food and eating medicine. The sorrel flower is sun-dried and boiled to make a refreshing pink lemonade-like drink called *wonjo*. That I really liked, especially when sweetened with wild honey.

A favorite pastime was watching the goldsmith at work at his foundry. The way he worked the bellows to fire the foundry; how he gripped the precious metal with slim metal tongs before putting it in a dish and plunging it into the blazing flames, his face aglow in the dancing waves of flames — all that held me entranced for hours on end. From the blue flames flowed the precious liquid that at once turned into patterns and forms too wonderful for words. It was magic. At the end the smith produced gold trinkets of different shapes and sizes, from the finest filigree-braided bracelets and rings to fluted pendants to exfoliated, conch-shaped ear-rings that are worn through the lobes on suspended strings to carry their weight. Appropriately, tradition ascribed a magical reputation to goldsmiths who used to be purveyors to kings and princes. The town was a transit point for gold and silver that still trickled through in my youth.

Smithing *(numuya)* is the occupation of people belonging to the *nyamakala* caste, with its own system of status and prestige. Gold and silversmiths lead the guild, while cobblers and leatherworkers are at the bottom of the ladder. Similarly, music is a caste occupation, with *kora* and *balafong* players considered as the elites, and drummers and others below them. The *kora* is a twenty-one-string instrument that is a cross between a harp and a lute, while the *balafong* is the African xylophone. The *kora* is the older of the two, but both instruments, constructed without metal parts, have their origin in ancient Mali. It is there that the *jeli* bards, the poet-raconteurs of Manding princely families, have their origin. The *jelis* are described as the troubadours of cherished valor by Djibril Tamsir Niane in his famous account, *Sundiata: An Epic of Mali.* With its roots in the sixteenth-century Kaabou Empire, a successor state of the Mali Empire, the *nyancho* Sanneh royal lineage has an established musical line maintained by practitioners of the art. For some three hundred years the Sanneh royal lineage were the rulers of Kaabou and the patrons of custom and tradition, including music. Their fall from power is memorialized in legend and music. The classical repertoire includes

Kelefa, a song about the late imperial hero, *Janke Waali,* named for Kelefa Sanneh's general and vizier, and *Tcheddo,* the signature theme of the Sanneh lineage. Thanks to the global music industry, the music of Manding is widely available, with versions by such well-established names as Basirou Kouyate, Toumani Diabate, Sunjulu Cissoko and his wife, MaHawa Kuyate, Jeli Nyama Suso, and Jeli Fode Musa Suso.

Yet in our family, much of this musical tradition remained on the margins. The secular roots of the music offended my father's religious sensibilities. His own father and older brother were professional clerics. Father's grandfather, Malik, who converted as a consequence of the jihads that achieved the end of imperial Kaabou, was the first Muslim of the family. Yet Father's mother, Nnamunta Jebate, was adopted by one of the country's leading musical families, Banna and Dembo Kanute, who were masters of the *balafong.* Prominent women musicians like Nano Sakiliba grew up in my paternal grandmother's neighborhood. Nevertheless, Father would not allow the *jeli* into the household. His wishes were ignored on the occasions of naming ceremonies, when the women invited the *jeli* to participate. And we would slip away to attend musical exhibitions the bards led in neighboring compounds.

By its nature, *kora* and *balafong* music is chamber music, unlike drumming. For that reason, *kora* and *balafong* music looks to patrons of established households for sponsorship. The concert hall venue and the campus audiences of American vintage are relatively new and artificial, for they cannot replace the role of individual patronage; in fact, they risk creating the mistaken impression that the music is fair game for study and practice by people outside the guild of traditional musicians. I remember my shock at seeing a CD of a *kora*-toting European woman, and feeling that only supreme cultural ignorance or willfulness could make someone commit such a blunder. Women led in music, but never as *kora* players. As a family tradition, *jeliya* has its assigned place in creation, and is not simply a whimsical art form. In the song that is an ode to music, for instance, the *jelis* speak of *jeliya* and *mansaya,* rulership, as sharing sanctity because God created them together: *allah meng ye mansaya da, wole nata jeliya da.* The ode is at the same time a claim to royal favor.

Father's strictures against the music were consonant with the standing stigma of the mosque. Even though they are Muslims, and even though their music is liberally sprinkled with Qur'anic Arabic phrases, the musicians are forbidden to carry their music into the mosque. Even the extramural activities surrounding the observance of the *mawlid* birthday celebrations of the prophet are forbidden territory, violated only from ignorance. The musicians maintain their Muslim reputation by observing the canonical obligations, including the pilgrimage to Mecca, as the price for saving their art from complete cultural quarantine. Along with that has come a certain stigma on the *jeli* performers, who are decried as beggars and parasites, and are resented as such. For that reason, except on occasions of marriage and naming ceremonies, people give the *jeli* a wide berth in the ordinary course of business. Islam is both the *jelis'* safety net and their trap. Their compounds, called *jelikunda,* are separated from those of free families, and intermarriage with members of free families is considered taboo. But the *jelis* are not a slave caste.

In my childhood I did not understand such crossed signals, but later I thought that one way forward for the tradition would be to break it open and to let the musical art stand alone without the shibboleths of caste separation, pedigree, and patronage. On the other hand, as the Guinean writer Djibril Tamsir Niane contends in his account, society depends for its memory and self-understanding on the *jeliya* tradition, and without that a rich heritage risks being diminished along with a great musical art. The need for patronage, and for the safeguard of Islam, in that combination, has revealed the nature and scale of the challenge *jeliya* faces, as well as the acute cultural options confronting the Manding heritage.[2] Our family put little faith in that heritage, preferring instead to range itself on the side of Islam. Still, in moments of cultural flashback I would sneak away from home to attend performances. My parents could always tell from my face what I had been up to, and I thought that was because they had extra-sensory perception. Innocence is a child's alibi.

2. A major international conference and festival held at the School of Oriental and African Studies in the University of London in 1972, with exhibitions at the British Museum, examined aspects of the Manding heritage, and resulted, among other things, in the creation of the Mande Studies Group within the African Studies Association of the United States. Penguin published the epic of Sunjata by Bamba Suso and Banna Kanute as *Sunjata* in 1999. It was based on the SOAS version first published in 1974.

Father once fell out with my stepmother, and threatened to throw her out of the compound, which was her worst nightmare. I volunteered impishly to follow her into exile, scarcely knowing what I was thinking. I can only put it down to an early intimation of my pacifist inclination, but whatever it was I must have been relieved when the threat didn't materialize. My stepmother recalled it many years later when I visited her with my wife and children — I had totally forgotten the incident. She told her daughter, who had not been born at the time, that it showed how much I loved her, little suspecting that I probably did it more in panic than in love. Her memory had grown more generous with the years, bless her, inclining her to fancy me as a child throwing down a welcome gauntlet in her defense. It's the kind of grandstanding childish innocence would encourage, unaware of the foolhardy risks. A piece of folkloric wisdom says that those children who want to wear adult trousers must tie them at their throats. The outsize discomfort of it all and the pang of self-preservation explain why it fled my mind. Society teaches that filial disobedience is a character defect, and carries the stigma of *danka,* the Kafkaesque ill-fortune that haunts and tracks you in every subsequent venture. Only the threat being promptly withdrawn saved me from that fate.

My younger half-sister, who called herself Maïe, picked up her own gauntlet and forced my now flat-footed father to pawn to her his embroidered tribal gown, a family heirloom. Many years later, long after I had been handed a life raft in the form of my government scholarship to Armitage High School, and long after my father had died, Maïe offered me the gown. I was surprised and confused. What happened after all these many years? What was the bargain with my father? How long ago was it? Who else knew? Why hadn't she sold it if money was the issue? Had anyone declined before me? How much baggage was the gown carrying by this time? The family seemed to be running away from it; was that a warning? I thought long and hard. Clearly, the garment should remain in the family, but it had obviously acquired the aspect of a haunting nemesis. I finally declined. I would look and feel odd in it, I thought, but I must confess that I thought it might jinx me. Fingers would point, eyes stare, and tongues wag. I still do not know who cast lots for that last family exhibit and took possession of it. Perhaps it's best not to know.

As for Maïe — God rest her soul — she died prematurely in her fifties. She was not too ill at the time I came on the scene and offered help, but she refused medical treatment, and her condition eventually took a turn for the worse. She refused medical treatment not for religious reasons; it was simply because of her insistence that it is unnatural to recoil at the prospect of death and to pretend that it would never happen. She had *nyanchoya,* the proverbial code of fearlessness the Sanneh clan reputedly personified — code that somebody neglected to pass on to me. I was informed that her illness was aggravated by malaria that she later contracted. She never recovered.

Maïe's loss much grieved family and friends, for, in spite of all her quirks, she was tireless in maintaining contact with all and sundry. In an odd way, she was a staunch defender of the old pre-Islamic tradition, including drumming performances in which the women dominated as singers and dancers. She told me with pride her efforts in that cause, saying she and another woman, Tida, had organized many memorable performances in Georgetown in defiance of religious objections, objections that led finally to the demise of drumming there. "The men are too timid to stand up for the old order," she declared defiantly. "Without women the world would end on a whimper." I grinned weakly in response; I was no match.

Maïe chided me often, saying the West had made me successful, but only superficially. She pleaded with me to hold up my end of tradition by taking many wives, or at least by fathering many more children. I was being brainwashed, she insisted, to wait for Cupid's arrow to stab me before asking for a quiver full of children. When I replied that life in America ruled out such calculations, she responded somewhat dismissively, "I am talking about the eternal law. Even America cannot defy the law of reproduction, which is God's will." How could I make the unnatural natural? It did not matter to her that she had never been to America; neither, it occurred to me, would it have mattered to the ancient scribe who wrote, "Your wife will be like a fruitful vine within your house; your children will be like olive shoots around your table" (Ps. 128:3). Maïe finally gave up on me, thanks in large part to the huge distance, physical and cultural, between us. She was, however, always warm and kind to my wife and children. With her gone, the family fabric simply shrank and looked worn out. Her death made me feel lonely, even when I was not alone.

CHAPTER 3

Second Wind

❀   ❀   ❀

I do not remember being a fast runner as a child, although like most others I could manage a burst of speed when fleeing a bully or when offered an incentive like a marshmallow. I slipped away often to be with boys my age. With the bush full of all sorts of unexplored nooks and crannies, and with abundant wild fruit in season, I joined playmates in adventure seeking. A pack of monkeys on the prowl for fruit and nuts would often beat us to it, but we learned their feeding habits so we could hit the bush trail before they got going. Timing was crucial, and so we had to be careful not to let our innocent enthusiasm get in the way of smart planning. The monkeys being clever and unpredictable meant that we never knew where they might suddenly turn up, which added extra excitement to our outings.

The thrill of going in pursuit of monkeys would get us so excited that we would giggle ourselves stiff, staggering and falling to the ground, unable to help ourselves for the amusement of it. We learned that monkeys are social animals, travel in packs, use scouts to scan the field and sound the alarm when necessary, and fake an attack just to gauge or avert potential danger. Monkeys tend to band together, and even when taken by surprise they do not scatter helter-skelter, lest they expose one of their members to danger. We never came across a lone monkey in all the time we started tracking them; we had better, we thought, learn to stick together, too. Female monkeys carried their babies on their backs and hung them from their stomachs, with the males flanking and covering their rear for protection. They are born tree-climbers, and use the branches for excellent camouflage. That taught us never to loiter under the trees, in case they were ensconced up there. In what seemed like a game, monkeys would waylay us and stage a mock attack, halting and retreating after scampering after us for a short distance.

The bush abounded in snakes, too, but thankfully they got out of the way when they sensed us coming. Pythons and other big constrictors we seldom saw in the open. We heard reports occasionally that they had attacked a lamb or young goat, but that was too rare to deter us from going to the bush. We heard of pythons strangling calves, but attentive cowherds minimized such incidents. There would be great excitement anytime we saw a snake. Kekuta, my neighborhood playmate, who had a knack for imitating animals and creatures of all kinds, would close his eyes and make a wavy motion with his hands, with his palm open and raised to simulate the movement of a slithering snake, accompanied with a rising hissing sound. His eyes would suddenly open wide to signal the snake coming into view, at which point we would jump and scream, acting as if we had had a close brush with the dreaded reptile. I remember the awe of meeting a man who said he once fought with a python after the snake attacked him. My eyes popped as he described how after the python struck, coiled, and bit him, he bit the python back and twisted its tail. The python then uncoiled, at which point, instead of making a dash for it, as I would have, he recovered his machete and cut off the python's head. He skinned the snake and took the skin home as a trophy. That was hard to imagine, and so I watched closely for signs of embellishment. A walking legend, the man was the bodyguard of the senior chief of Fulladu, Cherno Kadeh Bandeh. A descendant of the chief some fifty years later married my brother Musa.

The person we regarded as the real master of mysteries was the Qur'an school teacher whom we called Cherno, the Fula term for cleric/teacher. He was trained by Fulbe masters in Futa Jallon, Guinea, the home of a centuries-long distinguished tradition of Islamic learning. Soon after the end of World War II, Cherno was chartered by the town to establish a school of Qur'anic instruction. For his services, the town paid and maintained him and his wife. As far as I can remember, he had no children of his own.

Cherno sported a pretty formidable reputation, adding to his mystical command of the sacred language the stern profile of a disciplinarian. For him, teaching was not a child-friendly craft. At first we were thrilled when at age five our parents enrolled us in the Qur'an school. We felt proud to be admitted to the inner circle of apprentices of the oracle of revelation. It is hard to put into words what that feeling meant. But at the same time we were afraid of him because of the certain prospect of being at the receiving end of the cane. As he wielded his cane menacingly, Cherno described us as God's mud walls. We knew exactly what he meant. We were made of inferior material and erected on shallow foundations, and since we were God's, and since he was the master of God's word, it was his to attend to us with the craftsman's devotion to structure and detail. With divine prompting, Cherno applied the cane to align us and to dig the foundations deeper. "Draw near, you rough clod, so I can chisel off a few more protruding bulges and angles from God's mud wall," he would thunder as he cracked the whip over and over again. Our parents approved of such harsh treatment because it conveyed the seriousness of learning God's word. But I secretly longed for the lessons to be over so I could go and play.

The attitude of our parents made it easy for Cherno to treat us as his minions. The Qur'an school was asylum from the world, and everything Cherno said and did there was beyond reproach. The testimony of holy scripture was his anointing and standing alibi. Accordingly, Cherno acted the part expected of him, prowling the grounds of the Qur'an school as master of all that he surveyed. His power unquestioned, he set out in pursuit of laggards and mumblers. For him both were guilty: laggards for inattentiveness, and mumblers for mangling the tones of the holy text. The mighty cane would make them answer to the Almighty. And so Cherno resumed the chiseling and smoothing and the thundering, as the offending children groveled in the dust, twitching, sobbing, and whimpering. Through their tears the children stuttered and stumbled as they groped for the words on their slates, careful not to smudge them with their tears. Cherno would make them pay for that, too. We could point to the text on the slate only with the right index finger. God favored the right hand, and woe to anyone who offered the left hand, even in compliment. If you were left-handed, as I was, your left index finger got smacked often enough to make you switch hands before you lost a joint and any merit from the holy exercise. I still bristle instinctively when people remark on my being left-handed, so fresh is the memory of the time when the cane was not far behind that observation. To claim that God made us like that was a useless argument. God made everything without making everything morally equal, as is evident to common sense.

The attitude that language was sacred and absolute made the Qur'an school a special experience. Knowing that the mother tongue was not fit for faith and worship, we had no esteem for the vernacular. We looked on it as a native leftover, rather than as a rock of ages. Even the little we understood made us realize that Arabic was special; that the words had a holy reputation and a sacred personality; that they never changed or aged; that we suffered for offending against them, for soiling them, and for tripping over them. We stood condemned for failing to master the sacred word, but were amply rewarded for memorizing the tone and sound. We didn't need any complicated doctrine to inscribe that view into our childish psyches. Parents, elders, distinguished visitors, pilgrims, and traders — all of them concurred with the view that learning the Qur'an justified subjecting children to the strictest discipline, and Cherno was ready to play his part. Practicing and performing the word of God raised it above the ordinary and mundane. Memorization, syllable for syllable, tone for tone, blocked any extraneous influence. In service to the word, Cherno was quick to anger and slow to be pleased. When he set out to praise a child's success he would halt in his prowl and pivot effortlessly, his favorite cane mounted across his shoulder, as he communed with himself in a tone half assuaging and half menacing: *al-hamdu li-llahi subhana-hu wa ta'la,* "thanks and praise to God the Exalted." No one but God deserves perfect, fulsome praise — certainly not a clump of mud wall. A translucent calmness suffused Cherno's face as he rocked and turned like a dervish. For a moment his edginess dissipated into calm serenity, making religion feel out of this world.

In principle and practice Cherno never looked us in the eye, except when he was about to come down on us like a ton of bricks. His was a singular temperament: no frivolous stories, no games, no gossip, no sense of humor, no smile ever, no expressions of emotion, no socializing. Cherno was so quiet in his movements that you didn't notice him until he was breathing down your neck, bearer of the limp words of the heavenly tablet. He was not a child's friend, yet only a childlike trust could endure such draconian mentoring. Surely, the walls of God's truth would not tumble because the untrained tongue or the disfavored left hand got involved, I would muse aimlessly. But I covered the odds by taking my chances in both hands: I learned to be ambidextrous in school.

The Western school that arrived three years later presented Cherno with an unwelcome dilemma. He kept a disdainful distance from the school, but he didn't stop us from enrolling there as long as we continued at the Qur'an school. He was concerned, but felt that the Qur'an school would overcome the moral corrosion of the Western school, that revealed truth would win in the end. "At the Western school they teach you the infidel tongue," he would sneer, "so that men may speak without speaking the truth. Arabic is fragranced with the musk of paradise, and is fit to bear truth; heathen dialects smell merely of the inkhorn, may God shield us." His scorn masked a real fear of losing competitive advantage, but Cherno never blew his top; he remained, instead, the impeccable avatar of sangfroid. We divided the day between the two schools, with late afternoons, evenings, and weekends reserved for the Qur'an school.

Our Muslim town had long resisted Western schools as a cesspool of infidel corruption. "School bewitches children and feeds them with the illusion that self is supreme. School makes you big-headed so you think you don't need God or tradition. Look at what so-called civilized schooling has done to civil servants and off-duty policemen who smoke joints and have loose morals," Father would say with rising disdain. "Religion must rout infidel delusion!" I didn't find that view entirely persuasive, because I knew that the civil servants and off-duty policemen did not let religion stand in the way of their corruption; telling children that it was because of infidel delusion made no difference whatsoever.

I do not remember my mother offering any opinions on schools and civilization, except her jovial comment that pretty soon we would be speaking the white man's language and leaving her out of it. What I did observe, though, was Mother's anxiety that her children succeed in life and her hope that they be spared the wiles of the Enemy, *jawo*. I do not pray that you will be spared *jawo*, she would say, but may *jawo's* satisfaction never be granted. (The sentiment is echoed in John 17:15, where Jesus pleads to God on behalf of his disciples: "I do not pray that thou shouldst take them out of the world, but that thou shouldst keep them from the evil one.") In her view, the moral imperative was too self-evident to be flouted with impunity; no one was exempt. You cannot sit on your hands and expect reward, or value it. She said that no effort went unrewarded. I would steal a look at her callous hands and wonder what had happened to her reward. "My children are my reward," she assured us, her words breathing with maternal pride. That made an impression on us, though any evidence that we were valuable remained for now only in the eye of the beholder. Mother let us entertain ourselves and trusted in whatever break came her way — of which there was not much, to judge by those calloused hands.

As Cherno well knew, the contrast with the Qur'an school could not be greater. Lessons were organized and phased in set periods, with a mid-morning break for physical exercise. Classrooms were partitioned, and the children arranged more or less by age, with tests and exams to determine placement. The classroom had a blackboard and boxes of chalk, with a wooden stick for pointing to things, not for beating us. We had copy books and pencils to write with, and chairs and desks. The purpose of learning was to acquire critical skills and to develop our understanding. We had nothing like that at the Qur'an school. It was thrilling.

We had no way, however, of replicating the classroom at home, which was pretty sparse and lean: no desk to work from, no chairs, no light, no place for books or papers, and often little food for strength. Homework was done in any available corner of the yard before sunset, dodging and eluding the sharp elbows of jealous siblings, and then tucking away the copy book under the mattress on your side of the shared bed to guard it. Thriving at school requires a corresponding supporting home environment, which in our case was assuming too much. As the first generation of my family to go to Western school, I had to guard my few opportunities.

Going to school often on a near-empty stomach, we came back to scraps of food like boiled rice, porridge, or mashed pumpkin. In lean times Mother foraged for food and pawned her jewelry for rice, with the thought of us being happy at school fueling her forays. With our heads full of thoughts of school, we could avoid noticing Mother having to scramble to make ends meet. When possible, we stayed late at school to do our homework. We would linger on the school grounds even after school closed, so mesmerizing was the idea of gaining an education, and one day being able to work and earn money to repay our parents. With great anticipation, our mothers watched as we laboriously assembled the letters of the alphabet to form words, then took the words to form sentences, then used the sentences to express an idea that could be translated back to them. They would hum and beam with pride just to see the transformation with their own eyes. God willing, they would share in the spoils of their children's achievement.

With that domestic backup, we threw ourselves with gusto into life at school. The nursery rhymes we learned charged us up pretty well. At the end of the lessons we bounded out of school, singing all the way home to impress our parents, as well as for our own amusement. Singing nursery rhymes was new and thrilling; it added palpable excitement to school experience. Our least favorite time was when school closed for the holidays. We counted the days before school opened again, and in the meantime returned to the school grounds to play games. We signed up for private tutorials with anyone willing to take us on. The teachers we regarded like magicians of knowledge, like *jinnis* of the mind. It was becoming impossible to imagine life without school, not only for us but also for our mothers, who for their own reasons saw school as welcome diversion from the grinding monotony of life on a shoestring. School made their foraging for food all that much more worthwhile.

Of course, school wasn't our only fun. Not having playgrounds or arcades for fun and games, we looked for various pastimes to fill up the rest of the day. The open river within walking distance was a standing invitation, and boys accepted it with reckless abandon, dodging crocodiles and hippos to compete by swimming to the opposite bank. Our parents knew the risks, of course, and they strongly disapproved, paddling us whenever found out. Yet we couldn't help it. Like the bush, the river was too mesmerizing and too close to ignore.

In the rainy season, when the crocodiles and hippos proliferated, we kept our distance — most of the time. The thrill of flirting with danger sometimes overcame the fear of crocodiles and paddles. We would sit on the river bank biding our time. At a moment's notice we braved danger and took a plunge before making a quick exit from the water, shaking all over with excitement. In the dry season, when the river was calmer and the waters less murky, we threw caution to the winds and congregated at the river bank. Before long we would be splashing in the water, submerging and surfacing abruptly to surprise an inattentive swimmer. The bigger boys would dare the younger ones to follow them out, but without a lifeguard, to swim beyond our range was foolhardy. Everyone knew that a mishap would cause the adults to ban all access to the river, and so we took care not to court that. Someone sold us on the idea that when we recited designated verses of the Qur'an over pieces of pebble and cast them into the river, the verses had power to muzzle crocodiles. So we would mumble the sacred words over the pebbles and then throw them as far out as possible, the distance being our margin of safety. It removed all fear of being eaten alive by crocodiles, letting us spend a long time in the water. I was a reasonable swimmer with stamina, but I was not an "amphibian," which was what we called good divers. Even today, swimming and beachcombing hold a special magic for me.

One unfortunate incident attracted the attention of our parents. It was a day of wonderful swimming. The tide had come in and crested, and the river looked inviting, with small waves breaking all over the surface. An unusual number of boys had gathered on the bank before taking to the waters. There was a lot of excitement in the shallows where some of the swimmers were, with the usual splashing and screams that one would expect from excitable boys. We observed some of the bigger boys striking out into the deep, content to watch them from our safe vantage point. Then we resumed our swimming, racing each other round the jetty, with bigger boys calling out to us, daring us to follow them out. One of them swam back to us and grabbed a smaller boy and pulled him further out with him. The boy kicked and screamed trying to resist, but was overpowered and dragged further out. He disappeared briefly before he emerged gagging and sputtering, pleading to be let go. He was frantic and threw his arms around helplessly, his cry for help interrupted by the mouthfuls of water he was taking in. There was panic among the other boys, who called for intervention to save the lad. There was a moment when the victim felt his strength weakening and feared that he wouldn't make it. He had not taken in enough water to go down, but he was clearly having trouble staying afloat. Before he passed out the bully let him go, and the other boys came to his rescue and pulled him to safety as he coughed and sputtered and cried.

We knew the attacker, but not his motive. Upset, the normally placid mother of the victim promptly fired off a complaint to the bully's parents. That ended any friendly relations between the two families, and also reminded us boys of the perils of socializing out of our league. The incident sowed distrust, and we learned to keep a safe distance from the bully. Bigger boys had the natural advantages of age and size; bullies went the extra step by adding menace to their arsenal. It made us see the world in primary colors without shades of uncertainty and ambivalence. In that world, smaller children were easy punching bags. We were expected to internalize that lesson and apply it to those down the pecking order. I couldn't imagine it would be any more fun for them.

Sometimes the pranks were good-humored and harmless. On April Fools' Day, the older boys had us running in circles on a fool's errand of carrying messages. Out of breath, we would return frustrated because nobody had a clue what we were talking about. Oh, the older boys would announce with glee, didn't we know it was April Fools' Day? We would swear never to be caught again, but to little effect. One time, however, we were forewarned, and when someone tried to pull a trick on us we pretended to fall for it just so we could turn the tables. It was exhilarating finally to fool rather than be fooled, and it made us eager for more victims of our own.

The April Fool jokes slipped in with the Western calendar, as did Christmas and New Year's Day, both of which we celebrated as secular festivals. Christmas was an opportunity to make money by adopting traders and civil servants as patrons of the paper lanterns we made. With lit candles safely placed inside the lanterns, and accompanied by drumming and singing, we made the round of village homes at night. We concluded the week of celebrations on New Year's Day when we delivered the lanterns to our patrons, receiving a cash gift in return. We also celebrated Muslim festivals by knocking on the doors of Muslim homes and offering prayers for money or for gifts in kind. We were supposed to turn in the money to our parents, but all too often gifts in kind ended up as personal hoards.

Muslim festivals are based on the lunar cycle, which is shorter than the solar calendar. Muslim festivals came upon us earlier each solar year. In a given year the pilgrimage festival might coincide with Christmas, and that would double the fun and excitement without the risk of conflation. When Ramadan and Christmas converged, however, it placed a damp squib on Christmas, and in time the calendrical conflict sharpened the contrast with Western values, and also with the customary practices. Along with the old New Year's rite (in Mandinka, *musukoroni salo*, or *musukoto salo*), Christmas has now virtually died out in Georgetown as Islam has taken over the feast cycle.

With time the Muslim religious calendar came to dominate much of our social life, with Ramadan a particularly potent rite that set the community on edge because of the accompanying month-long ban on all forms of entertainment. A public celebration is held during Ramadan on the night of the twenty-seventh day, called *laylatu-l-qadar,* the Night of Power, which the Qur'an celebrates as *khayrun min alf shahrin,* "better than a thousand months," because it is believed to be the night when the Qur'an was revealed to the prophet. *Laylatu-l-qadar* is Islam's version of the feast of unleavened bread, called locally *nán mburu.* We made the round of homes begging for charity that took the form of balls of pounded, sweetened grain that had no commercial value whatsoever, and without refrigeration had a short shelf life. Instead, their value lay in the *barakah* (blessings) they would bring to givers and receivers alike — though it was hard for hungry children to think of abstract *barakah* as the real motivation for hitting the begging trail all night. The next stage was the all-night vigil of Qur'an recitation *(tartíl).* We went to these vigils enthusiastically but unrealistically. We slept through most of the exercises, leaving us wondering about how much merit we earned there compared to begging for food.

As a small-town religious culture didn't give us too many options, we looked for excitement in other directions. Alcohol and girls were out of bounds, and we were too inhibited to challenge the rule. Marijuana was around, and we knew about it because it was the drug of choice for civil servants and policemen. But it was not a draw for youngsters. In folklore, marijuana was a drug of ill-repute; it had no intrinsic value and was devoid of blessing. The devil used the drug to lead astray. As proof, we noticed how the fumes made us sick. Even today I find the smell nauseating. Still, curiosity made us watch as the adults rolled leaves in thin paper into a joint and lit it; only then did we abandon the room. Afterward we could see the dramatic effect on the smokers, a happy mood oscillating freely between lassitude and loquacious bonhomie. Yet it was the kind of spacey friendliness that impressed us enough to make us want to look for an alternative way to get high behind our parents' backs.

We tried gasoline as a liquid substitute, inserting a piece of rag in the fuel tank of a vehicle and inhaling deeply from it. Within minutes we were walking on air. Egged on by more experienced boys, I tried it, only to find myself sputtering and coughing and sneezing as the gas and whatever else was in the filthy wet rag sailed up my windpipe. My eyes felt on fire. When finally I got the hang of it, it was difficult to say which was worse: the burning throat and itchy eyes from all the coughing the first time, or the mood of disembodied enhancement and the throbbing headache the second time. I knew then what parents meant about marijuana as the devil's weed of choice to trip the innocent. Enough of that experience, I thought. As children we associated no religious meaning with the feeling: the experience led to no epiphany, no moral insight, no ethical awakening, no discovery of hidden powers of the mind. It was mischief for mischief's sake, pure and simple. Being high was strangely arid and transitory, with images and shadows silently flitting up and down and in and out. It could not be God's will that we should be enticed and let down all at once. We merely set ourselves a-tingle with ephemeral excitement, the secrecy of it adding a euphoric mystique.

Smoking cigarettes was an entirely different matter, though it never quite caught on with me, either. My father smoked quite a bit, and got himself into debt for the habit. I became fairly certain he was addicted when I came to understand what addiction is. If necessary, he would pawn a valuable possession to get cigarettes, and the anxiety of going without made him very moody. I would run errands for him to neighborhood convenience stores with a request for a loan of cigarettes to be paid at month's end — if even then. Many times the store owners would refuse because of a pattern of non-payment. I would feel disappointed for Father's sake, and embarrassed at the cost to the family's reputation. The experience contributed to my strong dislike of indebtedness; I would live within my means when I grew up, I would tell myself. At any rate, it was in this environment of filial susceptibility that my brothers and I started to smoke. Little by little I could light up and inhale without sputtering and coughing. I found the smell of tobacco nauseating, but I was duly persuaded that with practice the sensation would go away. We tried to neutralize the smell by chewing on the leaf of the lime tree and rubbing our fingers with it. That gave us the illusion that we could hide the odor from disapproving adults, who insisted that smoking would stunt our development. It was an expensive habit, too, as I saw with my father. Besides, the school banned smoking, making us fear being punished if caught. Since I was interested in neither adult disapproval nor punishment, disliked the tobacco smell, had no money, the charms of smoking did not prevail.

Shortage of money became a much more serious affair in the years when the crops failed, usually from drought. I recall one year in the early 1950s when we faced the threat of mass hunger — the path leading to the abyss. I was eight years old. Facing the hard choice between starving the children now and risking a future without a new crop to harvest, the women raided the seed-corn to feed the children. They looked for a compromise, if you can call it that, eating half the seed-corn and half-starving, waiting for the first rains before committing the other half to the ground. That year the first rains came late, by which time the planted seeds had turned to dust. When the heavens finally opened, rain drenched the fields and suffocated the remaining seeds waiting to sprout. The point of no return was the month of August, the median point between sowing and harvest. August packs a fearful punch for cultivators caught in a drought. By then rain only compounds the problem, with the blazing sun scorching every sign of life in nature. The dry months of October and beyond would be months of scandalous scarcity, and everyone knew it.

Hunger ruthlessly dispenses with polite ceremony, even though habit leaves people observing the rules. Mother would pick up her hoe and head for her fields. I would sometimes trot along behind her, partly out of curiosity and partly because of my innocent eagerness to be where the action was — in this case where Mother was. The field had turned dry from the drought, and Mother's energetic strikes with the hoe caused fragments of hard clay to fly in the air and bounce against her shin, her back arched, her face etched with streaks of perspiration. She was pre-paring to sow the small reserve of seed-corn she had saved, but wasn't sure the gamble would pay off. After working a couple of rows she took rest in the scanty shade of the surrounding trees. She would stare into the distance looking for an answer. "I know this is the will of God, but maybe God will relent just one time and send us rain," she would mutter to herself, almost as if I wasn't there. The hope kept her looking to the skies for the rain that would not come. She prayed that something would materialize out of the thin clouds. She would stay active in the hope of a miracle, and that hope constrained her to continue to till her field even if the outcome looked bleak. Her efforts might humor the powers of nature into relenting for once. The reward of hope is hope itself — and that never fails.

Meanwhile, waiting back in the house were hungry children, all on short fuses. But children cry only if they think the situation they are in is intolerable and can be changed. With its unrelenting grip, hunger has a way of stanching tears and draining emotions. We would fuss and fidget and be cantankerous, but we were too weak to carry on being a nuisance. Our mothers could forget about trying to keep us in line and focus on the more urgent business of keeping us alive.

If for adults August was the month of scandal, for children it was the grim daily reality of having to go without food. Adults measure time by ample, leisurely units: the annual cycle, the seasonal calendar, the phases of the moon, and the weekly routine. But such computations are much too abstract for children because they lack any narrative immedi-

48

acy. Rather, what kept us awake even more was the grinding question night after night: what have we done to deserve this affliction? We were reduced to imagining the sleep we could not have, so we laid still and twitched and turned and waited — for nothing in particular. The night air hangs heavy when there is little to fill or to defy it; an empty stomach is easy foil for empty thoughts. In vain we shut our eyes to keep away thoughts of food. At least with shut eyes we could feign the relief of sleep. But in the darkness of night we would see images and shapes with an intensity of vividness that, for all its loudness, the daylight spared us. Night was no refuge from hunger; vacant thoughts bounced and reverberated in it with a deafening echo. The insects and bugs marauded in the intervals of bedtime insomnia. And the prospects of morning without breakfast left us coiled up in bed, a bundle of despondent resignation. O that fate would whisk us away and spare us the indignity of living empty like this! O death, where is thy swift angel? Thoughts, not dreams, tormented us in the night.

We dragged ourselves out of bed in the morning and crumpled on the floor, looking pleadingly into each other's eyes. What stones had we left unturned? Were we not at this same point yesterday, and the day before yesterday? When it concerns the fundamental questions of life, communication is remarkably economical, often free of words. We knew where each one had been and was headed. A tight-fisted God had reduced us to the wretched of the earth, first making us dependent on the natural cycle, and then leaving us withering in the heat. Hunger discriminates not at all between men and women, adults and children — or, for that matter, between day and night. The same issues of life and death beset the hungry, the same grey monotony, the same blank indifference, and the same fate should the famine persist. Being related here meant hanging by the same slender thread, and Mother was the hook holding us up.

By its unrelenting nature, hunger numbed us to pain. We wilted slowly. We knew the world around us was changing when siblings annoyed one another without setting off temper tantrums. We were irritable, but without the fuel to stoke a fight. Also, there were fewer errands to run, and so fewer demands to test us. Hunger has a way of taking the edge off gripes and grievances with sheer fatigue. But misery loves company. The insects smelled an easy kill; for the mosquitoes we were twice the feast for the bite, too feeble to parry them and too numb to feel their bite until after the fact. The annoyance of it would paralyze us and leave us at the mercy of the pestering insects. It was hard to know where to turn for relief. Mother chewed kola nuts, a stimulant, to mask her hunger and give us hope. Her headscarf she tied tightly into a headband to block any headache. Thus suited for battle against forces seen and unseen, she would go days without food. We feared for her, and she for us.

I should describe eating in the depths of hunger. You discover that the appetite is tied to emotion. As the hungry season grinds on, hunger dims the appetite and disables the mealtime alert that normally sparks the taste buds. I read somewhere that taste buds die every ten days or so and have to be replaced to maintain the appetite. Chronic hunger interferes with that renewal cycle, leaving your body victim to a slow, debilitating decline. You don't go up in a flare; you simply fade by imperceptible shades of gray until darkness swallows you completely. The stomach shrinks with dwindling food reserves and the disappearing options. You lose weight gradually, so that even in your weakening state you can muster enough energy to hang around, but you never expend any more precious energy than you have to.

In time, a relief barge was sent from Bathurst. Mother boiled her ration of three cups of rice to last a day, with several times the usual quantity of water to produce her version of fishes and loaves to feed the household. She sprinkled sugar on the porridge, serving it in a calabash dish. In the silent huddle we set upon the brew without waiting for the customary invitation. There was little emotion, just a brief feeling of incredulity, succeeded by a vague worry that the worst might not yet be behind us. It is a caricature to think of famine as uncoiling the savage in victims and inciting riotous conduct. For that, you need to be better fed.

Finally relief supplies arrived in sufficient quantity to make us feel confident that the siege was broken. It took several months to get over the fear of starvation and to regain a semblance of self-respect. It had been a moral as well as physical crisis, kindling a burning sense of shame about going hungry and not able to help ourselves. People spoke darkly about hunger like a chain that reduced victims to psychological bondage: when self-respect went, so did the idea of self. Precisely for that reason the community took prompt measures to bury memories of the hungry season, now referred to only as that thing in the past. Elders chided us if we slipped and named the thing. Children like to brag about thrilling close shaves with danger, but grown-ups know better than to jest about flirting with disaster, and thus averted, the famine became unmentionable.

The days of relief returned with a festive air, as smiles returned to our faces along with a mood of charitableness and indulgence. The day was too short for our pranks, and the night far too brief for our favorite bedtime nursery rhymes. Running errands was not a chore when food awaited our return; in fact, we volunteered for them. The menace of August became a receding memory, its tattered reminders gathered up like a family secret and dumped into the lock box of folklore.

With the return of good times the community could return to its familiar cycles, which swept me up the following year. In the next round of the harvest season, when the new rice and millet crop started arriving at home, and with it the abundance of a well-stocked food pantry, the town began to organize the ritual staging of the circumcision ceremony. It typically involves sequestration in a part of the bush beyond the rice paddies. The rite was shrouded in stringent secrecy, which cut off any gossip and rumors about it beforehand. Boys and girls were divided between the circumcised and the uncircumcised, and although it was a pretty radical distinction, society behaved as if it was just a function of age. In a dispute an older boy might say to a younger one, "I'll have you circumcised," swiping the index finger across the palm of the hand to indicate a knife in the act of slicing. It's another way of saying, "I'll have you well beaten." But circumcision was not personal punishment. It was simply part of the natural order of growing up.

But it was hard not to feel we were being punished when a gaggle of us boys were scooped up in a coordinated move at dawn and marched off into the field to be circumcised. *Kuyang* is the name given to the surgical rite. We learned something terrifying was afoot only when the women jumped to their feet and raised the alarm, begging for their children to be spared the blood-rite. "Please don't take him away . . . please give him back to me," they cried. The women were several steps behind, though. Those boys who tried to resist were quickly overpowered with whips. The dawn surprise of the roundup prevented any delaying worrying about what was happening, and by the time the stampede roused us out of the deep sleep of the night we were assembling with hearts pounding under the baobab tree where we would make our home for the next two months. We were ushered to a spot behind the trees, where the man who was going to cut us was waiting. He cut us without looking us in the eye, and then we would be whisked away by the back door so the other boys being lined up would not see the tears. Throughout the day, blood-stained initiates in their grey baft cotton uniforms would whimper and drag themselves to the mats spread out around the tree. The young men who were the chaperones shouted commands at us like young athletes in a race for courage, praising the bravery of those who stopped crying as a way of shaming and motivating the others. I was about nine. I hesitated too long to be able to make any move to turn back. The momentum simply swept me along.

The surgical procedure was relatively quick and bearable. The knife glistened in the dawn light as it rose and fell in a twinkle, eliciting a gasp and a wince. The anxious moment was mercifully brief, and in a flash it was done. It was when the cut was doused with liquid iodine for antiseptic purposes, however, that I saw in the dancing skies shooting stars and flaming planets, with imaginary meteors colliding and splitting in my head. Through tears of pain we could bear no thoughts of manhood, as we were supposed to. Thoughts of bravery and valor were far from our minds. To little effect, our elders pleaded with us to hold back our tears, but we were too confused and frightened for anything else. Moaning and shivering as the fresh blood stained our robes, we begged for help. The chaperones told us that our bush tent, called *waana,* was surrounded by evil spirits, and that if we wandered too far the bad spirits would catch us. The idea made it unthinkable to contemplate running away. Fear combined with the cramping to swamp the homing instinct and pin us down.

As initiates we were allowed only the meager food given to us by our chaperones, called *kintang'lu;* the best food the adults kept for themselves. It lengthened the days of loneliness. The chaperones told us to ask our mothers to cook our favorite food, knowing full well that we wouldn't see a scrap of it. We groveled for crumbs, but even then a chaperone would order us to drop the crumb before it reached our mouth to show unquestioning submission. We were kept up at night by rumors that a dragon had smelled blood in the air and was on the prowl, ready to pounce. The contraption for faking the dragon's stirrings was the bull roarer, a bamboo blade with a string through a hole at one end and whirled above the head to create the sound effect. It reduced us to a shivering, frightened litter of puppies.

In time the ritual ordeal took its toll. Boys walked — actually dragged themselves — with their legs apart as they swayed and paddled their way about, trying not to irritate the wound. A number fell ill and some even died, while wounds turned septic, leaving scars. I began to experience a pain in my sides that felt like a branch of acacia thorns jammed into my lungs, making it torture to breathe. I lay in a fever, unable to sit up. The last I remember was lying next to the clay watercoolers at the entrance to the tent. I was told afterward that Father picked me up and drove me to Bansang hospital on the south bank to get a doctor to attend to me. He diagnosed me with pneumonia, thus saving my life. I don't remember anyone from the circumcision camp coming to visit — but at least I survived. I had glimpsed the last frontier without crossing over.

The circumcision rite concluded with a rousing community celebration. On the appointed day the initiates trooped off to the river to wash before sunrise to avoid premature contact with women. It took several cycles of washing to peel off the layers of grime: first a long soak, then a rinse, then another soak, and yet another rinse, then a soaking with soap followed by a scrub-down with an alfalfa sponge that left us tingling all over, then yet another rinse, and finally full immersion. We climbed out of the river puffing as from a cocoon, shivering and smarting in the early morning air. In our new skins we had a new birth, frisky like butterflies emerging from the chrysalis. We were given new, secret names, never to be divulged except to fellow initiates.

Finally it was time to return home. Suited for the battle of life, young athletes of courage were emerging as fresh young warriors, taking their turn to guard and defend tradition, and to do so in festive company. Hooded, wearing masks made of woven basketry, and carrying decorated staffs and shields, we lined up in ranks and moved in step toward the town. When we reached the town square, we began taking down our hoods and turning aside our masks to reveal our faces. Our spirits were high when the women came out to greet and welcome us, their long-lost sons, but we strained every nerve to control our feelings, just as we were supposed to. Their rapturous clapping blended with their singing and drumming and dancing. Mothers and aunts broke and streamed toward us, lifting us off the ground in rousing jubilation, forgetting for the moment our new status. They whisked us home and danced some more, their faces glistening with tears of joy. We beamed in the glow of it all as the bustle of the festive excitement swelled and spread wave-like through the town, subsiding only with the sinking sun.

Now we saw the two faces of the circumcision rite. In the bush, the rite had been a test of individual endurance under the ever-vigilant eyes of the elders. Back home, the circumcision was a communal celebration of our coming of age. We were pleased and encouraged by the delight with which our mothers and sisters introduced us to relatives and friends; their happiness at seeing us showed that we had not been alone or forgotten. The rite had merely added to our stature. This maternal welcome felt like the prize and reward of our initiation. The women were our allies and protectors, but now without them we had beaten the odds stacked against us and emerged valiant. Their tribute was ours alone to enjoy, making up for all the maternal attention we had been starving for in the bush.

We also began to glimpse the balance between religion and local custom, as well as the balance between the roles of women and the roles of men. The young looked up to mothers and male elders as they also looked forward to their own turn. Circumcision was the turning point, and afterward the passage into the arms of mothers and sisters affirmed their role as life-givers and pillars of custom. All of this would be a bonanza for Islam as a religion of submission, except that religion restricted the role of women in the mosque and at school. The formative role of women in societal tradition makes a striking contrast to their influence in canonical religious practices, where Islam has restricted women's participation. But custom, in turn, restricted the role of religion by excluding all religious observance from the circumcision, and established its own gender expectations in the process.

The rite was sacred but not holy, sacred in the sense of rules and precepts whose force was based on custom rather than on the injunctions of a deity or of a supernatural power. The justification of the rite was community practice and sanction, not revelation. The submission that is common in the response to the holy and the sacred conceals a real difference with our rite of circumcision. There was honor in circumcision, but it was honor due to society and custom, not to God. Honor, along with the corresponding deference, comes from society, not from submission to a supernatural commandment. Deference is the key to custom. Deference is custom's safeguard against instability; it allays uncertainty by prescribing conduct and obedience.

But custom is fragile, and any disruption or interruption weakens it, as happened in Georgetown. Thanks to the wind of change blowing from the West and then from the East, our circumcision rite was the last such event. Circumcision would be performed at the medical clinic set up by the colonial administration, not in the bush infested with the dragon's threats, and certainly without the enforced sequestration from family and friends. In the end, custom bowed first to creeping modernization, and finally to Islam. The songs, rhymes, riddles, fables, stories, music, and instruments of custom were effaced in one bound, as Islam closed in to strip the ancient baobab tree of its mystery as the magnet of tradition and custom. No transcript of this heritage exists anywhere as far as I know, which means we are about one lifetime away from forgetting it completely. Many of the last generation to undergo the rite have as men gone on to perform the pilgrimage to Mecca, and thereby relinquished their role as guardians of local custom. If the custom survives it will do so in scattered scraps and fragments, and but less likely as a whole. We would have to cobble from the shards of memory an approximate idea of its once vigorous life.

We grew up without feeling the need to pass judgment on other people's chances of salvation. In fact, we didn't worry much about our own chances. We had no atonement to perform, ate no tainted apple, and had no remorseful aftertaste to assuage. Sin was contravention of the code, for which restitution was full and sufficient remedy. We had no idea of sin as an intrinsic moral defect, and, therefore, no idea of moral goodness independent of custom and social obligations. Of course, this left us largely exempt from probing self-scrutiny, and therefore from the idea of individual responsibility. I was a pretty attentive child, but I don't remember ever hearing anyone say, "I am sorry. It's my fault, and I take responsibility." Admitting wrongdoing is normally done by dispatching a delegation in the cause, proof that being at fault is a social issue essentially. In my language, the concept of *guilt* as a moral disposition is nonexistent, whereas *shame* as a social breach is well known.

In the world in which I grew up, individual thoughts and feelings had a marginal role, as evidenced in the circumcision ritual, where coming of age meant schooling our feelings so as not to make a spectacle. The chaperones said that the circumcision would teach us not to be cowards by confronting us with naked fear. It was useless to ask why. Our initiation was driven not by a false hope of taking on the sword of faith to slay demons, with diabolic monsters to be gagged and bound in a final victory, but, rather, by the need to disarm fear.

What was missing in all this was a dimension of self-inquiry, a quest for the interior light, a spiritual rite of passage with atoning possibility. We donned our stiff uniforms as a deterrent against idle thoughts. Custom shielded us from individual speculation by clipping our wings so that there would be little risk of losing our heads in the flaky world of personal spiritual liberation. The decisive site of value and meaning was not touchy-feely impulses or the vagaries of mystical cultivation, but society and received custom. Society was the source in which we lived, moved, and had our being. Society circumcised the outward man, rather than the inward self. As a child I never understood feelings and emotions as having any moral merit, even though I was conscious of myself. That forbidden ground in time would become my destined haunt.

Our elders drew firm lines of behavior and conduct that children could not cross, while they themselves talked freely about all sorts of things except in the hearing of children. In our presence many subjects were off limits: girls, suffering, death, taking God's name in vain, swearing by your mother, calling your parents by their first names, offering the left hand instead of the right, looking elders in the eye, and so on. Society in turn kept faith with children by not belittling them or confounding them with inconsistent advice. Being circumcised while we were still children meant that we were entitled to the respect of our elders without being entitled to their deference. Their respect encouraged us while their status humbled us. That was the lesson the initiation rite tried to impart to us by cutting it into our skin.

Custom had a spiritual side to it, which was this sense of obligation without feeling put upon, with boundaries emphasizing limits as well as latitude. That perspective changed our understanding of our place in society, giving us the idea that we belonged to society by the roles we filled. Family *jelis* recounted our sagas to challenge us to take charge of our destiny. We watched our parents dwell and reflect on the natural world and our puny place in it: the open skies, the low, drifting clouds; the ceaseless ebb and flow of the tide; the luminous night sky; the two main seasons of dry and wet; the incandescent dawn sky; the noonday sun and the twilight tinge that soon gave way to night. All these attuned us to the well-regulated rhythm of nature, like a promise offered, then withdrawn, only to be offered again with the same reassuring undulating regularity. It settled our spirit by affirming our fixed and fleeting place in the natural order.

We marveled at the fire-flies that greeted the first rains, flickering in the silent night air; the velvet bugs that stirred on the wet ground like ruby gems; the butterflies and the birds of rich, diverse plumage that filled the fields with their unhurried rotation; the smell of corn freshly plucked; the taste of new rice at harvest. We reflected on livestock breeding with fretless regularity, how the sheep and goats were driven to pasture, and how toward evening light they wended their way home. It is hard to calculate what effect all this had on our mind. I am sure it turned us inward, or, better, it turned us on. We sat before nature like willing novices.

In spite of being hemmed in by nature, we never entertained in any sense that vernal rapture, as Wordsworth describes it, of the sounding cataract haunting like a passion and nature becoming an appetite, a feeling, and a love. Quite the contrary: the wonder of nature lay in the outward composure of its sweeping cyclical regularity. Nature drew its boundaries with ample, ungrudging lines. The river flowed with teeming life, and followed its course with quiet constancy. Even when the tinge of twilight flecked the horizon each day it was as often quenched in the smothering evening hue. We watched and marveled at nature's scale, detail, and balance. Nature was there when we rose and when we went to bed, its measured constancy the background of our activities. The Qur'an teacher forbade us to make a picture of any living things, saying if we did God would demand that we breathe life into them on the Day of Resurrection. Nature is wonderfully rich and ample furnishing for language and mood, but we did not account to it. In primary school I learned this poem by William Brighty Rands, the nineteenth-century English poet called the "Laureate of the Nursery." It begins:

> Great, wide, beautiful, wonderful world,
> With the wonderful water around you curled,
> And the wonderful grass upon your breast,
> World, you are beautifully dressed.

I didn't dare recite that to the Qur'an teacher, and as for Mother she had no idea what I was jabbering about, she who lived with nature's fickle moods through thick and thin. Nature didn't milk cows, build houses, make clothes or tools, or carry loads for us. Indeed, as in the hungry season, nature seemed malevolent, with a grim message. We were taught that in the Qur'an the only miracles of nature are those that are intended as lessons for us, as God's way of calling us to account here and in the hereafter. The poetic imagination is no match for that formidable display of God's iron will. Even the Sufis are careful to observe the rule that nature is a quarry only for moral instruction. So I developed the taste for poetry undercover. Outside school, other children would tease me if I ever made a show of it. It is a safe guess that my taste for poetry made me suspect.

Compared to the natural order, society was a lot more demanding by how it imposed rules and norms of conduct and observance. Those rules defined relationships that were by their nature unequal, relationships of age, rank, fortune, and role assignment. The norms of society were the creation of its leaders, and they acted the part by directing us. People lived in society by rules and norms, with sanctions for infractions and disobedience. In nature, on the other hand, we are all on an equal footing: we come into the world and leave it on equal terms. We are one because we answer to one moral law. This sort of reflection enabled me to transcend natural limitations without flouting nature's laws. People left their imprint on nature while they remained subject to nature. The fragility and uncertainty of life together dissuaded us from romanticizing the natural world. Rands's poem rejects the false security of nature worship and asks, instead, that we take moral responsibility for the world:

> The wonderful air is over me,
> And the wonderful wind is shaking the tree;
> It walks on the water, and whirls the mills,
> And talks to itself on the top of the hills.
>
> Ah! you are so great, and I am so small,
> I hardly can think of you, World, at all;
> And yet, when I said my prayers today,
> My mother kissed me, and said, quite gay,
>
> "If the wonderful world is great to you,
> And great to Father and Mother, too,
> You are more than the Earth, though you are such a dot!
> You can love and think, and the Earth cannot!"

Theater and drama never existed in my culture, and so there was no stage to give vent to our secret desires, no obsession with contrived thrills. The opinion attributed (probably wrongly) to Cyprian of Carthage, condemning the theater as a trap of sin, would resonate well with my parents and teachers. For them, too, the eyes are made for adoring the marvel and wonder of creation, not for feasting on spectacles of dubious moral character. Maybe this has something to do with the fact that all my life I have been visually underdeveloped while remaining morally on tenterhooks.

Yet I remember gazing at the starry sky and marveling at shooting stars popping like fiery bubbles as they streaked across the firmament, and Mother explaining that the shooting stars were bearing condolence before God for the passing of a holy person that night. Transfixed, I would hold my breath in awe, impressed that faith so intangible was powerful enough to jolt the remote stars as they cut a bright path through the heavens on their funereal errand. It brought on an acute sense of self-awareness. "When I look at thy heavens, the work of thy fingers, the moon and the stars which thou hast established; what is man that thou art mindful of him?" (Ps. 8:3-4). What theater built by human hands could ever compare to the awesome splendor of the Creator's handiwork? The fact that we can love and think, and the earth cannot, puts us on a higher moral plane, and proves our moral affinity with truth, so that we prosper by contemplating the purpose for which God put us here. My curiosity about nature was leading to curiosity about God.

I recall a distant relative my age saying religion was the path our forebears walked; we their descendants should not stray from that path. Had she spied on my thoughts? Her religious faith allowed her to go back and forth fetching water from the river and to the rice fields to assist her mother. In time she would get married, raise a family, and tend her own fields. That was God's will, and she would teach her children that lesson. I ached to ask her: is it also not God's will that we should be openly curious about Him? She brushed me aside, saying I was not worth her time, that she had urgent chores to attend to. I wanted to tell her, but could not, that the grinding routine of drawing water and growing rice does not have to be a choice between drudgery and thinking about God. I guess I was rehearsing to myself things I wanted to discuss with Mother. Father was too conventional to entertain what he considered frivolous questions, and so it never entered my head that I might talk to him. For him a transcendent God was too out of reach for humans to influence, and only charlatans would think otherwise. Spiritual questioning only irritated him.

But I saw the lowing herds treading the same paths in and out of their pens without the slightest curiosity about the world around them and felt that human beings were created differently. I used to accompany the family cowherd, the *ngainako,* as he shepherded his flock at dusk to be tethered for the night in an open field on the outskirts of the town. He would give me sips of the warm milk he had just drawn from the cows. Being there gave me a chance to watch and think as the *ngainako* belted out commands to the animals with confident authority while tying them to the wooden stakes. As Whitman says, animals abide "placid and self-contain'd"; "they do not lie awake in the dark" fretting for the fate of their soul. But for us, curiosity is the soul's reflex, the door through which we come upon our own company.

We learned at school Thomas Gray's "Elegy in a Country Church-yard," which seems an appropriate plaintive anthem to the anticlimactic innocence of pastoral life.

> The curfew tolls the knell of parting day,
> The lowing herd winds slowly o'er the lea,
> The ploughman homeward plods his weary way,
> And leaves the world to darkness and to me.

I went through many stages of understanding in learning that poem. First was the smug satisfaction of being able to recite it well. Qur'an school education was handy in that regard. Then I rolled with the meter, adding an African lilt to it and breaking into a step-dance with the poem's symmetrical two-plus-three beat. African children would dance to anything, including the patter and splatter of rain drops. I could stage the poem as a one-man act, concluding with a tilt of the head and a flour-ish of the hand. Finally I could attach the sentiments of the poem to events of daily life: ploughmen, end-of-day chores, and parting greetings resounding with the comings and goings of family, friends, and neigh-bors, sometimes with the let-down of long absence. The world of leave-taking, of voices and faces hovering, retreating, and bubbling up as fond memories, would evoke Elizabeth Browning: "Who knows but the world may end to-night?" Father's goings and comings touched off that feeling. I nuzzled up to him for warmth and assurance every time he returned home, relieved and pleased in equal measure. I am sure he was aware of my feelings, but I had to guess that. He was pretty inscrutable.

The repetitive nature of all this returning, leaving, and recalling sim-ply inscribed itself on my mind as gaining what I had lost, and losing in the next round only to regain it once again. The certainty of both evoked a sense of moral scale. Father returning home did not really solve my anxiety about his next departure; the relief and pleasure of his coming home triggered a feeling of hugging the thought so as to savor it for as long as possible. It was like a religious feeling, looking to God to protect us in our parents, and our parents in us. It evolves with our reflexive nature, and blends unobtrusively with our moral inclination. In the best of times and in the worst of times we overflow with our own company; religion distils that into the idea that there is company more and better than our own.

Having had Gray's "Elegy" for practice, I found ample space for a dialogue with myself. I imagined a fantasy stage on which to act out the drama of the goings and comings in which one person speaks as two people, one of whom acts and observes the other with close attention. St Paul emerges from the first stages of this self-inquiry with the verdict, "I know nothing against myself" (1 Cor. 4:4). Others, though, come up short. Seneca says that self-knowledge leads to the desire to wish to hide one's sins, whereas a good conscience loves the light. Self-knowledge is a moral catalyst, the kind of dress rehearsal that will prompt self-scrutiny: wishing to hide your sins presupposes that you know they are sins in the first place, and as such require attention.

I wondered: what if God is the hidden interlocutor, prepping us in a two-way conversation whose entire purpose is to guide us into making healthy choices in life? With one part of my mind I tried to weigh the difference between striving with hope of reward, and lapsing with threat of punishment, while with the other part I questioned whether it is in our power to exert ourselves in God's business at all unless there is reward for the effort. Given the limited opportunities at my disposal, I faced few distractions. What society believed about the will of God left no margin for procrastination or excuse. No stopgaps were available; consequences for action or inaction were immediate, personal, and irreversible.

All this faced me with simple, clear choices. With God's help, I had to take risks in order to live at all, and in risking I had to move forward with purpose. I might not succeed in *all* my school work, but unless I applied myself and turned down the appeal of idle fun I would not succeed in *any* of my school work. I would look for ways of enjoying the challenge, lest I begrudge the frolicking crowd. I had to believe that the will of God left room to strive, to labor, and to embrace the reward.

When you begin to live life from choice rather than on terms dictated by circumstances, you see things in a wholly different light. Living could not be a happy-go-lucky game, for one misstep could cost me dearly, while a single opportunity could make all the difference. I could not sit back and wait. It was becoming clear, for example, that I could not make the assumptions of my peers at school about family support. When I overheard conversations among the boys about how many heads of cattle or houses their family had and what portion would accrue to them by right, I felt envious but not necessarily unhappy. I knew that I was not prepared to risk life and limb for anything that might pass for a family legacy, because it would in all likelihood be riddled with tangled grudges and residual jealousy. I would rather be free to face the world without being haunted by simmering ill-will. I was never going to walk into a great inheritance, but that left me free to look for possibilities within my range. Some writers have pooh-poohed the notion of hope as unrealistically cruel, yet without it we are left only with arid skepticism, and I did not see how I or anyone else could make a living in that. And so I began to live in hope. I was haunted by a sense of impending change in which I knew I had a meaningful role to play. Instead of waiting for that change to happen, I looked for ways to bring it about. Everywhere I turned I imagined hearing someone urging me not to draw back. I felt myself not a stranger in the world, and so I turned to it with anticipation. High school was the next stage in the passage to the world of risk and possibility, and when it came, I was ready.

CHAPTER 4

Exile at Home

Having passed an entrance examination I arrived at Armitage High School in 1954, thrilled at the rare opportunity boys of my generation had of obtaining a secondary school education. Three-quarters of the boys from the primary school didn't make it, and that was the end of the road for them, educationally speaking. I escaped that fate.

Armitage was a strictly-run government boarding school in Georgetown with between 80 and 100 students drawn from all over the Gambia. The school had five grade levels, or forms, and even though there were end-of-year exams, the school operated an automatic promotion-to-the-next-form system. It meant that no matter how badly you performed in the exams you had five years to finish school. Only in exceptional cases would the principal expel a student for being a habitual failure. I was determined to finish at the top of my class — two other boys, Kebba and Makang, both now deceased, competed with me for that honor. We became close rivals and good friends by virtue of our identical interests, and our friendship reinforced my sense that academic work suited my temperament. The demand for places made it a highly competitive school, especially since everyone there was on a full government scholarship that covered fees, tuition, uniforms, food, and supplies.

With its five times of worship at dawn, at noon, in the late afternoon, at dusk, and at night before bedtime, the mosque commanded daily life.

Worship was mandatory, with punishment for delinquents. School lessons occupied the first half of the day, with the rest of the time spent on class assignments, chores, and running errands for our teachers and the senior boys. The highly regimented life of the school left little time for individual interests, or even for personal recreation. Sunday afternoon between two and four o'clock was free time, except we couldn't leave the premises. For those of us from Georgetown the restriction was particularly onerous, to be so close to home and yet not to be able to visit. On Fridays we joined the community for the early afternoon worship at the town mosque, and it was tempting then to try to slip our handlers and steal a visit home. But the threat of punishment if we were caught was deterrent enough.

My pack leader in mischief, Njagga, admiringly known among his friends by the sinewy, ranging name of Jini-jini, was a fun-loving fellow who dazzled us with his nimble ways around prohibitions. So many times he slipped the dragnet of rules that trapped the rest of us. I was not alone in foraging in the heap to which he adroitly reduced prohibitions and restrictions. He lived in a different dorm, but in the dead of night he would crawl out of bed, come over to the window over my bunk bed, tap-tap me out of sleep, and have us tiptoe out of the school compound. He would open a hole in the fence at the back of the school yard allowing us to bolt, our hearts pounding as we headed down the bush path for town. Once there it occurred to us that everyone was asleep, and our daring getaway was for nothing. But absconding became a game of its own. Intrepid rule-breaker that he was, Jini-jini calculated our gambit differently, insisting that we had beaten the odds, and that the experience had toughened me, wimp that I was. Next time we would do better and go further, with the practice run an asset. Jini-jini took the same attitude to other school rules and regulations. Even people he offended yielded to his guilelessness. For a boy his age, he was well versed in the ways of the world; the girls adored him, much to my envy. With an itch for adventure, Jini-jini was not one known to stint on his zest for life.

Yet for all his effort at trying to pull me into his extrovert world, Jini-jini could not change my introspective disposition. Three years into life at Armitage, doubts and questions assailed me. I faced my assigned tasks with growing faintheartedness, wishing I didn't have to do them. Unlike

Jini-jini, I could not escape from doubts and uncertainty about my purpose in life. In me Jini-jini saw an opportunity to put his talents to work by rescuing me from abstract preoccupations he considered futile. The concrete, tangible world was a magnet for him, and he couldn't wait to embrace it with passion.

Jini-jini couldn't understand what my problem was. God cut us slack by turning His back on us so we could have fun while He wasn't looking, Jini-jini would say with a chuckle. He knew that I didn't relish risking God finding me out. The ground of his moral daring — that transparency was not a requirement for being human before an inscrutable God — was the very reason for my plight. Because the Muslim revelation taught us that we could never hide from God, the All-Seeing (Qur'an 17:26), the mother tongue left us without cover. I knew that God would not stoop to speak to us in it, but He could still know our thoughts. The issue never bothered Jini-jini, who insisted that God didn't have to know everything we said or wanted to say.

Jini-jini saw Islam as eminently sensible: it demands no monastic asceticism to mock and torment the flesh, and no demons of the emotions to make us fear the sensuous. There is no heroic merit in cleaving to the straight and narrow when we can take the scenic route in life. The fact that God is far away Jini-jini saw as our advantage: it is license to use the gap to pursue our desires without being spooked by the thought of someone snooping on us. Temptations are ordained for us, as is our appetite for them, he said, and could I not see that this is God's will? Rather than being scandalous, our natural desires are what make us human. Religion acknowledges that by making provision for our senses and giving us the palate for a world full of wonderful flavors. If we allow impossible ideals to tie us down we will make religion our enemy, and scandal our companion. That would be the end of religion, and then we would truly be miserable. Jini-jini's inscrutable God was not an accessory to the sins of the faithful, allowing Jini-jini to dispense with any idea of nemesis. "Accepting Islam," according to Jini-jini, "means sin cannot pursue us nor haunt us. We prosper, if we prosper at all, by doing so as God created us, not by dividing and condemning ourselves as spirit or matter, as mind or body." Jini-jini's *joie de vivre* shines through the words of the poet:

You promise heavens free from strife,
    Pure truth, and perfect change of will;
But sweet, sweet, is this human life,
    So sweet, I fain would breathe it still;
Your chilly stars I can forgo,
This warm kind world is all I know.

                  William Cory

I would grin and agree with the primal sentiment of Jini-jini's reasoning even though I couldn't take my mind off the issue: it is also God's will, I felt, that we stand unmasked before Him. The angel of light is set loose like the nemesis to whisper in our ear: "Even before a word is on my tongue, lo, O Lord, thou knowest it altogether. My frame was not hidden from thee, when I was being made in secret, intricately wrought in the depths of the earth. Thy eyes beheld my unformed substance" (Ps. 139:4, 15-16). Where, then, can I hide, O God of my life?

My questioning was only enhanced by the demands of competing languages. From the religious point of view, it is not difficult to establish mother tongue inferiority. The language took root nowhere outside the walls of those who spoke it; it had no written literature to advertise and promote it; no orthography for written communication; no forum of shared ideas; and no organized, institutional means of transmitting knowledge beyond the oral medium. The idea of language as God's gift is odd in respect of the mother tongue, because the God in question is none other than Islam's God, who shut the door on it. To be religious required listening to God in the revealed language, and that demoted the mother tongue to the religious black market of juju and nocturnal rituals. Brief as the worship was, its regular, routine nature gave it exclusive, daylight merit, and assured the demise of the mother tongue. It is not possible to conceive a divine role for the vernacular against the transcendent Arabic, thus making worship a ban on the mother tongue. My own language was at best mundane and vain. I could plead and pour out my soul before God but, with odors of the inkhorn, it would be without the merit of worship. In the tones and sounds I learned from my mother, lively thoughts of God formed in my mind, only to dissipate with the worship. To make matters worse, the school instituted English, and placed a ban on the vernacular by imposing as penalty carrying a metal plate on a string slung from the neck — with taunting to shame offenders. The language of school and the language of worship together tied my tongue up. But it was hard to turn my back on the language my mother had taught me.

Behind Father's back, the diviners Mother secretly consulted claimed that they could bargain with and outwit the invisible spirits and, for a fee, work their knowledge to our advantage. I was in turn inquisitive and skeptical, eager to see a marvel, but knowing you can't cheat reality in the final analysis. People possessed by the spirit of divination must snap out of it while they could and collect their fee, or else lose their minds and forfeit all, whereas faith in a personal God connected you to the light of day. Messing around with invisible spirits was a risky habit, and that was why good diviners worked only for limited hours at night. It led me to marvel less at the diviners' arcane powers than at why they didn't solve the enigma of life: where did we come from and what are we here for? Humanity is a question to itself. I heard St. Anselm whispering: "Woe is me, one of the poor children of Eve, far from God, what did I set out to do and what have I accomplished? What was I aiming for and how far have I got? What did I aspire to and what did I long for? O Lord, you are not only that than which nothing greater can be conceived, but you are greater than all that can be conceived." I could hear pursuing footsteps at night, as if my thoughts could walk.

The sequestration of boarding school was not entirely new, given the comparable separation of the circumcision ritual. What was new was the five-year duration. It did not offer the pain and intensity of the initiatory circumcision rite, but boarding school made up the difference in other ways. For one, there were the five-times-daily prayers that began with the dawn devotions at 5:30 and ended with the night prayer after dinner — seven days a week, year in, year out. There was no point in counting the number of required prayers, as the students were prone to do, since the prayers never got fewer. Chapel at school had nothing of the convenience of the once-a-day or once-a-week routine of educational institutions in America, where religion simply is about finding your comfort zone. I wished my devotions were up to me; I would have bagged and abandoned them at a moment's notice.

Missing the prayers carried a penalty of chores — cleaning toilets, sweeping floors, tending the lawn with endless bucket-loads of water drawn from the well, tending the vegetable garden on the river bank, and in general being reduced to carrying out menial tasks of all descriptions. It was hazing by standing order. Other infractions carried requisite sanctions as well, making school feel like a remand center. Few students faced all these sanctions without appreciating the rewards and advantages of toeing the line. It was really a simple calculation. Which activity would I rather spend my time doing: carrying out my religious obligations, however onerous, or doing unpleasant tasks? The choice was no longer about my freedom; it was about doing what I was told. Yet cowering before obligations or groveling under sanctions was not a good basis for undertaking my devotions and lessons. We were taught that punishment had divine merit, and that in the hereafter God would punish us for being remiss at prayer. The owl in me shivered at the thought of the endless rounds of dawn raids whose ogre as *jinko,* "doziness," stalked me for the rest of the day.

Religious observation reached its peak in Ramadan, the Muslim lenten season that forced the gluttonous among the students to search their hearts. The month-long fasting requires abstention from food and drink from the dawn prayer to the *maghrib* sunset prayer, about fourteen hours. In the tropical heat, observant students were physically drained by the Ramadan demands. You could opt out by obtaining medical exemption, though you were not credible if you requested exemption for all of Ramadan; it revealed your malingering intentions. Not surprisingly, Ramadan never deterred Jini-jini. Rather, singing the praises of the kitchen staff for their gourmet dishes, he placed a standing order for the full ration of breakfast and the other two daily meals, suitably seasoned and generously provisioned with meat. The aroma of the food, as well as his own amusing company, would entice me to join Jini-jini for a week or so before my conscience hounded me into returning to the lenten life, with my bedraggled resolve as suitable tribute. My reputation tarnished by my temporary indiscretion, a nagging sense of guilt dogged me for the rest of Ramadan. How I regarded my own lamentable performance felt more damning than the disapproval of my peers.

The first week of Ramadan was brutal. Gastronomic spasms erupted at meal times, leaving us gasping and panting. The thirst was unendurable, and only the prospect of breaking the fast at the end of the day kept me from the water coolers. We tried to conserve energy by reducing the need to exert ourselves. Going without food long enough allowed our appetite to decline in stages, making the prospect of going without food and water less unbearable by the week. The school offered no respite from chores, for that would be cheating Ramadan of the heroism it demanded. In fact, there was an unspoken rule about who looked the cheeriest while fasting. I would douse my face with water to rinse the fatigue out of it, gladly leaving the high stakes to the others. To be really hungry and thirsty not because food and water are scarce, but because of religious obligation, taught us that truth could not be rationalized away. Ramadan is the pre-ordained visitor you don't have to entertain; we greeted its prescribed departure with feasting. God brought Ramadan, and God would take it away, which encouraged us to persist. Food was a big deal at school, and only Ramadan could make us turn away from it. It made the idea of paradise as a never-ending feast for the faithful irresistible. Braving the fast made that jackpot an enticing dream.

In the meantime the road there remained steep. We earned extra bad marks for dozing during school lessons, which attracted the threat of additional sanctions. That compounded things considerably. Dozing made me late for things, which left me with only crumbs at breakfast and at tea breaks, and with little water for ablutions at prayer times. The much-feared principal felt my abject helplessness, fortunately, and relented finally when I had turned up once too many times before him for sleeping in class. Knowing that I did well in my exercises, he gave me the benefit of the doubt; he wouldn't punish me just for the idea of it. He simply dismissed me from his office, saying only I should go back to my lessons. It was like manna from heaven. I idly hoped that God was like that, knowing our will was inclined to do well but seeing that the flesh was weak.

Could God deal with us not according to our just deserts but according to His sovereign grace? Would He? If God was a relenting God, what a boon that would be for the laggard in me. Oh, please, God, be like that, I would say to myself every night when I went to bed — until the next dawn raid. I would feel pounding on the bed frame, and sometimes on my back, followed by a booming voice rousing me for prayer. The rough dawn handling had the threatening clatter of coming judgment. God, "robing day with beauteous light, hast clothed in soft repose the night," now created the dawn prayer to foil sleep. Why?

The issue followed us into the classroom, where three teachers of Islam awaited us. The teacher of Arabic, Ustadhi, saw the students as stray and misplaced parts of Arabic grammar, and he took it upon himself to prod us into position. He had little sympathy for our shortcomings. The fact that the students spoke several other languages didn't count; our multilingual skills proved merely our addiction to heathen tongues. Arabic is the friction for stripping native alloy. He turned on weak students with sardonic humor, wondering how in heaven's name the students ever came to him. His cane twirled and trembled as he locked eyes on the students. For him God made Arabic the perfect, preordained language, and like God, Arabic was its own first and last justification.

The lessons proceeded to the nominal sentence, which the teacher wrapped round us like an ill fate. *Kalbun jahilun fi-l-bustan,* "an ignorant dog is in the garden," he would begin, with a meaningful look at the culprits grinning at the back of the class where they were consigned. After all, stray weeds must not clutter the garden of knowledge, Ustadhi would mutter audibly. Heaven's language must stifle such worthless undergrowth, and it was his job to show how. I don't think it mattered to Ustadhi whether the students he considered mere distraction made the grade in carrying out their religious obligations. Religion is not just collusion with ourselves, with prayer a pious exercise in self-motivation. Ustadhi sneered about blissful ignorance as a vicious circle.

Perhaps the teacher of theology, *kalam,* would reassure us on that point, and so to him we next turned. A man of solid build and always neatly dressed in a manner that did not impede his quick, almost jerky movements, Karantabi carried his arms crossed behind his back as he paced up and down delivering his lecture. He folded his hands and held them over his head as he pondered a question. The joining of hands was in fact an appropriate metaphor of the task of theology as the teacher saw it, so that the right and left hands ceased to be two contenders of the truth without being a divided representation of it. There was no risk of contention in a situation where there was no risk of separation. God is one, and we have two hands to defend and serve that truth. Our hands may not be detached from the God who created us, but they cannot grasp God, Karantabi would insist. Only the delusion of language would make anyone think that God fits our measurement and reckons that to be insightful. Human beings misconstrue the truth because their short-comings blinker them. "Don't think for a moment your shortcomings count for exculpation," Karantabi would declare impatiently. "What clods of ignorance," he would spit out. "But who made us like that," we would think impishly without daring to say so. He could intuit our thoughts, but was content to let the silence drown them out.

Coming up short against Karantabi, we next turned to Séringe, the teacher of ritual and liturgy, for whom the habits of religion belonged with speaking truth to the limbs of the body. Séringe was tall, lean, and looking "the shadowed livery of the burnished sun," with an upright, stately carriage that emphasized his proximity to higher things. The mystical glint in his eyes accentuated his generous mouth, with his sweaty forehead conveying a hint of inner toil. He sported a colorful scarf, symbol of his rebirth, and used it to mop perspiration. He wore a crimson fez hat with a pointed middle but without the customary tassel down the side, an embellishment he considered bordering on the frivo-lous. He was officially also the imam of the school, and taught liturgy based on the pastoral practices.

An avatar of religious experience, Séringe had once been a police-man who confessed to drinking alcohol, taking drugs, chasing women, and generally living a carefree life of *dolce vita* before the hound of heaven that was nipping at his heels finally snagged him. He shook his head in feigned self-disgust but with the hint of a secret relish as he re-counted how alcohol made people feel, using "people" as a foil for him-self. The sensation in his voice about how alcohol and weed induced a buoyant mood had the echo of a secret. Evidently, this man was in touch with his shadow self. On his way down from one of his customary highs, he received from an unknown source strong intimations of a higher reality. He yielded, giving up the pursuit of lawbreakers for the pursuit of the spiritual life. He found sanctuary on the Sufi Mouride path in Senegal and there he surrendered. (The Mourides [from the Arabic *muríd,* novice,] have their base in peasant society and increasingly among mobile urban youth. Their leaders stress and benefit from hard work and material gifts from devotees.) So much reminded him of what was unredeemed in life; it made him bristle with the cop's instincts, his guilt-burdened conscience pricking him into finding restitution by pursuing carnal offenders of God's law, whom he recognized as his own kind. Séringe affected redemption, but the fresh scars of his battles with the flesh left him a wary penitent.

Séringe had a nervous twitch that his religious sensitivity bent into a twinge of conscience; it inclined him to keep watchful vigil lest, sleepwalking, he stumbled unawares on marks of God's displeasure. A friend of God who shunned worldly friendships, Séringe's conscience provoked him into bouts of self-preoccupation, convinced that the world was a snare, and that only vigilant watchfulness could cut its seductive attachments. We couldn't help wondering if Séringe hated in the world what he knew firsthand of its sweet spots, which would explain his seeming inability to accept his deliverance without always checking with himself. He would be scandalized to know that it was not his conversion to faith that riveted his students, but his earlier life of worldly pleasures, which was much closer to where the students were.

With his signature chuckle, Jini-jini would bound out of the lessons buoyed and jubilant, not because Séringe had found God, but because Séringe had tasted forbidden fruit with no damning aftereffect. For Jini-jini it was pious sophistry to say that conversion was God's reward of faith; conversion was the fruit of life lived to the full, with the path to faith ripened by carnal knowledge. Women and the hint of alcohol in Séringe's testimony cast a spell on Jini-jini. Séringe showed that indulging in worldly pleasures did not foreclose on God's favored visitation at a future date, Jini-jini pointed out to me smugly. Consequently, Séringe's testimony of faith was not the intended deterrent he wished it to be. It simply titillated the students who were in his presence without being in his confidence.

I could not help noticing when he mounted the prayer mat to lead the worship that he would be emotional, his voice cracking as his eyes filled with tears, something religious teaching explicitly condemns. In the rulebooks uncontrolled emotion voids the worship, requiring doing it again. Séringe's explanation, however, was that the thought of him as a once-hardened sinner now permitted by God to be a prince of worship simply overcame him. Yet we could not help wondering if that was another case of the sinner's thrill dressed up as humble penitence.

Still, awareness of our own moral weakness dogged us, and made us wonder whether God had shortchanged us. If God is good, why are we bad, the "we" being a surreptitious reference to him, too? Séringe brushed aside the questions with an accusatory stare. How dare we interrogate God? he bristled, his eyes turned down as if he was trying to banish the thought of his sinful past. If divine transcendence is so impervious, why are religious people so prickly about God? we wondered impishly. Why do human beings think they know God enough to set themselves up as arbiters of His mind? The answer is straightforward: because we have the Qur'an as God's infallible rule book. But that prompted another question: why even trust us with that?

Here Séringe turned to fear. For him fear was the great motivating impulse of the religious life. In the pure light of God, human beings would simply be incinerated to nothingness, because in their radical core they were offensive to God, not just unintelligible by the rules of linguistic perfection, but too twisted by youthful impetuousness to be able to follow with steady feet the straight path, the *sirat al-mustaqim,* to God. Only the Prophet's intercession could save people from the wrath God was piling up for them. In that light, even the fear of God was not a mitigating virtue; it was merely an index of the coming inferno. Religious fear actually cripples the moral impulse: one prays because one fears retribution. For Séringe compliance under sanction proved that religion is necessary to the social order, for how else is society possible if it is just up to the pleasure and whim of each individual? That's why the holy law teaches that personal feelings are dangerous as criterion of public order. Still, all that left me paralyzed in the clutches of an implacable, terrifying omnipotence; it turns God into our enemy, stipulating compliance without responsibility. (I have wondered whether religious extremism and terrorism have their source in the enmity the divine law foments. Show no mercy to the enemy because mercy has the precondition of total capitulation.)

Listening to the experience of a school friend I knew as Madi made me look at the will of God in a new light. Madi arrived in school fitted out with a battery of amulets his mother procured for him at great expense and trouble. The amulets were sewn in cloth and leather pouches and tied on his body under his baggy gown, with a few stuffed in his pockets. It must have increased his weight by a few pounds. While in the mosque once, Madi bent down to pray, only to have some of his amulets spill out on to the prayer mat. The sight of the amulets distracted him, and he could not concentrate. Then a thought ricocheted in his mind: where, honestly, did he put his trust, in God or in amulets? In the standing position, when he was looking straight, Madi's thoughts were God-centered. But that moment of clarity receded when in the next motion he was bending down to get on his knees for the prescribed *sujúd,* prostration. At that point he was much too close to the amulets on the mat to overlook them, which kindled the question about ultimate trust. It was unsettling to be that close to the offending amulets and not to be able to scoop them up, thus ending the distraction once and for all. On the other hand, worship in the mosque is not about cleaning up amulets.

So here was Madi, reeling between attending to his godly duty and covering up the amulets, between standing up for God one moment, and in the next stooping down close to the incriminating amulets, his devotional intention in tatters. If only he had left the amulets at home! If only he had secured them better! If only he had picked up the stuff immediately and prevented further exposure! Madi was trying to cut his losses long after he had lost the game. Even if they are only a second line of defense, are amulets good or bad for faith, he worried?

The question Madi had been postponing all along he no longer could evade. Trust is unimpaired moral commitment, and Madi could not make it into a matter of mere usefulness. He tried to comfort himself by thinking with one part of his mind that the amulets contained potent Qur'anic verses, signifying trust in God, while, with the other part, he saw that he was hiding the amulets to avert the charge that he was merely being superstitious. He had reduced religion to wagering between the God who created him, and a sacred object made for him and which he carried around concealed. In worship Madi acknowledged God as his Maker and Lord, but with the amulets he hedged his bets. He had never thought about amulets in the mosque that way before. Amulets are a contract with the spirits as amenable to our agency; the mosque, on the other hand, signifies submission with no strings attached. Amulets are of the shadowy world, making daylight God's exclusive domain. True religion robbed amulets of any daylight legitimacy. The Qur'an is only disputably an individual's private hoard as medicine; before all else it is a public rule of life and conduct. Carrying fragments of the holy text in sheaths and pouches may not substitute for obedience to the holy book. The will of God cannot be sewn up in arm-bands, Madi acknowledged.

It was a conundrum. He mused: "If amulets as contract do not work, and resignation to the will of God being in any case so vague and without any content to be worth anything, how else can faith in God flourish? What symbols or signs may serve as tokens of divine aid? My fate in the hereafter requires every help I can get. But amulets may distract by focusing on self-advantage, leaving me to wonder if I can be religious with a mechanical view of the will of God. Is the will of God about personal advantage only? Trust and devotion, I reckoned, should be expressions of gratitude, not a hedge against ill befalling us."

Like Madi and Jini-jini, the idea that I could love God in any credible fashion had not entered my mind — the code had turned me into a devotee for hire, my faith for a stay of execution. For very practical reasons, the religious canon does not make love of God motive for fulfilling the standing obligations, and that gave love of God no role in our life at school. If it was allowed, I would have led a troop of delinquent boys before the authorities to plead love of God in mitigation for being remiss at prayer or at fasting. But it was not allowed. In effect, religious obligations left me reaching for a retreating God.

Although not a religious school in the sense of being owned and run by a religious organization, Armitage worked with theocratic dedication. Non-Muslim students were conspicuous by being sidelined in "splendid isolation." Not for the unredeemed are the sacraments of praying and fasting. One of the students was a Protestant; his community had died out, and his Muslim stepmother, having sensibly secured her rights to her Christian husband's pension, promptly turned the boy over to the imam as soon as the boy's father had died and been buried. The lad had his head shaved to bury his Christian past, and was given a Muslim name (Al-Husayn) as sign of his new life. Three other students came from a pagan background, and the campaign to have them baptized was unremitting until they too capitulated. Once they were allowed to graze with the Muslim flock, the converts assumed a new standing, and we stopped speaking of them in the third person. It was proof that, whatever my ambivalence, I would do well to guard my Muslim name and status as a matter of survival.

To take my mind off the subject, I found temporary diversion in the palpable excitement at school when a new consignment of books arrived at the beginning of each academic year. The school's tight budget required rationing the books among us. We returned the books when the lessons were over. In study period we borrowed novels to read in the classroom; they included *Pilgrim's Progress, The Cloister and the Hearth, Black Beauty, Vanity Fair, Eothen, Silas Marner, The Mill on the Floss, Barchester Towers, Tom Jones, The Wind in the Willows, Robinson Crusoe, The Scarlett Pimpernel, Wuthering Heights, David Copperfield, Oliver Twist, A Tale of Two Cities, Tom Brown's School Days, Treasure Island, Tom Sawyer, Around the World in Eighty Days,* and several poetry and prose anthologies that included essays on subjects such as Isaac Newton, the Copernican Revolution, and Charles Darwin. I remember with fascination reading a book on Mendel's genetic discovery in 1855-56 about the ratio of hereditary transmission of genetic traits in hybrid plants. The theory about the orderly sequence of life captivated me, making me realize that reality as such conforms to the hidden law of life even when we take no heed — such, too, being the will of God. There was little competition for the books, and given my penchant I had more or less free run with them. It made school life under the heavy hand of authority bearable.

The questions that rattled my superiors continued to rise from all directions: from study, from prayer, from chores, from reflection, from books, from personal experience, from Madi and his amulets, and from Jini-jini's rationalizations, and I turned to them with an obsession. The complex demands of an extended family life, the vagaries of a young life, and my growing inclination to introspection focused my mind. On that wavelength I suffered few breaks in concentration or in continuity of thought — except in the company of Jini-jini and our illicit escapades. I had the introspective waveband to myself. I wrestled, brooded, and pondered, trying to gauge how to match strategy and options, and where to look for help. The modest education at my disposal offered the prospect of gainful employment, but, without being unrealistic, I could not stop there. I didn't know for certain, but I had a hunch that there was more to aim for. It made little difference that those who heard my musings dismissed me out of hand, saying there was little precedent for what I was thinking. Regardless, I persisted in believing that my curiosity and eagerness would be rewarded.

In cycles of observer and observed, of hunter and the hunted, I mused with myself. God made us all, and, once born, no one is exempt from death. We are all equal on that front. Either that fact is meaningful or it is not, depending on your moral intuition. You build on it if that fact is meaningful; otherwise you live with it as a cruel joke. The struggle of life makes not a scrap of difference to the underlying reality if that reality is meaningless. By the same token, a meaningful reality makes all the difference to the struggle of life. That struggle brooks no excuse from assuming responsibility for ourselves. When I thought I was alone I would be reminded that people around me shared my interests and feelings; that would pull me back from being lost in my own thoughts. Awareness of others was the spur to being considerate. Community as mutual need and mutual recognition was always there, I discovered, though the coming of Western schools and better communication were eroding many of the easy assumptions of custom and tradition. Yet the roots remained sound.

In my final year at Armitage, in December 1958, my anticipated relief at the prospects of graduating and going out to seek opportunities in the wider world took an unexpected, sad turn. The wear and tear of domestic strife finally took their toll on Mother, and when Father took early retirement and moved out of town with his new bride, Kaddi, and the small pot of money that was his gratuity, Mother yielded to pressure from my grandmother and aunts to divorce Father and remarry. It did not have a happy outcome, however. During school holidays I walked barefoot the twenty miles of bush to her new village to be with her in her illness. I remember counting my steps by the thousand, and accompanying myself with many encores of nursery rhymes. Mother's symptoms of swelling in the face and limbs concerned me enough to raise the alarm when I returned. I reported it to the headmaster and to the chief, hoping they would intervene and get her medical help. I was despondent when no one moved. I knew full well the dreaded outcome.

That left me with the goodwill of strangers to turn to. I knew only too well the harsh reality of a life of foraging for food and for goodwill, and so I set out each new day looking for a sympathetic stranger. Sometimes these strangers gave me both food and company. A Wolof trading family in the town adopted me as one of their own, and the memory of their Benedictine kindness is imperishable and still deeply cherished. Aziz, a resident civil servant from Bathurst, became a close friend and helped me out with food and token pocket money. He studied part-time for a British exam, and from time to time loaned me his course materials. Sadly, Aziz never made it, as his family and career crumbled. He was more than a brother to me, and I admired and cherished him more than he would ever know. I became acquainted with the British district commissioner, who introduced me to the poetry of Keats, which was among his small collection of books helping to keep boredom at bay. Better that than drinking oneself stone cold, I guess. The local women were too simple for the DC's taste and station, I gathered, yet I didn't know why he thought I made a likely kindred spirit. I didn't quibble. When the mail boat arrived from Bathurst on its regular monthly round, I made sure, even late at night, to be awake so I could visit and talk to the crew, who were by then brimming with mariners' tales, reports, and stories. The sailors plied me with eye-popping accounts of their travels, opening horizons for my keen imagination to explore. I pined to go where they had been and would be going. How did they come to be what they were, traveling and experiencing the world in its incredible range and diversity? I wondered enviously. What was the secret for their exciting lifestyle, and how could I have it? They didn't talk about books, and yet their lives read like thrillers. If only I could be like them.

My father did not encourage such thoughts because he said the reality out there was a lot less romantic than gullible children were inclined to believe. Perhaps for that reason, he spoke little of his own regular road treks. But boyhood imagination is much too lively to be tethered to distrust of the unknown, and so, following instinct, I sought out strangers. They were company well suited to my mood for adventure of the social kind as well as the intellectual kind. If I climbed to the top of the tallest tree in the town I would still not be able to see the nearest village a few miles away, let alone all the remote places I was hearing about, but if I climbed on the shoulders of travelers, I would be able to share in the thrills of others. I was sold on the company of strangers.

The world lay before me like an open book, but because I did not know how to decipher the script I came upon it none the wiser. Yet there were enough hints to show that in another realm life was packed full of promise. I fell back sentimentally on the ad hoc accoutrements of my first quest for literacy: the empty boxes and cartons with writing on them showing what they contained and where they came from. I recalled the "Palmtree" safety matches that came from Sweden, the "Peak" brand evaporated milk and bales of cotton fabric from the Netherlands, and the candlesticks made in France, and tried to imagine what life was like in those faraway countries. If only I could see the children there and learn their names. I wondered if they knew about us, or even if they knew about Africa and would like to meet us. I imagined they wore shorts and shoes to school where they learned English, and, like us, ate meat and rice, only a lot more of it. My imaginary envy was tempered by the thought that pork was in all likelihood regular fare in those countries — if only the people there knew better! Still, I was dying to know what games the children played, what they did during holidays, and if they traveled to other countries. I didn't know what snow was, except that it was like rain, fell like white flakes, and covered the ground for the "winter," whatever that meant. It was hard to imagine anything like that. How did people keep warm? I wondered. Did Muslims live there?

Thinking like that made the world feel so big and so wonderful, with my curiosity letting my imagination roam free. Perhaps one day I would visit other places, learn a new language, and make friends. Taught by A. A. Njie, a charismatic senior teacher, geography was one of the most popular subjects at Armitage. There was palpable excitement learning about the boy Pablo in Argentina accompanying his father to the family cattle ranch, Olav in Norway joining his family on a voyage among the fjords, and Simon, whose family and neighbors worked as lumberjacks on the St. Lawrence River in Canada. Human geography was the way we were taught about climate, soil, terrain, and rivers. So many things I wanted in turn to tell my imaginary friends about, things we were good at as children, things we liked to eat, our homes, our parents, our brothers and sisters, our schoolmates, our favorite pastimes and stories, and what I would do when I grew up. Daydreaming like that brought with it a special thrill. The fact that the world was so big and so diverse meant that there was room for all my dreams. That world of the imagination was as big as it was wonderful, and I would skip and jump for the delight of it. That thought was the secret motivation that made me want to persist against the odds. I thought thinking like that, and wishing to see that world, would make it happen one day. The disposition to think positively landed me in the imagined world of Pablo, Olav, and Simon before I experienced the reality of it. I would reach their world soon enough, but first there would be unexpected stops along the way.

CHAPTER 5

Knocking on the Door

I finished Armitage in a state of high intellectual turmoil, and I hoped that turning my back on Georgetown would also help me leave behind my restlessness. I moved to Banjul after doing well in the annual competitive civil service exam and landing a secure job there. Banjul was the biggest town I ever lived in up to that point, and, compared to Georgetown, it felt like a different world. One may recall what, by the mouth of Tityrus, Vergil describes of his first impression of Rome:

> I thought the city called Rome, Meliboeus,
> Was like this one of ours, fool that I am,
> Where shepherds often take their sheep's offsprings.
> As puppies have the look of dogs and kids
> The look of nannies, I compared small with great,
> But she lifts up her head among cities
> As the wild cypress does above the ditch-rose.

As the colonial capital, Banjul had paved roads, street pumps, telephones, electricity, and cars. It had the country's main hospital. But the drainage was nothing to speak of. The town is blessed with a natural harbor for ocean-going ships, and there was a modest international airport some fifteen miles away. The Catholic and Protestant missions had their headquarters there. The town itself is situated on St. Mary's Island, linked by a bottleneck of a bridge to the mainland. Women and men worked as civil servants or as teachers on equal pay. There were several schools, many of them co-educational. There was a modest entertainment culture, including cinema. The town was within range of many beautiful beaches, mostly deserted by local folk, partly because of various fears, and partly because of religious inhibitions about nakedness.

Soon after my arrival in Banjul, the husband of Mother's sister broke the dreaded news that Mother had died on January 31, 1959, leaving behind a six-month-old baby girl whose father, it turned out, was too adrift to care for her. The family agreed that my mother's older sister, who was childless, should adopt the baby. I didn't have any say in the matter in any case. A busy social life of dance parties, neighborhood events, beach picnics, and weekend country jaunts were a welcome distraction from the grief. The subject seldom came up in conversations because friends and acquaintances didn't know my family or my childhood background. That provided space to heal privately and to keep my thoughts to myself.

I knew that the situation of my brothers back home could not be more precarious. Ebrima, also known as Janko, was eight, and since Mother's second marriage he had become a *de facto* ward of our stepmother, who had her own children to tend to. Kebba was ten, and was attending primary school, but Ebrima, a mere sapling, was left to lie fallow. Musa, I think, was enrolled at school, and would later enter Armitage, so at least he was at no immediate risk. Besides, he had been adopted by a family relative, giving him a home of his own. Adoption is a tried and proven practice, often providing simultaneously the answer to the problem of orphans as well as to that of childless families, as in Musa's case. It was a convenient solution, but one that came with significant emotional cost. I had a brother who was now not one of us. Blood ties existed, but without the flow of daily contact to feed them. Having had siblings at home, Musa was reduced to being a single child in a strange house a few yards from us, and the dual status must have been difficult for him to reconcile, as it was for us. In the end, his birthright of being a sibling he had to shed for a new family. It complicated relations across family lines, with Mother having to bear the brunt of it. How would Musa grieve for the loss of his mother without loyalty to his adopted mother being strained? Did that draw and split his emotions? How did it fill the brooding hole of the introvert in him? Could we reach him now?

I returned to Georgetown briefly to visit the family: my brothers, aunts, and grandmother. It was clear life would not be the same for any of us. Too numb for words, my brothers just stared at me and at one another, while Grandmother simply turned her eyes downward, as if the pain was right there under her feet. I tried to meet Father, but I can't recall what happened, if anything happened. Relatives engaged in their own coping strategies: they invoked God's will, saying God ordained it, and that her time had come — *wato le sita.* They believed that fate is a blind alley, and resignation, not defiance, befits it. An ancient poet drops the gauntlet here, defying anyone to do better:

> We spin about and whirl our way through life,
>> Then, rich and poor alike, at last seek rest
> Below the ground in hollow pits slate-covered;
>> And there we do abide.

I turned to the words of the poet John Masefield to express the feeling buried under the root of my grief:

> In the dark womb where I began,
> My mother's life made me a man;
> Through all the months of human birth
> Her beauty fed my common earth.
> I cannot see, nor breathe, nor stir
> But through the death of some of her.

Mother used to say when someone died that the silk cotton tree had fallen on its weight, setting off the nestled birds to scatter to the four winds. I wondered how many stars fell in her memory. Each of us as children was searching for a gem in the debris of Mother's death, and all we could come up with was a crutch. Still, it was better to have that than to limp off in denial. Mother left her children very few options when she remarried. We could not have followed her to her new home in a strange village far away, nor did we have any claim on the former co-wives who ran the household with their own scores to settle. Having run out of money, Father had returned a few years later with his bride, who had by then become dismayed and left him. With nothing more than the pittance of his government pension, he was down to his first and by now much-riled wife, though he pretended nothing had changed. He offered no explanation for these dramatic changes as the household contracted, switching to survival mode. It was not an encouraging setting for farming out the new burdens Mother left behind.

Grandmother's reaction to Mother's death was one of stunned disbelief, I suppose because it destroyed her well-laid plans to have the last word against Father. With malice aforethought she had masterminded the breakup of her daughter's marriage behind Father's back and steered her into the arms of a stranger. The whiplash from the backfiring of her plan took its expected toll. Now she had to cope with both the unpleasant fact of her daughter's children being abandoned to the mercy of a slighted and resentful co-wife and the harsh truth of her daughter's relocation and eventual death in a remote village away from her children.

I had seen my grandmother on earlier weekend school outings, and it had become clear to me that the months preceding Mother's death had been weighing heavily on her. She had rescued her daughter from a hard but known risk, only to lose her in an untested gambit. In place of the old eccentricities of jovial slights and idiosyncratic affectations there were now only desultory hisses and sullen regrets. Her spirit deflated and her fury quenched, the volcano was extinct. Grandmother could not bring herself to talk about Mother, and she died of grief exactly a year to the day after Mother — January 31, 1960. She just felt unable to live with her herself after all that. God's will takes no hostages.

With his own complicated reasons for not wanting to talk about it, it was impossible to get through Father's defensive shield. I was left to forage for solace, to muse on "the outworn world's decay" and to nurse my "rankling hate of God." Cornered, I watched and listened closely. By tradition the elders were solicitous of our welfare, but the options for expressing that were very limited. Their greeting, liberally sprinkled with pious phrases and Qur'anic references, was the typical form of expressing condolence. Even there, boys and girls were not supposed to express such sentiments, and were reprimanded if they tried to do so. Society kept a tight lid on emotions, with age an additional safeguard. Society was much better at adding flavor to life by dispensing anecdotes and amusing stories for entertainment and diversion. This was not the place to deal with grief, I reminded myself. After briefly mentioning their sorrow, people were reluctant to discuss bereavement at all. I was home, but my grief left me a stranger there. People who did not share my disposition simply held their nose and looked the other way when they saw me coming. I had the door shut in my face when I visited friends, with their parents saying I was not good company. *"A mâ fansung mó-lèti,"* they would say, literally, "he is his own person," with the pejorative sense of someone who rejects society for the solitary life.

After returning to Banjul, I continued to rehearse to myself the events and incidents of my young life, with little pattern emerging to guide me. The setbacks just kept mounting, and I didn't know what the future held in store. It was hard to contemplate it. I turned my attention to people I could look up to for their aptitude and achievement, lingering on the examples of those who did well in life and what it was exactly they had in common. I concluded that whether they were hippo hunters, traders, schoolteachers, carpenters, tailors, goldsmiths, bakers, musicians, or builders, all such persons exerted themselves and took risks, convinced that their effort and dedication would be rewarded. Society commended such enterprising individuals by saying it was God's will, though in that case it was so after the fact, making God's will here diagnostic rather than prognostic. In effect, good luck comes only to those who have been industriously engaged. That helped define where I should look for help. Traders and civil servants I found generally to be more sympathetic, in both cases perhaps because they saw the world in more than one color.

The Thompsons, a Creole family, accepted the part of host family while I went job hunting in Banjul. I felt very fortunate indeed to have the Thompsons for sanctuary. They were practicing Anglicans, I believe, and had another son living in the United Kingdom who was married to a British woman. I don't think the Thompsons had ever lived that close to a Muslim before, even though they lived in a Muslim neighborhood. The sanctuary turned out to be short-lived; in time, my early morning prayers and devotions unnerved them, and they asked me to leave. There was not really any spare space in the house, for that matter, but the way Mrs. Thompson put it was simply that the Muslim prayers frightened the family. She said the God of Islam was not the God of Christianity, and vice versa, and so she decided that the strange experiences of the household since my arrival were an expression of the displeasure of the Christian God. This coincided with having my food served in the same dish as the one used for the house dog, a scandal to Muslim sensibility, and an appropriate revenge of the Christian God. So I moved on. I rented a one room nearby and repaired for food and drink to the home of a new friend who became my social companion. His mother would save me food even when I was too shy to keep turning up for such favors.

I accepted a job later in 1959 at the government-run Royal Victoria Hospital in Banjul as a nurse's aid, thinking that might lead to a career in medicine. After a year of grueling rounds of working the wards and attending weekly lectures I decided on a change, and, accordingly, applied to the Secretariat for a job in administration. The following year I received a transfer to the Treasury Department doing daily abstracts. It was a tedious job, I found, but I didn't know where else to turn. All I knew was that the working life that I was experiencing did not fit well with my hopes, and it seemed too premature a step for me to take at that point in my life. I wasn't alone in that position: many other young people in the office were enrolled in British correspondence courses, and, in their spare time, working toward higher certification. Work as such was a stepping stone for them, too.

In the continuing uncertainty of my life, I began reassessing the Christian religion — or what little I knew of it. In my brief and rather untypical encounter with Christians thus far, I did not know what to make of the religion except that it was a contradiction of Islam. Christian colleagues at work were the soul of camaraderie, and little of religious matters entered or soured our conversations. Indeed, the deputy accountant general, also a Methodist lay leader, was known and admired as an Islamophile; he was unhappy with my Christian inquiries when he found out. For their part, the Thompsons were generous to begin with, but I was confused and embarrassed by the abrupt turn of events there. The

Christian religion remained largely a mystery. In Muslim teaching, Christianity is a corrupted faith, endowed with the truth but unfaithful to it. Beyond that Christianity made only a superficial impression on me. What I observed of Christians did not make me stop and think. Christians did not appear to possess a revealed language, unlike the sacred Arabic, and the talking points for Christians were for the most part secular. Europeans did not seem particularly religious, I imagined; their outlook seemed this-worldly, with a liberal permissive bias. No one told me they ever saw a European other than a priest on bended knee at prayer, I thought, suggesting Europeans had turned their backs on God because of Christianity, rather than in spite of it.

In these circumstances it was positively heady to fancy myself a flag-bearer of Islam. I recalled the teachers at school who in their lessons strained for the deliverance of Christians from error and blindness. Then when I saw Christians drunk on Christmas Day, the birthday of Jesus son of Mary (peace be upon him), I felt stirring in me the iconoclastic resolve to purge Christians of their sinful habits, including the demon of alcohol. I thought Muslims were right to think that Christianity had lost its right to be considered a religion and should do us the favor of going out of business altogether. I discovered in time that Christian fundamentalists shared this view, though their remedy of scriptural stringency may simply be evasive, confusing the symptom with the cause. When I came upon the book *How to Be a Christian Without Being Religious* (1967), by Fritz Ridenour, which sold over a million copies, it left me puzzled by its promotion of Christianity without metaphysics. Salvation is full and complete now, and this life — or the American uplift version of it — is all there is to the religion, the book claims. Muslim friends and jaded Christians warned of such experimentation in Christianity as proof of a concocted religion.

It is worth thinking about the fact that, even without much exposure to Christians or to Christianity, Muslims' negative impression of the religion should abound. Proximity did not seem to improve the impression, while familiarity appeared only to deepen it. Again, this was no different for me, except that it gave prickly cover for the secret doubts that left me restless and unfulfilled. I speculated inconclusively: if Europeans are nonbelievers, perhaps it is because Christianity fails as a religion. If the religion does not avert wild behavior, can it save? I wondered. Drunken indulgence quenches the thirst for knowledge of God, I gloated all too readily. However lukewarm and profligate, Muslims would never dream of engaging in drunken revelry on the birthday of the Prophet Muhammad, or take their rowdy behavior into a place of worship, heaven forbid. The stringent form of school Islam that I knew made Christianity seem like weak stuff by comparison. The fact of congenial friendships notwithstanding, I was convinced Christianity was a deluded creed. I found out later that St. Paul wrote, "let us conduct ourselves becomingly as in the day, not in reveling and drunkenness" (Rom. 13:13). Similarly, St. Peter: "Be sober, be watchful" (1 Pet. 5:8). Yet despite being clear and well-known, these exhortations apparently made no difference to Christians, perhaps because the words lacked revealed authority. It might explain why the Qur'an claims that Jesus is the posthumous false creation of his misguided followers. May God assail them! (Q 9:30).

I felt roused to do battle by the belligerent view that someone else's religion was my business, nay, was my mission, forsaking my conciliatory African ideals. The idea of Christians as Catholics and Protestants I found offensive. It didn't matter the difference between them — just the fact of it provoked me. Muslims as Muslims were right to reject Christianity, though the people who called themselves Christians could be tolerated for not knowing any better. Claims about the divinity of Jesus, about the Crucifixion, about the Trinity, and about the authenticity of the Bible at best simply left Muslims bemused. Such claims, says the magisterial al-Ghazali (d. 1111), show only impudence towards God and are a disgrace to religion. Only by biting with their wisdom teeth — i.e., by stubborn willfulness — could Christians persist in making those claims, protests al-Ghazali. On any standard of religious integrity, theological seriousness, moral consistency, and social decorum, Muslims rated Islam by far the superior religion over Christianity. Islam held competitive advantage, and was the ideal religion for revealing misbehaving Christians as the scandal they were. None of this required a word about Christianity itself, but that was not necessary. Simply the idea of it was enough to attract outright condemnation. I had reached the point where it was not enough just to be religious; it had to be at the expense of someone else's religion.

Yet all this left me with a flea in my ear, with nagging questions about true knowledge of God. The Qur'anic picture of the moral life was good as far as it went. Teachers had said that God rewards obedience with success, and sheds His favor on believers. The Qur'an says the fate of the unbelievers is unenviable torment (Q 50:18-30; 70; 88; 101). If God punishes the disobedient, does that mean that failure and suffering are signs of divine displeasure? Would we suffer, then, if we did not displease God? Similarly, why do we suffer while we try to please God?

I persisted: if suffering is so widespread, it must be because either disobedience is rampant or suffering is indiscriminate, afflicting good and bad alike. Where does that leave God? Success does not raise awkward moral questions, but suffering, on the other hand, kindles with smoldering queries about how a sovereign and omnipotent God of goodness can allow it, or allow us to allow it. The question dogs us at every step.

If the prophets suffered and were afflicted, maybe God is sending us a message. "Take, my brethren, the prophets, who have spoken in the name of the Lord, for an example of suffering affliction, and of patience. Behold, we count them happy which endure. Ye have heard of the patience of Job, and have seen the end of the Lord; that the Lord is very pitiful, and of tender mercy" (James 5:10-11). The Qur'an also testifies: "Even so We have appointed to every Prophet an enemy among the sinners; but Thy Lord suffices as a guide and as a helper" (Q 25:32-33). The picture of the cross-bearing Jesus trusting in God sprang to mind here. Jesus submitted, and, while obedient, suffered and was afflicted. He endured the Lord's trial faithfully (Q 25:22). If, after all that, Jesus did not look the part of God's favored prophet, we have to ask where else his prophethood resided. "For he hath no form nor comeliness; and when we shall see him, there is no beauty that we should desire him . . . and we hid as it were our faces from him; he was despised and we esteemed him not" (Isa. 53:2-3). "Not by might, nor by power, but by my Spirit, saith the Lord of hosts" (Zech. 4:6). The verse echoes the Muslim equivalent: *la hawla wa la quwwata illa bi-llahi* ("There is power and strength in none except in God.") If God accepted Jesus' suffering and failure, it would require us to judge him and God by a different rule, thus giving hope to suffering humanity; it was proof that God would not abandon us in the desolate experience of pain and loss. If a God-anointed Jesus suffered, as scripture claims, that fact would trump all theory; it would give us new knowledge about God and about us: God is in suffering to transform us. It would be crucial to affirm that truth. "For who hath despised the day of small things? For they shall rejoice" (Zech. 4:10).

Although I could recognize the logic, it was a different matter to submit to it. I had no experience of a corresponding community of faith to be able to imagine how one would live life on those terms. Living is conceivable only in concrete terms, and religion shares in the vitality of tangible, palpable life.

I was in a quandary. Without a God of suffering, life would be like a mirage, undependable in spite of all appearances. The God of my official instruction promised victory, and yet struggle and uncertainty dogged me: I knew so little, had so little, saw so little, and could do so little. Why would God do business with me? Just measuring up to the mundane demands of everyday living was enough to defy my best effort, let alone taking on the high calling of the hereafter. If suffering was alien to God, I reasoned, life as we know it seemed all but senseless and pointless. It seems unfair to be brought into the world, to be saddled with the ups and downs of life, and then to be on trial for having to account to a higher, unseen power. God had the help of angels; we had no such backup. But if suffering had divine merit, Jesus' ministry would vindicate it in a unique, definitive way. It would require me to reckon with God as Jesus had made God manifest. I was unwilling to do that, but it made me restless. The questions kept simmering, with youthful energy stoking the embers.

Having foreclosed any exit strategy from Islam, I was reduced to plowing over the same ground. In retrospect, agnosticism could have been an alternative, but it didn't seem viable: it offers only ready-made objections to truth claims. To say you object to God because you do not know sounds like a dying quail, and leaves you beholden to Pascal's wager: placing your bet on the possibility that God does not exist risks the whole of eternity if you lose, whereas your risk that God exists costs you nothing if in the end God does not exist. With so much at stake, it is imprudent, according to Pascal, to rely on the argument of uncertainty rather than on the wager for eternity. You risk only the inconvenience of forgoing the fruits of an unethical life if you are proven wrong. As Shakespeare puts it in *Hamlet,* what if there is sentient life beyond the grave, where "dreams may come when we have shuffled off this mortal coil"? It is enough to give one pause. This is not the same as banking on the lottery for your retirement, as some critics have objected, because retirement is not in doubt; only the lottery is. With or without a winning lottery, you will get to retirement sooner or later. A better analogy would be expending your winnings here on looking after the poor in the name of God in the hope of obtaining God's favor in the hereafter. You would have lived ethically even if God should elude you. With life's challenges as they were, I calculated that it would be far better to be found cleaving to the sunnier side of doubt.

Those who have objected to Pascal's wager have adopted a nihilist position as the next logical step of their agnosticism. In this nihilist philosophy where everything is in flux, commitment to truth is a delusion, and that gives the ephemeral primacy over any notion of ultimate truth. What matters is the search, the quest, not the goal or destination, and that is what should have the primary claim on our efforts. But this is trying to have it both ways, trying to say that our sense of values is important even though we cannot attribute any true value to ultimate reality. Both cannot be true. Belief in our thoughts concerning progress cannot survive if purpose or the destination has no intrinsic merit. If ultimate reality has no value, any sense of value must ultimately be whimsical, and that would knock the ground from under any idea of value. As Oscar Wilde contended, being in the gutter is not all we have; some of us are looking at the stars.

In any event, at my stage in life I thought that way of dealing with life's challenges was taking huge risks with my future. If my feelings, moods, desires, and impressions were all I had to explain why the world existed, there would be no point in committing to truth, or in taking responsibility in society. The fact that I was engaged in such a reflection was a vital clue that I was more than just a solitary hormonal byproduct of a bio-chemical process. At any rate, I didn't feel I could safely entrust myself to an impersonal chain of causation. As Dostoyevsky puts it in *The Brothers Karamazov,* if there is no God all bets are off, and you haven't seen the worst of it yet. In real life, the imperative of striving is more compelling than the abstract case for *I think, therefore I am.* In light of the few opportunities I had, being confined to my own thoughts was not viable or credible.

Islamic critical thought helped me make a distinction between an argument for argument's sake and one of substance. The *silsilah,* the chain, supporting an argument is more than a matter of the elegance, the *sahih,* of its links; it depends on the substance, the *matn,* of what the chain conveys. Faith gives reason the substance worthy of it, so that reason grows by contemplating the subject of its life. Reason is sound to the extent of its being in harmony with the truth of its nature. Reason is not for its own rehearsal, but accounts to the true source and purpose of all being. That is the light in which we see all light. I had no name for that Reason, still less a certainty of where I might find it. At night I looked to my guardian angels to bring me light, only to be no more enlightened when morning came. In the day there was light all around, but, alas, none to guide me, and so I would brace myself for another round of groping and stumbling. In their distress my pre-Islamic forebears, buoyed by the brew of choice, patronized concrete emblems in shrines and altars, but, apart from fragile memories, left no vindicating testimonies. Their legacy, alas, has dissipated into the mists of time. It is no consolation to reflect that the fathers were born under one law but left their children bound to another.

The only sensible choice here was to return to lessons I learned at Qur'an school and at Armitage, and to look for possible connections with my present condition. It was, I realized, too much of a jump to Christianity from my scanty knowledge of Jesus and his blessed mother in the Qur'an. Speaking of Mary as God's chosen model of womanhood, the Qur'an says: "Mary, God has chosen thee, and purified thee; He has chosen thee above all women" (3:39; also 19). Such knowledge, however, is swiftly overtaken by Islam's preemptive claim that it holds the key to the meaning of Jesus. Among themselves, Christians are split about who Jesus truly is, but not Muslims, which shows where the truth lies. Few Muslims were more confident about Islam's superiority over a fractious Christianity than I was, and my teachers praised their protégé with delight without realizing the nature of the moral storm that tossed and left me "toiling and turmoiling through want of truth," in the words of Augustine.

Having never attended a mission school, I asked repeatedly why I of all people should be drawn to Jesus. "They make them like that in mission schools" is the dismissive Muslim view. "They will not make you like that because you never went to mission school," I told myself defensively. There were countless Muslim children who had received the benefit of a mission education and who fitted the bill as admirers of Jesus better than I did. They owed a debt to the church as beneficiaries of consecrated Christian labor, whereas I patently did not.

I tried many ways to shake the monkey off my back. The small change from my small pay packet I distributed as a votive offering, asking for prayer that I would forsake Islam never. I used the Thompsons' withdrawal of hospitality as a weapon in my arsenal of anti-Christian resentment. It happened that the neighbors who came to be my Good Samaritans by sheltering and giving me food were a Muslim family; their generous kindness to me as a stranger I used to belittle Christianity. I bragged about the munificence of Muslim neighbors, parading that as evidence of the moral superiority of Islam. All that indulgent partisan righteousness I cranked up to trash Christianity. Yet I was rattled. For diversion I joined a neighborhood youth group that made the rounds of dance parties and entertainment events. We made out to be attending religious vigils, only to get diverted into pursuing girlfriends, our real motive. Omar (not his real name), the plucky leader of the pack, reduced the rest of us to admiring spectators as he picked off girl after girl, night after night. We admired in him what some of us patently lacked: sheer chutzpah with the opposite sex. Yet not all of us envied Omar in the least, because his conquests left him insatiate and cynical — and how I devoutly wished this was not more than simply crying sour grapes. I noticed that Omar was broken when I next saw him years later. Epicurean indulgence drove him to desperate measures, taking a terrible toll on him. It was truly sad to see. His eyes flashing and his hands shaking, he barely recognized me. He had the classic symptoms of mental illness. I was moved that his family let me see him in that state.

Unsuccessful at those evening forays into idle fun, I would return to my rented apartment deflated and confused. It was a standard expectation in society that young men should go out and have fun drinking sweet mint tea while chasing girls and rocking at discos, and in general leaving their mark on their corner of town. The only mitigating factor was that no alcohol was allowed. Yet I was miserable at those games. I had a secret illness that returned at bedtime. The company I wanted and sought deserted me, but the company from which I fled dogged me. In my thoughts I was preoccupied with questions about God; in my actions I looked for worldly diversion.

If only I had been able to talk to the Catholic and Protestant missionaries in town, whom I didn't know at all, having only recently arrived there. Yet they wouldn't know what to make of me either, bless them. No one like me had ever showed up on their radar. Careful not to offend Muslims, Christian mission in a Muslim society is very different from the stereotype of mission as a rambunctious charge into strange people's homes to kidnap boys and girls for indoctrination in schools. The mission schools active in the town officially abjured even the desire to convert Muslims, and instead offered education and guidance to their pupils with no strings attached. Missions represented an enlightened Christianity, too sophisticated for Africans to take in one stride, and yet too well endowed with material gifts not to share with Africans, such being God's wish. For Muslims, however, missions were the shield against defections from their ranks. Thus conceived, missions were allies of the colonial government's policy of support for Muslim institutions. Government provided subsidies for Muslim children attending Christian schools on the condition that they did not convert. It was an ironic way to do mission at all, but there they were, these consecrated men and women, leaving home to give their lives to the cause of promoting Muslims. It would have taken a quake of seismic proportions to shake this settled policy, as I would come to understand later. This three-cornered alliance of state, Islam, and mission would prefer that someone on my sort of quest disappear in a hole. I had no idea what I was digging myself into.

If I could have kept things to myself rather than let anyone into my thoughts, I would have done so gladly. On both the Christian and the Muslim fronts, the odds stacked against me were considerable. Friends soon noticed, however, that I was straining at having fun, that I gravitated toward religious-minded people, that I was attentive when discussing religious questions, and that I no longer frequented venues where boys converged to have fun.

I could not afford to buy books, so I spent my spare time in the local British Council library — what a boon! The books were begging me to pick them up. It felt magical. I wondered whether I was strange for being attracted to books while my peers sought each other's company. It didn't matter. With books it was easy to overcome distractions.

The question that crumbled my partisan wall of presumption came from a Christian acquaintance, John T. On a late weekend afternoon he found me sitting outside the gate of my apartment compound. Given my mental state I think I made the first move, telling him that claims about the crucifixion were willful fabrication, and wasn't it time Christians came to their senses and admitted the nonsense? In that case, he said somewhat offhandedly, if Jesus was not crucified, who rose from the grave? I recalled that the Qur'an denies that Jesus was crucified, and, having inwardly taken in and digested that, I assumed the question of his resurrection to be moot. The Qur'an makes only an oblique reference to it, and in a symbolic way. So I never dwelled on the subject — until then.

By tying the crucifixion to the resurrection so directly at a particularly sensitive point in my life, John T. set bells ringing in my head. Was I living in a haunted neighborhood? Was the truth of the resurrection my issue also? Did I live in a world awake to that truth, and yet I was kept in the dark about it? How could something like that happen without my ever having had the slightest curiosity about it? Why did conventional teaching about the world omit even the slightest whisper of it, if it was true? How could an explosive fact like that be that well contained? Were Christians that smart to perpetrate such a brazen hoax on the world with a disappearing body, and yet be so dim as to think that God could have a son? How could a trick that simple uphold a faith that old? The question of the crucifixion that I raised with such rambunctious confidence now boomeranged with the unsettling enigma of the resurrection. There seemed no viable way to evade that inconvenient truth, nor was retreat feasible.

Thus I wrestled and tussled and agonized. I remember asking an

Englishman who worked in the colonial service and who was a self-avowed atheist if it was true that Jesus died on the cross. He responded that it appeared to be a settled fact of history, but added promptly that it proved nothing about there being a God at all. How strange, I thought, that an atheistic disposition could face and dismiss the crucifixion that Jesus did not survive, making atheism seem all too willful. By pointing out the resurrection as the sequel of the crucifixion, John T. made the connection that compelled bringing God into the picture in a way I had never done. John T. unleashed a torrent of questions that shook my moorings and scrambled my landscape, leaving me tossing with confusion. Even before I understood the import, the crucifixion and the resurrection together disrupted my mental picture of religion and of the world, and it upset and frustrated me that I had to face the question at all. I regretted that the Muslim in me didn't have the last word. Where was John T. coming from? I puzzled. Had God sent him?

He left me reeling and clamoring for an answer. The challenge implicit in his words commanded attention, and I realized I could not go on playing the same old game of beating up on Christians to make Islam look great, parading my piety to tweak Christian friends and acquaintances, and trusting in time to rout untruth. I persisted in attack mode for several more months, dismissing the crucifixion, while, meanwhile, I was unable to shut it out of my mind. I was a disarmed rebel, a sorry heap of crumbling zeal. I resented it that religion in the form of Christianity had me nettled in that way. Christianity was not what I was looking for, yet Christianity's slain founder had risen from the grave and was threatening to pursue me in my thoughts. When and where might I find the answer? I was frantic.

At this point Terry Iles, an Englishman who had recently arrived as a high school history teacher, took me under his wing. It was a brief but consequential event of my life. In Terry's company I met in late 1960 Irene Bednall, a senior nursing sister at the Royal Victoria Hospital. A charismatic evangelical Christian, Sister Bednall had served as a faith mission worker in China, where she was a disciple of Gladys Aylward, a famous English charismatic Christian missionary to China. Sister Bednall eventually became an employee of the colonial administration in the Gambia, and in her spare time evangelized among her mainly

Muslim hospital staff, who treated her kindly while rebuffing her evangelistic efforts.

I was introduced to her during one of her one-woman evangelistic forays at a tea event she hosted in her flat, but I couldn't make sense of what she was saying. With a bubbly, outgoing personality, Sister Bednall pumped a Bible into my hand that I never opened — I thought no such thing existed, and here she was thinking her sunny, hugging disposition could pass off a fake as the real thing. I didn't know if I should wash my hands for touching an unclean thing. I should state here that for penance, I kept in touch with Sister Bednall long after she retired and went to live in West Yorkshire to tend her ailing father. Until her death we maintained a faithful annual Christmas exchange of cards and gifts. In all that time Sister Bednall had no idea how strange charismatic religion was to Muslim society, and to the end she remained baffled and befuddled by the firm rejection of her message in spite of genuine affection for her. With holy figures, Sufi brotherhoods do make use of charismatic ideas and teachings, but they do so by investing in institutions and structures of family and corporate life, rather than in individualistic notions. The gregarious Sister Bednall viewed religion as experiential exuberance, and, without a family, she made religion look like a novel, solitary business. I knew religion only as faith with boundaries, markers, and structures, and so was unable to relate to religion simply as goodwill unbound. Mood uplift alone is not enough to make religion — that only looks to us for validation.

Still, after about a year of treating Sister Bednall as an improbable, if friendly, spectacle, my mind now turned to her with new purpose. Her breezy remarks about following Jesus started slowly to come into focus and to grow into a recognizable picture, even though Sister Bednall's language about salvation was atmospheric and hazy. God — Christ — sin — atonement — salvation: it was the same lofty idea in repetitive abstract language. Though too disembodied for Muslim ears, the reference to Jesus alerted me to the idea that there might be important sources on his life outside the Qur'an, though I was unwilling to go to those sources, whatever or wherever they were. Since the idea of following the prophets of God is well established in Muslim teaching, following Jesus made sense to me as a Muslim.

What I didn't know was what Jesus could or would do for me or, in-deed, for anyone else. The Islamic curriculum places the prophets of old in the iron grid of dogma, with the Qur'anic Jesus bristling with Islam's subpoenas. Yet here was Sister Bednall saying that Jesus was a living presence. The thought stuck with me, although I never raised it, or thought of raising it, with Sister Bednall. As I dwelled on the idea of fol-lowing Jesus, I returned in my mind to the crucifixion and the resurrec-tion, and was drawn once more by the power of their logical conver-gence. Yet, even after granting that Jesus was crucified and rose from the grave, I still did not know if and how that affected me personally. It upset me that I had overlooked those facts, but I did not have a theological ex-planation for them. What did I have to do with the crucifixion? And as for the resurrection, it might as well be as real as the distant clouds. It was like receiving dramatic news that someone had walked out of a burning house without any indications that I had anything to do with it — and if I did, what I should do in response. Was this person any relation of mine? Did I have any moral obligation to him?

In the standard Qur'anic account, the mysterious ascension of Jesus was how God intervened to rescue Jesus from the shame and humilia-tion inflicted by his enemies (4:157), and the symbolism of that divine in-tervention has priority over the historical fact of the crucifixion. But I could not get away from the feeling that a historical fact so potent could scarcely be so easily obliterated by making Jesus disappear in a mysteri-ous ascension — a story motivated by the view that it would be better if the crucifixion had not happened. The post-facto solution of the ascen-sion seemed still to concede the gravity of the anteceding historical cru-cifixion, rather than to make it vanish.

This is where the empty tomb juts in to solidify the idea that Jesus' embodiment of death and resurrection was a necessary and designated landmark of the God of history. The ground is God's own by design and choice, and it compels engagement and response on our part because the historical events in question are laden with moral import for us here and now: not the import of our natural and commendable desire to rescue Je-sus, but the import that his death and resurrection speak solicitously to our estrangement and reconciliation with God — on God's terms. God has chosen that way to speak to us, and dispensed with any need for an emergency rescue plot to confound Jesus' enemies and foil them. In Jesus God shows forgiveness and redemption to be more divine in their radical comprehensiveness than the impromptu disguise, illusion, and diversion we might conjure up. The issue is not a word-game at all; it lies heavy on God's heart. Jesus, crucified and raised, was the outcome. "It was the will of the Lord to bruise him; he has put him to grief." All this "because he had done no violence, neither was any deceit in his mouth" (Isa. 53:9-10). "Ought not the Christ to have suffered these things?" (Luke 24:26). He "endured the cross, heedless of the shame" (Heb. 12:2).

But what did all of that have to do with me? What part did I have with victim or victimizer? I learned that I should take it one idea at a time; after all, the cross and the empty tomb are hard to scale by natural means. First, the crucifixion. I worked up an attitude toward the enemies of Jesus: why did they treat God's prophet and a good person that way? Then I begged for God's mercy for the heartless cruelty that took the life of Jesus. I paused at this point, stumped by a suggestion that I could not grieve for Jesus without assuming personal responsibility, too. But what did it have to do with me? The fact that I was driven to ask for God's mercy for the tragedy of Jesus meant that I could not do so credibly from a remote, uncommitted position. It required personal proximity, in fact personal solidarity with the enmity that targeted Jesus precisely because it was enmity against God. If the enemies of Jesus sinned, we had all sinned. Their guilt was ours, too.

The next step was to face the resurrection. There any pity for the plight of Jesus was upstaged and rendered moot by his being raised, leaving me to grasp at pious straws. God did not need my pity. God could, and perhaps did, forgive Jesus' enemies, which would leave me stranded with a holy grievance God dissolved in the atonement. The thought reduced my grievance to self-incrimination. It would be better to be a forgiven enemy of Jesus, I reasoned, than to be his unforgiving defender.

My zeal for Jesus prevented me from seeking the benefit of the forgiveness his crucifixion achieved and his resurrection affirmed. It was not my role to defend Jesus; God had defended him already in the resurrection. His enemies could kill Jesus, or, to take the Qur'anic view, they could cause him to be removed from the scene, but only God could exonerate them and raise Jesus. My blindness instigated my enmity and placed my guilt before me as a barrier. I had to lay down my arms of resistance and give up any thought that I had a heart large enough to contain the anguish of Jesus. Instead I needed to put myself in the hands of God and ask forgiveness for my wrongheaded role as defender extraordinaire. I was fallen, yet I was acting the part of Jesus' rescuer. My devout bid to treat Jesus' tragedy as an illusion was a barrier against recognizing my part in his death, placing me in need of God's exoneration, too. I didn't need a complicated theology to appreciate that our hates for God need God to forgive. Still, how I wished for trained and solid Christian instruction at this stage! I was caught in a tide of confusion when the path to faith lay open before me.

In my fumbling steps I came to realize that there was a sure road to fellowship with God and I should take it without hesitation and without deviation. I could postpone the decision no longer. I used to go to bed thinking that the issue would go away by daybreak, but it didn't. By morning it simply revived in intensity. When night came around, the clamor would subside, only for the day, once more, to rekindle it, with night and day in their alternation as two contestants pitted in a tug-of-war.

Then as if prompted, on a solitary walk on the ocean beach one April afternoon I could not silence the voice begging for a yea or nay — begging, indeed, for night or day to decide the issue once and for all. But the morning light was already shining through. In the haunting words of the old spiritual:

> My Lord, what a morning!
> When the stars begin to fall
> 'Cause there's a new day come about

It was as if I heard a solicitous whisper, a simple, clear call borne on the wings of infinite forbearance to answer the summons of life: "Do not be afraid. Jesus surrendered to God. Won't you?"

Many words in my language represent the idea of surrender, of walking into the light: *dankeneya,* faith-filled certainty; *song,* to concede; *tubi,* from the Arabic *tawbah,* for repentance; *fang-dio,* to hand over oneself; *nyo-yi,* to kneel down; *kang-dio,* to give consent, and so on. Handing oneself over, kneeling down and giving consent — these carry a social connotation. But the other terms, including the Arabic-derived *tubi,* carry explicit religious meaning. On that day the boundary between these worlds merged to compel a decision for faith and trust. It produced the state of mind for which the word *dankeneya* is most apt: a providential process that brings one to encounter with unshakeable truth. The calm waves echoed the absence of any duress in the call, only that truth should make me free.

Suddenly I felt unable to continue with my stroll unless I persisted in defying the relentless nipping at my heels. A momentary pause was enough to set the new course. I had no idea what I was doing or why. The short, small step I took to suspend my seaside stroll and head home turned me in a new direction: I had to follow Jesus as the crucified and risen One. Like a gentle nod, a wave of anticipation rose in me as I responded feebly to a long delayed invitation, like rejoining a journey begun before my mother conceived me.

When I turned to go home I realized I had also yielded to the mystery pursuing me. I remember the sense of a door opening and a reassuring presence sweeping into my life. With my guard down, I had the feeling of giving myself in trust. By the time I reached home my legs were heavy, and the next thing I knew I was tumbling to my knees in prayer to Jesus, pleading, imploring, begging for God to forgive me, to accept me, to teach me, to help me — everything a child looks for. The cross flashed in my mind, making me think of redemptive solicitude. I was in tears, but not for long. After all, my formation was by the canon, not by subjective feeling.

I got up from my knees with the feeling that I was waking up on a new day. The late afternoon was infused with a grace-tinged soothing flare, and with a hint of the luminous freshness of new creation. Awakened, all sense of struggle, fear, and anxiety vanished. I felt bound and confused no longer. It was a new feeling of release and of freedom, infused with a sense of utter, serene peace. I could speak about it only in terms of new life, of being born again.

CHAPTER 6

Challenged

❋   ❋   ❋

In the aftermath of my conversion, I faced two challenges. I needed to slip away from my old moorings without raising a storm, and if I was to be a follower of Jesus, I needed to join a community in his name. After all, religion as mere mystical self-fulfillment had little appeal for me.

Rumors began to spread like wildfire among my Muslim friends that I was thinking Christian thoughts. It surprised and puzzled people, so outlandish was the idea. Wishing it not to be so, Muslim friends asked why God should allow such a fate to befall me. Some wondered if, given the spurt of a hormone-driven adolescence, alcohol or a girl might have seduced me. But they relented when they met with me and heard me out.

I asked to meet Salifu, a classmate who was leader of a gang of boys who were pursuing me with sticks and stones because they were angry about my conversion. I told Salifu I was joining the church not because I was abandoning Islam, but because I had learned as a Muslim to honor God, and now I wanted to love God. Islam had not repelled me; only the Gospel had attracted me. In surrendering and giving myself to this God, I was also acknowledging the goodness and kindness of others as so many material tokens of God's unfathomable and unstinting generosity, and that fact evoked grateful memories of old associates and associations, and a lively hope for new beginnings and commitments. My respect and appreciation of Muslim friends had never been more heartfelt, and I pledged to them my undying loyalty. I assured Salifu that I cherished our continuing friendship, and said gang violence was completely alien to the spirit in which we knew and valued each other. At this point I pleaded with Salifu to drop the stick he was carrying and, instead, to shake my hand, which he did.

I was not abandoning faith. Quite the contrary, I had embraced Jesus because I could not keep him down in my thoughts of honoring God. I recognized his voice as the same one that used to entrance me when as a child I watched, listened, and imitated the adults keeping silence in the mosque as they waited patiently for guidance from above. I felt constrained to embrace the truth of God because I had seen my parents and teachers fall on their knees and on their faces in sublime adoration of the Creator, and their example was the unspoken witness that commitment to God was its own rule and justification. My restless religious life had a power shaping it: God was there. I was drawn to the church because I was raised to value the truth that God was not owned by any tribe, class, or rank, making me aware that truth was not our possession alone.

I was shocked, however, by what I found out next. I might be drawn to the church, but as it turned out, the church was not drawn to me. It was as if somebody had been carefully watching my every move and promptly showed up to bar the way as I tried to speed to my desired objective. The pastors I approached, both Catholic and Protestant, deftly wrapped me in a blanket of good-mannered assurances, effectively smothering my declared intention of seeking baptism. I waited for the blanket to wear thin, poking here and there for evidence of interest, and hoping church officials would relent and welcome my decision. But they were wary, even nervous. It was as if I had roused them from a deep sleep.

Eventually, with prompting, someone moved, though not without first issuing a torrent of caveats. Yes, I was welcome; yes, I would be baptized; yes, the church would give me guidance; and yes, the church supported my decision; and so on. But there was no need for a change of names, no need for long-term commitment, no requirement to renounce Islam, and no need to feel bound to remain in the church. Officials went out of their way to say that the church could not give me employment, or allow my wish to study theology. I should look for something else to study. I would have little trouble landing a scholarship somewhere, I was assured.

I was obviously slow in these things, but in the end even I got the message. How could I not? Muslim friends joined in: "I told you so." "I know," I answered feebly. My unorthodox path to the church meant that I was never done giving explanations to scandalized Muslim friends and to incredulous Christian observers. Coming from a royal lineage, and as such not in search of social status, I did not fit the logic of classical Christian demography. Nobody was willing to believe that I would risk a *fall* in social standing for a religion so unconvinced of its own truth.

The key to understanding the situation lies in its political context. Everyone acknowledges that Islam encourages conversion — just not *from* it. Too often this position is conceded by the implicit consent of the churches in Muslim lands. In return, the churches receive permission to convert and to absorb the animist remnants Muslims regard as specimens of a defunct pagan tradition. Muslims retain entitlement to Christian deference as well as to Christianity's liberal reputation. Muslims honor and celebrate their converts as trophies of faith, while Christians take their converts as charitable ration with a pinch of shame. It forces Christian converts underground to keep their faith quiet, or else makes them propitiatory tokens of a grateful church for Muslim forbearance. This arrangement gives Muslims the confidence that they hold the high ground vis-à-vis Christians; after all, only an inferior religion would agree to such terms.

In the final analysis, Christianity has the status of a lower caste in Muslim lands. The idea of caste Christianity is not as far-fetched as it sounds if we bear in mind that the original core of Christian communities comprised freed slaves, liberated Africans, disbanded foot soldiers, and client families of European merchants. On such terms, interfaith relations are borne on the back of individual Christians, who are placed in something like a witness protection program.

Still, as the Egyptian-born Muslim convert to Catholicism Magdi Allam puts it,[1] conversion as a Muslim right of way makes the church ap-

---

1. Magdi Allam was baptized by Pope Benedict XVI at the Easter vigil at St. Peter's, Rome, on March 23, 2008. It was met with an international Muslim outcry for a variety of

pear not so credible in anything or anywhere else, including on its own turf. By the law of simple economy, religious diplomacy duly contracts to diplomacy as its own rule, so that fear of offending Muslims easily determines how and where to be the church. It seems a high price to pay for the Western guilt complex. To amend St. Augustine, people with an assortment of reasons would repudiate the truth of Christianity; it would be *flebile ludibrium,* a sad mockery, if churches were among them.

The free mission education given to Muslim children served the calculated purpose of granting Muslim demands, and Muslim appreciation for that in turn committed the churches to maintain their schools for the benefit of Muslims. As long as the churches observed the rule of forbidding conversion from Islam while educating Muslim children, they would be tolerated. Keeping school became valuable collateral for being Christian openly. Muslim society threw a few crumbs to the churches by permitting fringe elements of the dwindling non-Muslim residue to convert, but on the whole the churches were required to collaborate with Muslims in maintaining the sealed borders with Islam, and even to turning a blind eye to Christians crossing over. The border crossing with Islam was a one-way street, with Christian guards on sentinel duty — guarding their entrance, not their exit. I was moving against the flow of traffic, and in the process setting off alarm bells all around the ramparts. However well-intentioned, when the churches spoke about freedom of religion, they did so by straining language. Freedom of religion was a euphemism for a prickly status quo, code for observing the rule of causing no offense to Muslims. The churches could not afford Christian converts, for they upset that status quo. To the relief of the churches, however, that happened only rarely, if ever.

Yet however crass the church might be in its understanding of its mission, it probably had not forgotten why it was in the business of religion at all. Surrounded by supervening evidence of Muslim witness to

---

inconsistent reasons: it was insignificant except for the public nature of the event; Allam was free to convert except at the hands of the pope; Allam was free to renounce Islam except that he should not have embraced Christianity in such a high-profile fashion; he should have converted privately to avoid antagonizing Muslims; the Church should have turned him away as a goodwill interfaith gesture, and so on. On such terms Islam would vet the Church, with the pope as interfaith apologist.

one God, the church could not present itself as nothing more than a goodwill enterprise and pretend that personal faith was secondary. Muslims gave the church no such excuse. So there was in fact more to interfaith relations than unilateral Christian disarmament, more to mission than a demilitarized zone. Indeed, Muslims might have unwittingly redeemed the church from a thoroughly calculating, expedient attitude to its mission.

In any case, in spite of the challenges I faced and presented in my desire to join the church, I accepted it as God's will that my path should meet the way of the cross, and I remained transfixed by its gravity. The signposts directed me to fellowship with the people of God, whatever the stigma society attached to them. God's righteousness overcame my prejudice against caste Christianity.

When she heard the news, Sister Bednall was reportedly jubilant, saying it was an answer to prayer. She didn't know I had not opened the Bible she gave me. The Irish Methodist minister of my first approach was also outwardly enthusiastic. His support was immensely assuring and deeply appreciated. It is difficult, however, to square that with reservations he confided to a mutual friend and his subsequent inaction. With no further movement from him, I repeated my request a year later to his colleague, an English Methodist now returned from furlough leave. He echoed the enthusiasm of his colleague, but added an unexpected twist. Did I know that there was a Roman Catholic Church just a couple of blocks away? I stared at him blankly. "You are free to go there, you know," he added.

In my innocence I blissfully trotted along to the Catholic church, and for almost a year I tried in vain, in spite of earnest attempts, to get the attention of the young Irish priest there. I reckoned that since the Methodists and the Catholics were my only viable options, either would do — denominations had never loomed large in my inquiry, and I imagined ignorantly that that would be an advantage. The third option was the Anglican church, the establishment church, as it happened, but I ruled that out for fear of courting the political-motivation charge once more.

The Methodists and the Catholics, by contrast, could make no such claim to establishment entitlement. In fact, the Catholic church was in many ways the church of the poor and the marginal, and, for what it was worth, that appealed to me on its own merits. But the Catholics also parried with a host of reservations, qualifications, and caveats. I concluded that the doors remained shut there, too.

So, with my tail between my legs, I returned to the Methodists, who had heard by then what had transpired at the Catholic church. Still, the English minister waited for me to broach the question one more time. (In these matters, I learned, there were subtle social rules about not punching above one's weight.) Would the Methodist church please baptize me, seeing that I had come back empty-handed from the Catholic church? I asked timidly and pleadingly. "Absolutely," was his prompt answer, but he followed it up with a question: Did I know that the Catholic church recognized the baptism of the Methodist church? "No, I didn't," I answered acquiescently. I wondered why the Methodists were so keen on clueing me on the Catholic church when they had me at their beck and call. Didn't they have Methodism to offer?

My conversion was beginning to feel like managing an ecumenical hedge fund, with the Protestants and Catholics agreeing to share the risks of accepting a convert from Islam but neither being willing to take them on alone. I was back at square one — so much time passed, so little distance traveled. "Are you dim?" Muslim friends asked impatiently, but also solicitously. "The Christians do not want you! What possesses you not to see that? Come back to where you belong." They were not the only ones left incredulous. Yet I was too confused to think to go back to the church to demand a yes or no. Truth be told, I could not take no for an answer.

In this state of limbo I turned to books on Christianity. They were not easy to find. In town there were no bookshops to speak of, only one supply depot that served one or two small schools. There were no newspapers, either, and no reading public of any kind. When people finished high school, they stopped reading. The general attitude was that reading was for children. They outgrew books when school lessons were over, and active religious practice dispensed completely with the need to read books, so my interest in books only added to my reputation as a misfit.

There was the British Council library, which had a limited holding of books on secular subjects. Necessity, as the saying goes, is the mother of invention, so I made my way through what they had to offer. My curiosity led me to a hodgepodge of unlikely suspects. In the library I stumbled on the writings of Aristotle, Plato, Isaac Newton, Bertrand Russell, Harold Nicolson, David Daiches, Ivor Jennings, Leslie Paul, T. S. Eliot, J. Dover Wilson, C. Day Lewis, Lord Macaulay, Lord Chesterfield, Winston Churchill, Arnold J. Toynbee, Lord Acton, Iris Murdoch, the New England Transcendentalists, and French novelists like Guy de Maupassant, Victor Hugo, Gustave Flaubert, and Alexandre Dumas. This motley collection of the tried and proven had little explicit religious orientation as far as I could tell. Aside from Toynbee, there was also little awareness in most of these books of the world of Islam, which was my background. But to the starving, such fare was manna from heaven. In spite of the cultural gulf, I gorged myself on these books, happy to find myself close to books so neatly displayed on the shelves. Given my isolated background, all this was exhilarating in the extreme. I became a naturalized citizen of the world of books.

The world of the novel intrigued me. Here was proof that men and women crafted and launched ideas allowing the human spirit to soar above physical barriers and cultural restrictions, and to inspire pure action in the name of high human ideals. From the debris of World War II writers were calling us to rise from the ashes and to lay claim to the future. I read avidly, if not instructively. I tried none too successfully to coax faith out of my reluctant company.

Bertrand Russell in particular tantalized me. A Nobel laureate in literature and a militant peace activist, Russell was an elusive advocate of the committed ethical life but a sworn enemy of its religious roots. I was drawn to him like the moth to the flame. When it came to how to think, Russell was exemplary, but that was no index of his authority on how to live ethically. In spite of Arnold Toynbee's tribute to him as a leader in the campaign "for the survival of civilization and of the human race," I could not figure out how Russell could be a philosophical Puritan and an ethical antinomian, and whether the discrepancy between philosophical rigor and moral relativism could be anything but crippling. Russell seemed slippery, one time a model of intellectual stringency, and another a figure of moral obfuscation. Yet his philosophical brilliance, as demonstrated in his *Principia Mathematica,* written in collaboration with Alfred North Whitehead, gives hint of the shaft of light that is the source of all intelligence. Russell was proof that the reality of a higher intelligence was connected necessarily to the ethical life, and that one might no more doubt that than reject the ethical project. I received assurance in that regard from reading about the life of Isaac Newton, though I found out later that Newton treated the Bible like Muslims treat the Qur'an. Russell showed me that sovereign reason had its one true inheritance in the noble light of God's truth. Learning could only seek and serve that truth, or learning would serve demonstrably less worthy ends. Evil would be unfettered if truth, goodness, and honor were just opinions.

The world of literature revealed the power of the narrative creativeness of the mind, an existential clue about our origin in God, the warp and woof of the narrative fabric of life. The depth of the treasures that the creative writer plumbs cried out for celebration, indeed for sacramental acknowledgment, to invoke Flannery O'Connor. In spite of his neo-pagan instincts, even Thomas Hardy could not preclude that possibility.

With his sweeping mastery of historical detail, Toynbee soared above the clutter to glimpse something of history's moral impulse, with a built-in vindication of underdogs. When he looked back it was to wish that his contemporaries would follow where he pointed — beyond wars and devastations and the power-grab mentality of elites to the cause of victims. Suffering had taken its toll of human life and misery, and human hubris more than its share of wrong and injustice, Toynbee wrote.[2] The study of history was also the study of human nature and its tragic record, and the historian could not observe that grim reality without addressing its source in the human agent flawed by innate sin. Toynbee had seen too much to be carried away by promises of a utopia on earth. God's work of love was our only hope of earthly rescue, he argued.

Even with this jumble of ideas and thoughts, I was going somewhere

---

2. Arnold J. Toynbee, *An Historian's Approach to Religion* (Oxford University Press, 1956), and his *Experiences* (Oxford University Press, 1969).

rather than simply standing still. I had the sense that I had an obligation to improve myself without waiting for a *deus ex machina*. Thus, with the church still dragging its feet on my baptism, I took the bull by the horns and organized a debating society in the British Council library. Interest was abounding, and I had no trouble signing up volunteers; I even received support from the colony's attorney general. We debated topics as varied as press freedom, the value of education, the role of women in society, and the value of books. The parliamentary rules of debate we adopted ensured that opposing views could be canvassed without threat or grudge. Vigorous debate turned out to be good sport.

The debating filled an important social as well as a personal need. The topics we debated were fundamental to fostering a climate of tolerance and respect. We learned not to impugn the motives of others, and to laugh without mocking. Friendships formed there changed perspectives for the better. Debates could be important antidotes to caricature and distrust; it was a wonder they had not been widely adopted for boys and girls in strife-ridden communities. Such debates could be a vital asset in the search for a common future.

By a remarkable coincidence I chanced upon the writings of C. S. Lewis. The Kingsway Supermarket in Banjul had shipped to it a small consignment of popular paperbacks, including works by D. H. Lawrence. In one consignment I came upon C. S. Lewis's books *Mere Christianity, Miracles, The Problem of Pain,* and *Surprised by Joy,* among others. No one ever said a word about Lewis, but I was entranced by his compellingly clear prose, the force of his reasoning, his scrupulous candor, his unsparing self-scrutiny, and his towering faith in the God who had beset me all these many years. Lewis was proof that God's grace was unmerited and without bound, and that such a God demanded and deserved our free and unfettered consent. We were made for such company.

It puzzled me, however, to learn that the church leaders I knew had no interest in him whatsoever. The Methodist minister made the comment that Lewis never did get a chair at Oxford until Cambridge elevated him into one — a chair in Renaissance Studies, as it happened. You would have to be a cultural snob to understand the subterranean slight here intended; the putdown for me was wasted breath. I had more momentous issues weighing on my mind.

❋   ❋   ❋

Even with my growing disappointment in the church, I still felt a deep need to become a part of it. Tired of the stalemate, I devised a plan. I was off to Germany on holiday; perhaps the Methodist minister would baptize me right before I left. I would take any adverse consequences of my conversion to a picnic somewhere in Europe, and he wouldn't have to face local objections.

The unusual idea of a holiday in Germany was not mine but that of an American friend, Douglas McKinnon, with whom I had a chance encounter on his whirlwind tour through Africa while he was building Investors Overseas Service (IOS) into a global financial empire. I found Douglas one day, map in hand, wandering the streets of Banjul trying to find street names, of which there were few. He looked worn and lost. I asked if I could help, and I ended up escorting him through the town for the rest of the day. He purchased some local fabric and left the parcel with me to mail to him after he returned to Germany. That began our correspondence, which led to his generous invitation to spend my holiday with him in Europe.

With this news of my imminent departure, the minister relented gracefully. "Congratulations," he declared. "You should have a great time in Europe. Will you be coming back?" Yes, I responded deferentially. I could almost hear him thinking: I will be a trooper and do by the book what this lad has asked.

And so, one hot Sunday evening in June 1961, the minister set aside his scruples and administered the sacrament of baptism. I had wrung it out of him, I remember feeling. I was overcome by a mix of emotions: nervousness at cutting loose from the old moorings, uncertainty at what lay ahead of me in church and society, concern for hurt feelings. Mainly, however, I felt relief and a sense of unspeakable joy and inner peace. I knew without a shred of doubt that I had answered the call of the One who, with sovereign freedom, summons us for the march of life.

I felt renewed and challenged by the baptism. I was now a member of the family of God's people transcending all barriers of space and time. It was a new experience to think of God in those terms. Yet after the initial shock of recognition, I found that it sat well with my every hunch and premonition about the nature of truth. The realization it sparked had the ring of lifelong credibility, not just the thrill of a fleeting moment.

The minister was satisfied that I had read and "inwardly marked and digested" the lessons of historical form criticism of the synoptic Gospels of my official catechism. Form criticism is based on textual analysis of Scripture by tracing the history of its contents by forms: parables, proverbs, myths, sayings, and other genres. It is related to redaction criticism, which is the critical editing and rearrangement of the text to align it with an authoritative source. That kind of critical inquiry is the acid test, but to the minister's disappointment, the test failed to deter me at all. In his impatience with a question I once asked about the physical resurrection of Jesus, he appeared to bristle at the thought that I did not seem to be completely reconciled to the modernist project in theology. He made a mental note of that, and held it against me when subsequently I applied to study theology abroad. Nonetheless, in her somewhat idiosyncratic memoirs, his wife referred to my baptism and that of two other candidates baptized with me as a high point of her husband's mission, though she could not bring herself to mention my name in her account.

I found myself having to mark the occasion of my first Communion when the church would not do so. I wrote down a hymn of Charles Wesley that seemed to be in strange harmony with the truth of my individual faith journey. I return to it here for the first time since I sang it at my baptism. It struck me then, and still strikes me today, as evidence of the perennial universal spiritual prompting that defines the moral quest:

Thou great mysterious God unknown,
Whose love hath gently led me on,
Even from my infant days,
Mine inmost soul expose to view,
And tell me if I ever knew
Thy justifying grace.

If I have known only Thy fear,
And followed with a heart sincere
Thy drawings from above,
Now, now the further grace bestow,

And let my sprinkled conscience know
Thy sweet forgiving love.

Short of Thy love I would not stop,
A stranger to the Gospel hope,
The sense of sin forgiven;
I would not, Lord, my soul deceive,
Without the inward witness live,
That antepast of heaven.

If now the witness were in me,
Would He not testify of Thee
In Jesus reconciled?
And should I not with faith draw nigh,
And boldly Abba, Father! cry,
And know myself Thy child?

❁   ❁   ❁

I was eager to make the trip to Germany. It offered me an opportunity to see and reflect on the world and how that might help advance the goals of my eventful religious life. Douglas met me in Marseilles, where my ship, *m.v. General Mangin,* had docked.

After initial visa hassles I disembarked to join Douglas for the hair-raising alpine drive to Munich. It was Douglas's way of introducing me to his favorite wintertime ski slopes, little suspecting my newly discovered phobia of mountains. Douglas, as it turned out, was a mountain ranger at heart. The phenomenon was unknown to me, since there are no mountains in my part of West Africa, and it made me appreciate all the more how terrain could shape one's attitude to the world and to people. The small morsels of food I was able to eat fortunately reduced the chances of any paroxysms of car sickness that would have soiled and slowed our journey considerably. Holding altitude sickness at bay, I eyed Douglas carefully to see whether his evident thrill with steep mountain passes and precipitous drops was born of proven experience or of a reckless sense of adventure, in which case I should beg to be returned to safer ground. Douglas would hum and exclaim in delight as a vista suddenly opened out before us, with a snow-capped range topping a picturesque lakeside town glistening in the sunlight below. He would stop at the lookout to marvel at the spectacle, confounded meantime by my unwillingness to join him at the viewing site. Even in the June sunshine, the banks of mountain snow made me shiver.

By the time we emerged in Munich I was in a state of grateful recovery, having overcome my lowland alarm at Douglas's alpine enthusiasm, but left now to face a summer that was cold even by Munich's standards, let alone those of my homeland. Douglas thoughtfully introduced me to American and German friends, which I appreciated, but I found their ideas on religious matters too triumphalist to be of much help to me.

Douglas was puzzled by my religious interest. He was frankly agnostic in religious matters, and he challenged me to sharpen my wits with his blunt, persistent queries. Theology bored him to distraction. If you wanted to hear a good sermon, he thought, you went to a Methodist church; if you wanted to hear good music, you waited for Christmas and then trotted along to a Lutheran church; if you wanted commonsense, rational religion, you went to a Unitarian gathering; if you wanted religion for yourself without others bothering you, you went to a Quaker meeting; and if you wanted festive celebration, you went to a Catholic church on a feast day. For that matter, Buddhism also offered you enlightenment without religion, didn't I know. There was always something for everyone somewhere, Douglas asserted with evident satisfaction. I should leave the books alone and get out and enjoy Europe — he would even give me pocket money for that. Douglas had the good intentions of a Western liberal who believed that I was part of the emerging leadership of Africa's future, and he invested in me for that reason. My religious questions seemed to him like needless distraction.

On the German trip I saw evidence of the bombings of the war. Munich's art gallery, the Haus Der Kunst, was under comprehensive reconstruction. Postwar Europe was in the midst of stirring from its nightmare, and Douglas's view was that Europe's awakening would come from the restoration of its great musical heritage, with opera houses at Bayreuth, Salzburg, Vienna, Geneva, Milan, Paris, and London, among others, serving as temples of the second birth. He lavished attention and resources in that cause. I tagged along dutifully, if uncomprehendingly. That world of cultivated refinement was a long way from the dreams of a schoolboy, Douglas's guileless confidence notwithstanding. I appreciated his American-inspired optimism that the treasures of the human spirit are the heritage of all humanity, and I marveled that my uninitiated incomprehension never dented his optimism.

I saw evidence of Christian decline all around. On reflection, it was unsettling to be a new Christian surrounded by old crumbling churches and empty, ornate cathedrals. It was hard to evade the fact that the church was in a state of transition from spiritual belief to social action, from truth as revealed reality to relevance as the modern imperative. Douglas took me to meet German families whose memories of the Second World War were still fresh and who seemed in turn both eager and reluctant to revisit the experience. They appeared to be in the grip of a strange disenchantment. They had been chastened but spared, and were unwilling to dream about new possibilities. At Passau, where three rivers meet, we had a meal in the home of some friends and then trotted off to the church to see what Douglas described to me as the world's biggest organ — I think that was the main draw for Douglas. He hovered over the multi-tiered keyboard beaming and humming to himself, just imagining the throb and pulse of the instrument vibrating through the church. He had the organist try a few notes just so we could see his footwork with the pedals and his hands at work pulling the stops. Douglas offered to buy him dinner afterwards.

I remember speaking with some young Germans my age; their halting English and my kindergarten German, covered over with good-natured laughter, carried us along fine. Still at school, they flinched at the thought of doing their *abitur,* the exams taken at the end of high school. I asked Douglas about this, and he said Americans took it for granted that college, what Europeans call university, followed automatically after high school, but European high school students did not make the same assumptions. I guess I was trying to understand why university would be such an uncertainty when young Europeans had so much opportunity at their beck and call, whereas I felt destined to that end even though my opportunities and means were laughable. I thought studying for a degree was what every young person dreamed of; I couldn't imagine what else there was to dream about. At Armitage, we regarded anyone with a degree as virtually god-like, so rare were our opportunities for more schooling. I was beginning to appreciate how the postwar generation of Europeans was caught between a past difficult to shake off and a future impossible to avert. Douglas said the students would grow to seize their opportunities and become wealth-creators and patrons of music and the arts. He would take a useful life any day over the intellectual life.

Douglas's calculations on these matters bypassed religion, and I didn't know if that omission was a fair reflection of the state of things, or whether it was simply his bias. I understood that the school curriculum in Germany did not take in religious knowledge; instead students attended special classes of religious instruction outside the school curriculum. That was a far cry from my experience at school, where religion held center stage.

I happened to be reading the book *Does God Exist?* by A. E. Taylor (1869-1945), a leading philosopher of the British idealist school. A stalwart defender of idealism as shown in his magnum opus *Plato: The Man and His Work,* Taylor stood for rightness and goodness in an age of upheaval and strife. I stumbled on A. E. Taylor at the Kingsway Supermarket in Banjul on one of my window-shopping jaunts. I was eager to learn what the issues were between belief in God and what is reasonable to believe about the world as we know and experience it. It is a reasonable hypothesis, Taylor writes, that if the order of things is a reasonable order, it is wholly consistent with that reasonableness that it should have a purpose which should disclose itself in patterns and uniformities of sequence. A world where there were no such regularities of sequence, where "anything might follow on anything," would not be a reasonable world. It would, in effect, be a world where life as we know it would not exist. The ancient writers gave it the name *chaos.* The converse of that makes a compelling case for belief: it would be equally unreasonable if the regular recurrence of sequence led up to no end with an inherent worth of its own, which is where belief comes in. Both the speculative and practical forms of reason, as Immanuel Kant rightly insisted, are functions of one and the same intelligence.

Faith, Taylor thought, is no more unreasonable than the world of which it speaks. Jesus came into a world of gravity in which Roman imperial power collided with Jewish religious truth claims to fuel deep-seated disaffection expressing itself in a politically-charged anticipation of a Messiah. Jesus stepped into a fraught world ripe for judgment, with his violent death showing that we are dealing with a God who cannot be "the hedonistic God of making His creatures as comfortable as possible in their present state of existence, without regard to anything beyond their capacities for pain and pleasure."[3]

Beside himself with frustration, Douglas would pounce to yank me out of my musings, fed up that I didn't have the good sense to ditch such books. "Here you are wasting your time and talents reading works of such tortuous logic when the matter is clear to common sense," Douglas would declare over dinner. "Isn't it enough that we are enjoying food to see that we don't have to argue God into existence to accept His gifts?" I agreed enthusiastically, especially since Douglas was paying for the dinner. I couldn't tell him that taking God for granted seems a lazy way of dealing with truth and with the fact of God's active, loving solicitude of us, that the world is too wonderful not to deserve a personal Creator. As we headed out to the Mozart festival in Salzburg via Garmisch to visit an old friend, Douglas would talk at length about how simple wealth creation was the answer to the world's woes, for enterprise alone spoke the universal language of demonstrable self-betterment. Money was the alchemy that could transform a drab world into one of glittering opportunity. A schoolboy still adrift even in his own country could scarcely argue with that fluent sentiment.

Douglas drove me back to Marseilles, where I boarded the ship that returned me to West Africa. It was a cheap and effective way to visit all the intermediate ports in between. Douglas thought the experience would be invaluable for me, his idea of a future African leader. I couldn't bring myself to tell him I would be thinking religious thoughts, an honest difference that seemed a small price to pay for our friendship.

3. A. E. Taylor, *Does God Exist?* (London & Glasgow: Fontana Books, 1961), 178.

Upon my return to the Gambia, I made up my mind to do everything in my power to pursue the truth of my encounter with the Jesus of history and faith rather than to allow the ground to be taken out from under me. I came to the realization that nothing had interested me more during my time in Europe than the role of religion in its life. It was becoming clear that the study of religion should determine the contribution I might make in life. It was impossible to suppress the thought and slip back into the old ways.

I was faced with a choice, and so, with the encouragement and invaluable support of my friend Terry Iles, I took the unusual step of leaving my secure government job and returning to school. Friends and relatives thought it was crazy to give up on early marriage and raising a family for what seemed to them a retrogressive, risky step. Yet, given the opportunity, I made that change without a moment's hesitation. Obtaining higher qualifications was the only way I could assume responsibility for myself. It was also the way to pursue the path of an open future, with all its hazards and possibilities. Nothing ventured, nothing gained.

I loved my studies at the Gambia High School, and loved being with classmates once again: Ayo, who went to Wales to study political science and eventually become president of the World Bank; the three Ebous (short for Ebrima) and Modou, who chose study in Latin and French literature; Jack, Kabba, and Halifax, who all went into medicine, with Halifax becoming a thoracic surgeon in the U.S. Army; Wally, who ended up heading the UNDP in East Africa; James, who studied civil engineering at University College, London; Samba, who went to Cambridge; Satang, Faith, Gladys, Mam Silla, and Vicki, who studied mathematics; Dan, who made the challenging switch from Latin to science; Malick, the physicist and engineer; and Alieu, Baba, Geof, Moulaye, Bakary, Ousman, and Ghanim, the Lebanese-Gambian, who joined me in studying history. I was indeed ready for the change. It was a wonderful atmosphere at school, rigorous academic work combined with deep friendship and mutual respect among us. We so enjoyed one another's company. I guess that was because nearly all of us set our sights on high goals, and nearly all of us attained our ambition by succeeding in our exams and then going on to build a career for ourselves. The set of exams called Advanced Level, or "A" Level for short, constituted a formidable test of discipline and application. Perhaps this "A" Level system of education would not long survive the colonial administration of its creation, but for us it bred an effortless sense of confidence.

There were typically exams in three subjects, with a combined total of some twenty-seven hours, plus a comprehension paper of another three hours. The exams were written and printed in England and shipped out to Africa under strict rules of confidentiality. With the encouragement and guidance of Colin Eastwood, a very helpful senior English teacher, whose wife, Joan, was my geography teacher — both of them I much admired and maintained a lifelong friendship with — I chose scripture as one of the subjects for the exams. It turned out to be a tough assignment, consisting of the history of ancient Israel, the writing prophets, and the synoptic Gospels. Eventually Colin returned to England, leaving me to soldier on by myself. Sometimes I thought I was reckless to embark on such technical study by myself, but I was determined to do well because it was the way for me to catch up on knowledge of Christianity. History and literature were the other two subjects, and they involved a vast amount of reading. C. S. Lewis made a brief appearance in my literature class when we studied his book *Experiment in Literary Criticism* and excerpts from his study of Milton's *Paradise Lost*, which we read alongside C. Day Lewis. Keats was one of my favorite poets. Dickens, on the other hand, I found too lacking in subtlety to develop a taste for. His characters were in the main caricatures, and where he might empathize, he lampooned.

The demanding "A" Level track was designed for those preparing to enter elite British universities. Terry stressed the fact that we were competing with the brightest British students, who had the advantage of social capital going for them. We could not afford to slacken our pace. I also had some sense that if I did well in my exams the church might be impressed enough to revisit the theology and ordination option for me.

I did do well in my exams, but there was no second thought by the church regarding ordination. Instead my path turned in a totally unexpected direction. I received news that scholarship awards were being given out to qualified candidates by the education department on behalf of the U.S. administration. The principal of the Gambia High School announced this to us, asking us to submit our names to the education department. It was the first-ever such initiative in Africa, and it changed my plans abruptly and irreversibly.

Friends were delighted at the news of the award; the Methodist minister and his colleagues breathed a sigh of relief. They even managed to dodge my going-away party. I was able to squeeze all my earthly possessions into one suitcase, which was how I arrived in the U.S. I had no idea what awaited me. The warm, unstinting welcome shown by the State Department was a new experience. There would be many, many more new experiences to come.

Part II

Thy way was through the sea,

thy path through the great waters;

yet thy footprints were unseen.

PSALM 77:19

CHAPTER 7

New World

D ewy-eyed, I arrived in the U.S. in August 1963. It was at a time when
the country was heaving with giant waves of social unrest. It was
the era of the civil rights movement, and Americans my age were in the
vanguard of the struggle for justice and racial equality. It was the week
before the March on Washington organized by Martin Luther King Jr.
There was brewing at the same time the storm of the Black Muslim agitation, aggravated by the open rift between Elijah Muhammad and Mal-
colm X who, in his characteristically provocative style, called the March
on Washington the Farce on Washington.

To newcomers, not excepting me, America impresses with its sheer
size and its outsize appetite: the amazing highway system; the harbors
and airports knitting the continent and humming with traffic; the towering skyscrapers of Manhattan, where earth and heaven seem joined in a
triumph of indefatigable civic industry; buxom suburban cars and their
smooth suspensions that allow them to ride the roads like gentle waves;
the endless shelves of chocolate and ice cream flavors; the varieties of
fruit and vegetables; the extensive salad bars; the veritable thicket of
soda fountains that gush from millions of outlets across the country,
from convenience stores and hallways to lunch counters, bars, and vans;
the wide rolling roads; the massive tractor-trailers hauling their cargo;
homes with well-kept lawns and with their two-car garages; and a proliferation of colleges and universities that is the envy of the world. Here is a

consumer paradise packaged for cash-and-carry at the beck and call of people constantly on the move. America rewards the gypsy instinct with more space for wandering than there are gypsies in the world. Ask many Americans which state is their home, and they will wobble for an answer just to think of all the in-betweens that defy the singular idea of a fixed abode.

America's boundaries are evanescent, so endless and breathless is the vista in every direction over land, sea, and air, where it "spreads with crampless and flowing breadth," in the words of Whitman. The American outlook is upbeat, brooking no conceivable impediments. Unlike Europeans, Americans swing their arms when they walk to signify energy and unimpeded perpetual motion. As Arthur Bird (1899) put it, America is bounded on the north by the North Pole, on the south by the Antarctic, on the east by the first chapter of the Book of Genesis, and on the west by the Day of Judgment. America's landscape and skies beckon the adventurer as on a moral enterprise. Every sort of vehicle imaginable crisscrosses the country conveying passengers to destinations that serve as a thousand points of hope. A restless humanity has found in America its long-delayed homecoming, with plenty of room to make up for lost time.

Americans, I noticed, are wealthy, and yet do not appear awkward or snooty about money. Americans love to love money in the sense that they love money even if it's someone else's money. Americans not only suffer it when others succeed; they admire it. As an English taxi driver once put it, Americans lack the vice of envy, and, even better, they lack awareness of that as a virtue. They attend to the poor while remaining unsympathetic to the phenomenon of poverty; in their view, no one is predestined for that condition because all are endowed by the Creator with the means necessary for the pursuit of happiness. For Americans generosity and excitement have their springs in their boundless optimism that opportunity, education, and honest hard work will yield dividends. Wealth is a warrant not of class or pedigree, but of action, because ambition is the fuel of a healthy, industrious spirit. Americans look upon learning as the handmaid of a useful, productive life. Education is an industry, and even if the accountant is not the college CEO, the ledger book rules supreme in the counting house, which is the boardroom. Nowhere else has education been put to such fruitful use.

The media hold sway in America as in no other country, not primarily to educate and to instruct in a detached way, but to carry out the civic function of guarding the freedom of the people, including the pursuit of happiness. For their part, the media package the news as part reporting and part entertainment, with newscasters notable for their smiling voices. Accordingly, the entertainment industry is the most developed anywhere, and actors and actresses are cast as icons of the popular imagination. In America life imitates art to a degree unknown in any other part of the world, and so images of the silver screen loom larger than life. With the alchemy of Hollywood, reality breaks into visual electronic spin, dazzling and mesmerizing in its effect.[1] Appearing in a movie or on television is like being discovered, for it gives one instant celebrity.

Thrown into this world, an uninitiated African had to scramble to make sense of it all. The driving energy of America has little patience for temporizing or indifference. Resignation is not an option. I found all this exciting and energizing, if somewhat breathtaking. All manner of activist involvement in a life of busy chores assumes the force of a religious injunction. Indeed, activism is nearly a national creed. Calculations of money seemed to enter into everything, and nothing was done without first planning and setting goals. What was most striking about all this was the pragmatic spirit, the idea that what works should be promoted without regard to status, background, or cultural disadvantage. Tradition cannot be a justification for perpetuating economically disadvantageous practices. The notion of traditional societies, expressed in the formulation "this is the accustomed way of doing things among us," is entirely foreign to the entrepreneurial spirit of America. The rags-to-riches reputation of America is not just pure fantasy; it has its root in reality. Though understandable on its own terms, I was unfamiliar with this entrepreneurial spirit. It requires in the first place selling yourself for the going market rate for your qualifications, and that was too crass an

1. In his "Meditation on Broadway," G. K. Chesterton wrote that the kaleidoscope of colored lights arranged in large letters and sprawling trade-marks as advertising signs made Broadway feel like a glorious garden of wonders for anyone who was lucky enough to be unable to read. Chesterton, *Collected Works*, vol. 21 (San Francisco: Ignatius Press, 1990), 62.

idea for traditional notions of pedigree and position. At the same time, it opens society to healthy competition and to the removal of dead wood. Progress is a function of self-improvement.

The social life was unlike anything I had ever encountered before. In America women talk to men without being first spoken to, and it surprised and confused me. I was raised to be shy with the opposite sex, and that rule seemed to be flouted in America with harmless abandon. My host family in North Syracuse observed that it was preferred men didn't wear shorts, but that turned out not to be true. Called Bermudas, men's shorts abounded in stores in all shapes, styles, and colors. In any case, it made me wonder what kind of moral hang-up would give my skinny legs any hint of seduction. In my upbringing it was not men's bodies that seduced; rather the reverse, which was why women simply never wore shorts. Too, I had never encountered the word "dating" except as a matter of the calendar until I encountered it in America, where its use means something between chasing and courting girls. For young people, dates are a short-term upgrade without the high premium of permanent commitment. The world of mixed company of men and women fudges the boundary between the sexes: girls wear rumpled cut-offs, faded jeans, baseball caps, and logo-bearing T-shirts with the same freedom as boys. Not to be left out, grandmothers compete with their grandkids in the low-brow sartorial idiom. Being weaned on jumbo-size helpings of personal choice, children enjoy a degree of freedom undreamed of in my world. Oscar Wilde has rightly noted that the youth of America is America's oldest tradition; it has been going on for three hundred years.

I was struck by the thick proliferation of swear words and sultry colloquialisms. I found that in public company subtle ingredients were not essential or necessary for wit and humor. Language use observes no class lines, no age distinctions, few inhibitions, and certainly no religious codes. For adults and children alike, for believers and non-believers, "Jesus Christ" and "God" are common swear words, and even terms like "cross" and "sacrifice" have essentially a secular meaning. Putting up with a resentful relative is referred to as bearing one's cross, and distributing tracts and leaflets on community causes at street corners and in neighborhoods is seen as part of works of supererogatory merit. Devoting a weekend to mounting an exhibit at a community fair qualifies, too, as sacrifice. The Qur'an school teacher would have said about such use of language, "I told you so."

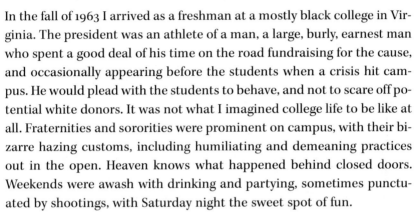

In the fall of 1963 I arrived as a freshman at a mostly black college in Virginia. The president was an athlete of a man, a large, burly, earnest man who spent a good deal of his time on the road fundraising for the cause, and occasionally appearing before the students when a crisis hit campus. He would plead with the students to behave, and not to scare off potential white donors. It was not what I imagined college life to be like at all. Fraternities and sororities were prominent on campus, with their bizarre hazing customs, including humiliating and demeaning practices out in the open. Heaven knows what happened behind closed doors. Weekends were awash with drinking and partying, sometimes punctuated by shootings, with Saturday night the sweet spot of fun.

Sunday was hangover day — and for the devout remnant it was a day to keep chapel, too. It didn't escape my attention that chapel was too casual to carry anything of the intimidating mandate of mosque attendance of my school days. In all likelihood, that force of old habit was what made me join it. I enrolled in the choir, too, and started a once-a-week student Bible study group in my dorm. John, my roommate from Florida, and Denis, an African student, helped me lead it. Jeff, another student, eventually discontinued his attendance; he was too spooked by memories of Ku Klux Klan cross-burnings in his family's yard back home in Mississippi to be comfortable with the cross. I had no idea what the KKK was, or why a Christian America did not stamp it out. The few of us left constituted the entire membership of the Bible study group. With the support of the assistant chapel minister, I tried some boosterism of my own by working the choir for recruits.

I remember stumbling on the fledgling environmental movement with the publication the previous year of Rachel Carson's national best-selling book, *Silent Spring,* which woke up a complacent nation. Her untimely death in 1964 created a national icon for the cause. I was taken by friends to pop music concerts, where I encountered for the first time songs of protest and resistance as the juggernauts of popular music hit their stride: Bob Dylan, Pete Seeger, Don McLean, Joan Baez, Peter, Paul and Mary, and so on. I learned and sang the songs myself, with pity for those within range of my off-pitch voice. I couldn't resist going just for the ride.

The Beatles, who crossed the Atlantic in February 1964 to blend their voices with youth rebellion, weighed in with songs of existential doubt best captured in their song "Nowhere Man," written in October 1965. I recall it well, living at the time in Washington, D.C., as hysterical girls greeted the Beatles everywhere. I was soon picking up on their lyrics and mining their words for the cultural message. "Nowhere Man" caught my attention. The song speaks of a real nowhere man sitting in his nowhere land making all his nowhere plans for nobody. He doesn't have a point of view and knows not where he is going, and in that way looks a lot like you and I. He is as blind as blind can be, just seeing what he wants to see, and yet, in spite of all his inadequacies, he has the world at his command. It was the ripe anthem for the "flower power" movement.

Meanwhile, under President Kennedy, America deployed fresh young peace messengers to cover the earth with American hope and goodwill as it had been filled with Soviet menace and ill-will. Hence the Peace Corps, the Alliance for Progress, and a phalanx of technical experts setting out to sow miracle seeds and to banish the specter of epidemics, disease, hunger, malnutrition, and other accumulated miseries that were fodder for communist revolution. But only a few months into my stay, the country was plunged into paroxysms of grief and confusion when President Kennedy was assassinated in Dallas in November. I was on my way to chapel choir practice on that fateful early Friday afternoon when the news of the assassination was broadcast.

As an international student I was constantly pestered with in-your-face questions about what chances I gave or did not give the Soviet Union to succeed in the Third World. "Tell us," my hosts would demand. George, a friend from New Jersey, said how disappointed his parents were when I sounded as if I was downplaying the communist menace in answer to their inquest. That view clearly was more about their phobias than about my expertise in Soviet grand strategy.

❁   ❁   ❁

The context of the civil rights movement in America accentuated issues of race with a disconcerting in-your-face directness; one could not ignore or avoid the subject. A group of us recently-arrived Gambian students met in a Washington apartment a year into our studies to compare notes. One was a fellow of Lebanese descent who was now a second- or third-generation Gambian, having gone to school with local children and speaking the language as well as they did. Living cheek by jowl with Africans and participating unselfconsciously in their lives, this Lebanese young man's race, while noticeable, ceased being normative. He obtained a scholarship under his Gambian identity, though it had never occurred to him that in America race was both noticeable and normative and would divide him from blacks, including his fellow Gambians. He suffered a severe mental crisis because suddenly his white skin was in conflict with his African cultural values. It affected his studies and drove him into treatment. I cannot now remember if he ever recovered or even if he returned to the Gambia. His experience was a vivid reminder that nothing in our background prepared us for America: we had no value system to deal with race, and no fund of personal experience to draw on for understanding or for self-preservation. We floundered and thrashed, looking for safety in unsettled waters. Then the feminist movement compounded the choices from which America did not spare us, in spite of the fact that whether male or female, blacks had few breaks in relations with the West.

We were also unprepared for tensions at college between Africans and African Americans. We found out that being black was not the same thing as being African American almost in the same way as being African American was not the same as being part of white America. This complicated triangular relationship turned out to be about establishing a pecking order between Africans and African Americans in which the color line faded into cultural grievance. Calculations of skin color now included a sidebar on foreign blacks, with the gradation extending from New World mulattos and their black siblings to Caribbean blacks, including those of Indian descent, and black Africans. In the contest of rankings, newly-arrived Africans came up suddenly against the black backlash of the race barrier and were at once disconcerted. They faced an awkward choice of identity.

The color line could not be drawn evenly because of the unique experience of African Americans. They drank from the bitter well of racism before black Africans ever did — and colonialism was a brief cloudburst by comparison. Martin Luther King Jr.'s call for justice and reconciliation was not an implausible moral option for Africans; in King's view, there were no gains or advantages that blacks wanted that they did not want for others, so that the struggle for civil rights extended more broadly. Racism was a multiracial problem, and victims and victimizers had a shared obligation and responsibility to undo it for the sake of their collective future. Nevertheless, American blacks could not exaggerate racism, and Africans could not appreciate it enough. Yet race would not exempt Africans, however much a homeland in Africa might offer psychological escape.

I discovered that the churches were centers of resistance to integration, which surprised and confounded me greatly. The Christian fundamentalists I met stood out for their jingoist fervor as an expression of their Christian faith. My fundamentalist friends inquired earnestly about whether I "knew the Lord," in their language. And precisely which missionary had led me to the Lord? Disappointed with the answers, they interrogated me closely to see if my faith was acceptable, the standard being mainly cultural. I wished to say, but couldn't, that I didn't know the Lord as well as the Lord knew me. They disparaged the civil rights movement, saying that while the goals might be laudable, the tactics and the methods of street protests and picketing were wrong. Indeed, the legal remedies being sought were an infringement of Christian liberty, because the gospel was about grace, not about law. I wondered, in that case, where that left the laws upholding segregation and discrimination, whether they too were an infringement of Christian liberty, never mind of the liberty of blacks as such. I joined some friends on a drive to integrate lunch counters in the Tidewater area, but the threat of violence impeded efforts in that direction. One Sunday a group of us students marched to a nearby United Methodist church to participate in the worship, but the stewards there refused to seat us, and we left without incident.

The fundamentalist contradiction left me uncertain about the proper order or merit of an *Americanized* Christianity versus a *Chris-*

tianized America, or about what hangs on the distinction. Is the Americanization of Christianity the primary fuel for the faith, with a commercialized religion pitched for optimum market share? What about the Christianization of America, so that justice and fairness might guide conduct and practice? Are the fruits of national ascendancy interchangeable with the fruits of the reign of God? Is national identity sufficient warrant of Christian identity? America's preponderant affluence is easily conflated with divine providence, but does that risk spiritual idolatry, rich in blessings but heedless of the Blessed One? Fundamentalists view liberals as a political faction, when, in fact, both share a common root in pragmatic activism. In both cases, too, religious officials are interest brokers for their side. Pragmatism fuels Christianity's commercial potential, making the religion a useful and politically expedient creed. The agenda of the churches supplies the pledge drive of politically mobilized neighborhoods. It's all about competition and besting others at the game. That's how we measure the extent of God's favor on our projects.

All this made me wonder whether the message of early Christianity that emerged so valiantly from the fires of Roman imperial repression could survive American domestication, and what merit there was still in the unconventional teachings of Jesus, the convicted field preacher. In that regard, I was intrigued to read in Frank Morison's brilliant book *Who Moved the Stone?* that the disciples resisted reports of the empty tomb because it was unexpected, and because it increased considerably their margin of public danger. Opponents could not gainsay the "physical vacancy of the authentic tomb of Christ,"[2] leaving Jesus' otherwise apprehensive disciples little protection from a public backlash. America, however, offered a different challenge, with Jesus custom-fitted in generous American proportions as an entrepreneurial avatar.

❁   ❁   ❁

Not exactly fresh from the jungle but still tradition-drenched, I arrived from Africa in the midst of all this throbbing ferment not knowing quite

---

2. Frank Morison, *Who Moved the Stone?* (New York and London: The Century Co., 1930), 102.

what to make of it all. I felt somewhat concussed. It was a tough environ-ment to try to look for the guiding hand of God — or at least for a God who was not consumed with the communist or liberal menace.

Still, I perceived that America offered a chance to leave behind the truculent issues of Islam and Christian self-understanding so that I could reassess my priorities afresh. I knew there was no going back on my decision, but also that there could be no barreling forward inexora-bly. I went into higher education for the purpose of preparing myself for a career, and I needed to be deliberate about that. Since I was feeling lost in my Virginia college, I endeavored to try something new.

By a combination of remarkable circumstances I had met Ted Lock-wood before coming to America. At that time he was dean at Concord College in West Virginia, traveling through Africa on a tour that hap-pened to include Banjul, where a group of us from school met him at the Reform Club. He had since moved to Union College in Schenectady, New York. Through his kind offices I was able to transfer to Union from my college in Virginia after one year.

I arrived at college on a weekend and checked into an assigned guest room of the house of the college president, Carter Davidson, a grey-haired man sporting a pair of wire-rimmed glasses who was retiring that summer. When I asked him about a church to visit that Sunday, his glasses nearly fell off his face. He stammered and groped for words be-fore finally sputtering, "Oh, look it up in the Yellow Pages." Suddenly I was as befuddled as he was: I didn't know what the Yellow Pages were. Was this a book? If so, where could I find it? Not wanting to seem foolish, I didn't press the issue, but instead retreated to my chambers to lick my wounds. I had clearly pushed President Davidson into a no-go area for him; he would not sully his reputation by entertaining conversation about religion, whatever his duties as my host. Not for him the mystify-ing rituals and mind-numbing exchanges that have bewitched primitive cultures. It was an ominous beginning.

When I finally figured out what the Yellow Pages were, I used them to locate the nearest Methodist church and introduced myself as a newly arrived international student from Africa — not a country but a conti-nent, I added defensively. I was met for an awkward moment or two with studied silence. Before I could repeat myself, under the misapprehension that the people had not heard me, I was told to help move a box of blankets for distribution to the homeless. "That is what we do here," a kind lady told me with pointed meaning, a hint that social action would have to do for being hospitable. "We are here for no other reason," I overheard people say. No one asked me back.

Since the Yellow Pages offered no meaningful guidance to my search for a church, I summoned the old reserves and resorted once more to legwork and word-of-mouth introduction. My next stop was a local Presbyterian church with an evangelical bent, which at first received me readily but with reservation. I happened to be the only black person there, and although the minister seemed uncomfortable about how precisely to welcome me, nevertheless he remained polite and courteous outwardly. In his eyes I seemed a contradiction of the black male stereotype, yet his instinct told him not to trust the evidence of his eyes. The cultural habits of a black male could not be wholesome, he suspected. He once remarked to me about blacks and weekend carousing, locking eyes on me with meaning. "We look down on that here," he spat impatiently.

Once again, the omens were looking unfavorable. It felt like I was repeating the frustrations of church-shopping from my earlier conversion days. The Gambia phase of my search had unsettlingly followed me to the New World. Here I was, once the bright new hope of Africa, floundering like a refugee on foreign soil.

The Presbyterian minister's hand was forced when, behind my back and without my prompting, the young adult fellowship unanimously elected me its president. When word of it reached the minister, he set out immediately to nullify the election, saying the church was not ready for such a step. Summoning me to his office, he said he meant no ill will, but that as the shepherd of the flock God had entrusted to him, he had to protect the interests of the church. He could not risk letting loose a lone black man among his white flock. Weekend carousing flashed before his eyes, I imagined. He took me shopping and bought me an expensive suit to demonstrate his biblical faith that "I was naked and you clothed me" — skipping the preceding verse, "I was a stranger and you welcomed me" (Matt. 25:35-36). I wondered secretly how he justified the split, but I was also reluctant not to believe the minister when he held forth on God's righteousness as necessary and sufficient for salvation. Faith, not works, he thundered from the pulpit. But now was it works, not faith? Was there any hint here that the minister held unspoken cultural dogmas as the frame of the gospel? I caught myself thinking that, perhaps, I misunderstood him, evidence that I also had fallen under his spell without realizing it. Quietly and tactfully I tried to gauge from members of the congregation how much support there was for his action. Many were openly friendly toward me, and yet no one to my knowledge took issue with the minister. It amounted to tacit approval, and left me in an untenable position. Befriending me seemed quite different from accepting me.

I knew in my heart that Americans are a warm, generous people; they would not countenance discrimination to a stranger in their midst. Yet no one moved, at least not openly. The minister had the congregation under his heel, and, even if they wanted to, no one would dare challenge his authority. I heard mutterings abroad about how America must act urgently to fix its racial problem, but little about what might be the specifically Christian answer. Race prejudice is a social problem that is a challenge to the nation, but is not an affront to the gospel as such, people seemed to imply. Yet the race issue intervened to determine who was and was not expected to be in the church. To general tacit approval, the minister acted to exclude me purely on the basis of race.

I resisted leaving because I dreaded the prospects of resuming the search for a church all over again, in case the outcome was no different. I began to muse on the solicitude of former Muslim friends. In Islam we were taught that we could never make mundane calculations the standard of God's justice without infringing God's sovereignty. In part, that was what attracted me to St. Paul's assessment that, if righteousness can be obtained by stipulations of human devising, Christ died in vain (Gal. 2:21), in which case the church preaches in vain and we believe in vain (1 Cor. 15:14). That was why, for both the minister and me, the expensive clothes could not dress up the shortfall. The minister made much of the *sola scriptura* principle, declaring at every opportunity that the Bible is the one and only authority of the church and of personal faith, only to veer and tack once I stirred the race current. One could adapt St. Bernard to say that the minister paraded a boisterous faith in the word of God, only quietly to sell the word of God for the shopping trip that money could buy. Al-Ghazali's dictum that the moral merit of a deed is determined by the intention behind it *(innama amal bi-n-niyah)* rang in my ears. I knew I couldn't stay.

Left to fend for myself, by this stage I worried that, with my exotic profile, news of my abortive sortie into the Presbyterian church would spread and precede or follow me everywhere else. I began to wish for the Islamic system, in which mosques do not maintain membership lists, which makes it straightforward just to drop in at the appointed prayer times without being subjected to any cultural vetting at the door. The mosque is where you carry out your duty to God; it is not a social niche for those of your kind. Islam's religious ethos is challengingly free of racism, even if Muslims have their share of negrophobia, as I know only too well from the history of Muslim slavery and from personal experience in the Middle East.

Still, none of that Muslim comparison could change my current situation, and so I decided to continue my search for a hospitable church. I went about it with a measure of instinctive trepidation. I ascertained upfront from the priest of the local Episcopal church, which belonged to the Anglo-Catholic tradition, that he had no racial objection to my visiting the church. Not only did he have no such objections, he offered me a job with the Sunday school class. With that he became my spiritual host and defender for the rest of my college years. I am fairly sure that even now, in his retirement, he has little idea that his gesture was the first of its kind in my experience. It felt like a godsend. Because of it I was able to settle down to my studies. Heaven knows what would have happened if I had run into one more church set to draw the fellowship line at fitting me out in fine clothes.

At Union College I had pillars of support. Ted Lockwood, who had single-handedly organized my transfer to the college, treated me like a member of his family. He had no idea what an inspiration and a refuge he was. In Henry Ferguson, a history professor, I met an intellectual mentor of formidable stature. Henry's reputation among students was that he did not suffer fools gladly, and yet he was absolutely devoted to students and unstinting in his attention to them. A Harvard-trained Europeanist, Henry had since switched to the history of China, Japan, and India, whose great intellectual treasures he opened to students, challenging us to appreciate these cultures from their respective primary sources. Under Henry, historical study of the religious traditions of Asia was eye-opening, for he showed us that the intellectual endeavor is connected to the value of intercultural understanding and respect. The study of history has much to teach us about our mutual interdependence and common moral footprint.

Overall, college was something of a mixed bag, wonderful for unlimited access to books, yet daunting for the limited opportunity to get to know fellow students. There were few international students on campus, and rare social occasions for meeting the majority of the American student body. Union was an all-male college, which meant that students went away on weekend dates, an idea entirely foreign and confounding to me. Furthermore, at Union fraternities were off campus, and they siphoned off the bulk of the weekend social events, leaving non-affiliated students like me high and dry. Union is the mother of American fraternities, though some professors thought it was well past time that Union outgrew its parenting obsession and threw the fraternities out on the street. At any rate, without a means of transport, and without friends who had cars, international students were virtually marooned on the campus, and it was a relief when the weekend was over and the college resumed normal activities.

College instilled in me important habits of frugality. I lived off-campus to save on food and amenities, and cooked on weekends when the cafeteria closed. Pots of stew would stretch to mid-week, and I filled in with cans of Campbell's soup, all varieties, except tomato soup and broth. I also stayed clear of chicken gumbo because of a childhood aversion to okra, my mother's cajoling notwithstanding. My favorite was turkey rice soup — it was the closest Campbell's got to my favorite food from childhood. There was limited space for cooked food in the small fridge, so the soup was an enormous help. Lunch-counter excursions I remember largely for the cheap way I could gorge on macaroni and cheese. I also relished invitations to Sunday lunch from ecumenically minded families. My beverage of choice was Kool-Aid, which to me demonstrated the brilliance of Americans in inventing a drink as appetizing as it was convenient and cheap.

After a year of stinting on food, I saved enough to purchase a record player and to buy records of classical and popular music. Several budget recording labels could bring classical music within range of the general public, among them Nonesuch, the Musical Heritage Society (MHS) at Carnegie Hall, CBS, Vox, and EMI. It was a great boon to have great music wrapped in frugal cover and chased down with discounted Campbell's fare to sustain the appetite for books. That was my appreciative angle on the Great Society of Lyndon Johnson's America.

I recall strolling through campus on winter evenings, the scene covered with fresh snow and aglow with the reflected lights shimmering in the distance. In the serene, quiet atmosphere I would think back to my African past before a gust of wind pulled me back sharply to the reality of a deep New York winter. Against the white of the snow I could make out the outline of rambling figures of hooded students shuffling back and forth among the buildings that seemed so still. The night winter scene filtered movement and stillness into ghost-like forms, and it stirred my tropical memories. Even though by now I had traveled too far to make going back an option, I still could not resist a few fond thoughts in the direction of my tropical upbringing. While I was not prepared for my first winter, eventually it became part of the rhythm of my life. I rummaged in my mind for lessons I could draw from my formative college education as I faced new paths before me. Winter still has that clarifying, rallying effect on me.

Chartered in 1795, with roots in the French Enlightenment, Union saw itself as a rampart against religion. The religion professor was a genial, bicycle-riding eccentric whose view was that the only religions worth studying were those that were historical relics, or were close to extinction. A dead or declining religion was a safe religion to study. Zoroastrianism topped his list here. He extended that approach to Christianity in America, indulging a comparable condescending curiosity in anyone who turned up as a Christian. Such survivals he regarded only as intriguing live specimens. Since there was not much evidence of Zoroastrianism left anywhere except in traces in far-flung places like Bombay, the professor turned instead to the Greek and Latin classics, where Christians did not fare too well, as the comments of Tacitus of the second century bear witness. "Christians," Tacitus writes, "were made an object of mockery: covered with animal skins, they were torn to pieces by dogs; or nailed to crosses, [and,] when daylight failed, they were set alight as torches to lighten the darkness." To make bonfires of Christians was too primitive for the professor's refined sensibilities; better to treat them with polite indulgence. Even though it was a small class, I felt certain he didn't know my name. His knowledge of Africa was restricted to wild animals in game parks — great stuff for a coffee table book or to do on a safari, but otherwise too unkempt and cluttered to drag into the study.

Strangely, the condensed edition of Alexis de Tocqueville's *Democracy in America* we read in courses cut out the sections on religion. It left us with a pinched view of Tocqueville's trenchant observations on American life and society, and when years later I had access to the unbowdlerized master edition I appreciated the force of Tocqueville's analysis. As he put it, in America, where liberty is celebrated, religion and liberal democracy flourished in mutual reinforcement. When people are free, Tocqueville argues, they believe; if they don't believe, they must obey. The state stifles religion to help spawn political tyranny; religion nourishes freedom by limiting the state's role in the moral life. Democratic freedom and religion are mutually reinforcing. To believe in that sense is to set moral limits to political power, and to govern without religion is to make coercion, not moral persuasion, the weapon of political obligation. The idea echoes a strain in Muslim classical political thought, I later learned. I regretted that I had not been able to read the complete Tocqueville in college; in retrospect it seems like one more example of the way the cultural high priests at Union put in place liberal safeguards against the contagion of religion.

It was not only the professors who had no time for religion. An African student colleague and a self-avowed atheist used to challenge us with his vigorous assertion that the idea of God is bogus, claiming Darwin as support, with racism in a Christian America his trump card against notions of Christian love. His name at baptism was James, a Western name, but in the era of cultural activism of the nationalist movement he dropped that name in America and replaced it with an African one, symbol of tradition. I still recall a memorable Saturday dinner at a Chinese restaurant on State Street in downtown Schenectady. He was rambunctious and in the mood for debate. Not sure if we had solved any of the big questions, James left the dinner having made no concessions to religion and feeling buoyant on account of it. His faith in science remained impregnable. On the other hand, he embraced African authenticity as the answer to Western imposition, and thus to Christianity. The fact that he didn't know much about Islam didn't prevent James from sharing the general sentiment that, unlike Christianity, Islam was closer to African culture by virtue of its endorsement of polygamy. His views had support in prevailing ideas of cultural relativism as well as in the decolonization movement, where Islam was often the beneficiary of subaltern sympathies. Even though there were prominent Christian figures in the decolonization movement, they did not prevent Christianity from being regarded as a villain in the politics of anti-imperialism.

James and I didn't have too many conversations after that dinner, in part because for him the matter was settled, and in part because our academic paths simply diverged. James was typical of his generation, whom the tide of Westernization left stranded in a no-man's-land of the polarity between tradition and progress, a convalescent still too close to the source of his discomfiture to be able to relax with his own native prognosis. He was proof that Western intellectual influence would penetrate Africa through the Africans who were meanwhile busy being proudly anti-Western. In contrast, I remained persuaded that Christianity persisted as a catalyst in African cultural renewal and in robust debate about race relations in America.

I took a standard assortment of liberal arts courses in college, which suited my eclectic interests even though the courses were not designed to make me expert in anything. On an exchange program at Edinburgh University in my junior year, the courses I took made me realize I had some way to go in my academic career. Spread out cafeteria-style on the syllabus, the courses required the veteran instincts of the forager to gauge what combination of courses was worth the pursuit. Often the hunt for good grades inhibited the appetite for exploration.

My interest in history led me in directions that were not incompatible with my religious interest. History as the study of change of temporal reality invigorated me; as I found out in my studies in Eastern religions and philosophy, I could not always count on my subjects to challenge me in the same way. I was spellbound by issues of movement and change in society, and felt that what happened in our past as a society would enhance us if we engaged it seriously. Knowledge of history should be a critical safeguard against repeating the follies of the past. We do not have power of foreknowledge; we should instead come to a sober reckoning with our past. History as a civic lesson we could not afford to do without.

This idea was not a standing dogma of my college history courses, but it seemed to me a deep truth about the nature of history. My economic history professor, a Jewish refugee from Nazi Germany, was passionate about history not being an idle pastime. If history is true, he insisted, we must act on it. In other words, the enterprise called for moral commitment of one kind or another to prevent history from being just mindless propaganda. I found history far more gripping than the world of pure thought, or the quiddities and sensations of symbols and images. Religion belonged in history, not in pure doctrine as such, but in the realities of people immersed in the struggle of life. God did not give us the capacity of hindsight without the intention for us to learn from it. Religion was not a warrant for indifference to the past.

In mild and easygoing times scholars and writers can afford detachment, disengagement, or even ambivalence, but in times of challenge and crisis, commitment and engagement are imperative. I decided that there was no better way to learn the lesson of history than to visit the Nazi concentration camps of my textbooks that stood as tragic monuments of decline and fall. (I was motivated by family history as well: my mother's only brother had died as a soldier of the colonial forces fighting against Hitler's armies.) So, with little money and a lot of youthful energy, I set out on my own for Germany. I obtained lodgings in a modest student hostel in Munich before venturing out to Dachau. Many years later I was also able to visit the Bergen Belsen Nazi camp near Hanover, on that occasion accompanied by a German Lutheran theologian.

The two visits concentrated my mind on the awful mystery of lunacy in an age of science and advanced civilization. My history courses described the details of the Holocaust that are as astounding as the scale of the horror. My religious inclination led me to the notion that when human beings are good, they are awesome, and when they are bad they are still awesome, but in a diabolical way. I saw the Holocaust as a judgment on us as human beings, not as a justification for pointing fingers at others. In the battle of good and evil, no one is immune and everyone is implicated. I recalled a Psalm of David to the effect that even with the best of accomplishments man is riddled with pride and vanity (Psalm 39:5). John Wise, a New England Puritan, echoes the idea when he writes that human beings must balance individual liberty against their common security so as to "guard themselves against the injuries men were liable to interchangeably; for none so good to man as man, and yet none a greater enemy." It is a reminder that we forget or evade the truth of ourselves to our peril.

I returned to college for final-year assignments. Protests over the Vietnam War were breaking out on campuses across the nation, and I was drawn into the upheaval. I read up on the history of Vietnam when it was French Indo-China and earlier. I took out a subscription to the *New York Review of Books* that published articles by antiwar activists such as I. F. Stone. I led student sit-ins. I later learned the meetings were bugged.

Still, in spite of my antiwar leanings, from my own remote vantage point I knew that it would be a gross misunderstanding of the activist students of my generation to accuse leaders like Lyndon Johnson and Robert McNamara of patriotic disloyalty. They were often motivated by the highest ideals of America. It was obvious that America makes war, but it was equally obvious that America makes peace — and is much better at making peace and feeding the hungry than it is at making war. In war America entered Vietnam; America would return to make peace, with John McCain, a former prisoner of war, appropriately leading the overture.

The senior essay required for the history major compensated somewhat for the jumble of jigsaw college credits students accumulated. The real trick was to obtain faculty interest and guidance, and that could not be taken for granted. I spent long hours over several months toiling away in the New York State archives in Albany and found myself gathering more documents and information than I had the good sense to know what to do with. My subject was the religious and economic sources of the eighteenth-century abolitionist movement. Not surprisingly, the result was disappointing. Just like choosing college courses, hunting down information and collecting it in files require an organizing, systematic framework to make heads or tails of it, and I faltered on that score. I produced a lumbering, uncoordinated essay that was generous on substance but, alas, meager in illumination.

In equal proportion I rose and fell under the weight of the senior essay project. I reproduced long sections of parliamentary speeches by the pro-slavery group known as the Planters, but failed to isolate the key points of turning moral arguments into arguments of economic self-interest — that procedure left very little to morality. I also overlooked the dogged defense of monopoly capitalism that looks to protectionism to serve the ideology of free trade. In that and other ways I failed to subject the quantity of sources to a quality of analysis that would make sense of the evidence. Here, the lack of supporting faculty supervision, and of a seminar setting, was telling, and I wondered how, for all their highly specialized training, professors could be happy with the state of affairs in which students went off in different directions in search of courses about whose relevance and suitability they had no prior knowledge.

As my undergraduate studies began to wind down, I began to consider post-graduate studies. My thoughts gravitated toward Asia, either Chinese or Japanese history, with summer language training if necessary as preparation. No one in the Gambia seemed eager to have me return. On his visit to New York shortly after Gambia's independence, Dawda Jawara, the president, was uninterested in my impending college graduation, merely saying that I should apply for a job at home through the normal process, assuming there was a normal process as such, and that I knew it. I took the president's rebuff, and the reluctance I had experienced from the churches at home, as signs that I should look elsewhere for a career. Henry Ferguson's recommendation that I pursue Islamic Studies persuaded me; he is responsible in large part for changing my direction and setting my career course. He based his recommendation on the fact that I had Arabic in my background. Thus the study of history led back to Islam, which had not been my plan at all.

My interest in theology, meanwhile, was rebuffed at every turn. I recall an American student guide at Union Theological Seminary in New York City pointing me to the study of African folk religion instead of theology in graduate school. That is where you can make a real contribution, he said. I encountered similar attitudes elsewhere. A prominent Methodist churchman based in London advised me against theology during his African tour, saying the church should better spend its scarce resources feeding the hungry than in supporting theological bursaries. An eminent African theologian of his day, Harry Sawyerr, expressed skepticism in a different way when I sought his wisdom: the vocation of theology, he said, should draw you in rather than being something you choose because of personal experience. I didn't see the difference.

In any case, I regarded the encouragement to pursue religious scholarship through Islamic Studies with relief. It turned out to be a wise decision, allowing me to combine history and religion in academic study. College, as it turned out, prepared me in unexpected ways for what lay ahead.

CHAPTER 8

Intercontinental Vistas

I finished college realizing that my education was much broader than the courses I had taken. My first taste of America had taught me about what America means, about the idea of America founded on the imperishable ideal of hope in a better future and "the mutual duty of all to practice Christian forbearance, love, and charity," as the 1776 Virginia Declaration of Rights put it. I bore these lessons in mind in relation to Africa, not forgetting that the countries there are not immigrant nations, and that America's founding Christian monotheist tradition had scarcely taken root in most places there. America's idea of power as flowing "from the uncorrupted choice of a brave and free people," which "is the purest source and original fountain of all power," in the words of Washington, still needed to cut channels in the new Africa, where the course of freedom faced enormous obstacles. I wondered, though, how Africans could have peace and security unless they understood that power is accountable, that it is constrained by the rule of law and by respect for personal freedom.

It was time to find out. In December 1966, a friend from nearby Rensselaer Polytechnic Institute accompanied me to New York City, where I boarded a flight to Lagos, Nigeria. There I spent several months studying Arabic while weighing my options for postgraduate studies in England. I considered enrolling in the Department of Religious Studies in the University of Ibadan, but a visit to the department, then headed by

E. Bolaji-Idowu, was disappointing. I received no encouragement as a prospective student.

To fill my time, I received private tutorials in theology, in which I learned a great deal, though I felt somewhat uneasy about being preoccupied with my own thoughts as a way of learning the lessons of faith and life. The dizzying disagreements among theologians meant there was no possibility of agreement about how to live, even though the imperative to live is unrelenting. I had to get on with life even when I had not solved the questions of theology. I was certain that the fate of people and societies cannot be less important than toying with words to chop logic.

After a brief stopover in the Gambia to visit my ailing father, I arrived in Ibadan in January 1967 to become an eyewitness to Nigeria's unfolding national drama. The weeks immediately preceding the outbreak of the civil war in July 1967 were marked by a bitter propaganda war in the press, which became the playing field of partisan protagonists. Cartoons were the chosen mode of discourse when words failed to convey the sense of scorn and vitriol of one side for the other. I remember being struck by the intemperate language and deliberate fabrication of intercultural misrepresentation. The country seemed to be sliding irreversibly down the slippery slope of mutual recrimination and dehumanization that led to hatred and terrible bloodshed.

The papers brimmed with news of impending cataclysm. A bloody military coup the previous year had toppled the first democratically elected government of Sir Abubakar Tafawa Balewa, who was killed, as was the immensely charismatic and equally controversial Sardauna of Sokoto, Ahmadu Bello. The mastermind of the coup was a commissioned Igbo military officer, Major Chukwuma Kaduna Nzeogwu, whose action opened the way for General Johnson Aguiyi-Ironsi to seize control. Ironsi ruled for only 194 days, from January to July, before he was in turn violently overthrown. Inflamed by the deaths of its prominent leaders, the Muslim North smelled an odious Igbo conspiracy in the coup, and Ironsi's promulgation of Decree No. 1 abrogating the federal constitution and replacing the structure of federal states with a unitary national state system seemed to confirm their suspicion that the minority Igbos were bent on taking over the country. It united the Hausa and

Yoruba communities in political opposition. Ironsi presided over a fractious and deeply fragmented army, and a faction led by Theophilus Danjuma pursued him to Ibadan, where he and his host, Adekunle Fajuyi, military governor of Western Nigeria, were shot and killed. Ironsi's army chief of staff, Yakubu Gowon, a Christian from a minority tribe in the north, became the new head of state. Gowon's major challenge was to take the country back from the edge.

At about this time Gowon was in the thick of negotiations with Chukwuemeka Odumegwu Ojukwu, the Sandhurst-trained Anglophile military governor of Eastern Nigeria, to thwart secessionist moves by the Igbos. These negotiations reached a crucial stage in January 1967 with the Aburi peace talks in Ghana. Gowon may have conceded too much, so that soon after he returned from Aburi he rejected the implications of the Aburi peace accord that Nigeria would exist as a collection of autonomous states knit together in a loose confederacy. In this Gowon was supported by Great Britain and the United States.

Gowon had given the peace effort everything he was worth. At the meeting his tone was conciliatory as he appealed to Ojukwu as a brother, a fellow citizen, and a fellow soldier. Ojukwu seemed to savor his moment in the sun, at least publicly. Whether accurate or not, press reports showed a cocky, intransigent Ojukwu in uncompromising mood as he played to the gallery. Prime Minister Harold Wilson of Britain and President Richard Nixon of the United States, however, both backed Gowon against Ojukwu, who tried unsuccessfully to frame the dispute as one between the Muslim North and the Christian South. In time, his Christian appeals notwithstanding, Ojukwu appealed to China for military help. Senator Strom Thurmond called on Nixon to defy the Nigerian blockade and fly in relief supplies to Biafra. Bucking expectations, the Soviet Union gave Gowon's federal forces strong military support, which he credited as the key factor in his side's victory.

Under its secretary-general, Diallo Telli of Guinea-Conakry, the Organization of African Unity (OAU) backed Gowon against the secessionists, to Ojukwu's bitter disappointment, particularly since OAU members Ivory Coast, Gabon, Tanzania, and Zambia recognized the Biafran state. Always the maverick, Charles de Gaulle also gave his support to the Biafran cause. Ojukwu's bid for Christian recognition impaled the missionary organizations active in Biafra on the horns of a cruel dilemma: either to stay on in Biafra as acknowledged traitors of Nigeria, or to leave as enemies of people who had once been their neighbors, colleagues, supporters, and friends. It didn't help that Gowon slapped missions in Nigeria with an automatic ban should they choose to remain in Biafra. Happily, the order, if not the residual distrust, was rescinded after hostilities ended in January 1970, though it took until 1974 before Catholic missionaries could receive entry visas. Rejecting calls for a Nuremberg-type trial of secessionist leaders, Gowon declared a general amnesty on January 30, 1970, which eventually paved the way for the return of Ojukwu from exile. For all the hatred directed at him by the secessionists, Gowon in fact prevented an all-too certain Igbo bloodbath, for which he deserves the gratitude of his country and the world.

One day, on a ride to Dugbe market in downtown Ibadan, my young taxi driver offered his opinion about the fate of his country and of Africa. "We have only politicians, not leaders; only factional chiefs, not statesmen," he declared. For examples of leaders and statesmen, he referred to Kwame Nkrumah of Ghana, Julius Nyerere of Tanzania, and Nnamdi Azikiwe of his own Nigeria. "Alas, their voices are no longer heard," he sighed. "The people have been abandoned. [Political] independence has not been good for Africa," he concluded ruefully. African intellectuals were largely tone deaf to the taxi driver's *cri de coeur,* with its hint of nostalgia for the peace and order of colonial rule. But it remained indelible in my memory ever since. Freedom without accountability was a sentence of misrule and mass suffering, patriotic wishful thinking notwithstanding.

I left Nigeria for Britain via the United States just weeks before the outbreak of the civil war. The outcome was never in doubt, only the duration and the cost — in human lives, mistrust, and broken relationships. The toll on all fronts was appallingly high.

I spent several weeks revisiting my old haunts at Edinburgh University before traveling down to Birmingham University to begin my studies in classical Arabic and Islam. The Methodist church agreed to sponsor me at this stage of my studies. The tutorial structure of the course was conducive to concentrated work, and was a great stimulus to careful research and investigation. Language study took the bulk of my time, with the rest of the time divided between writing essays and attending lectures and seminars. We had chapel every morning.

At this stage, the academic study of Islam was an eye-opener. Here was a religion whose history is deeply intertwined with the history of Europe and with much of the rest of the world, and yet whose cultural norms could not be more different, or more differently understood. On the origins of Islam, the works we studied included Ibn Hisham's biography of the prophet, the *Hadith* canon, al-Baladhuri, al-Baydawi, W. Montgomery Watt, Ignaz Goldziher, Richard Bell, Joseph Schacht, Arthur Jeffrey, and I. Filtshinsky, a Russian orientalist. The critical method of modern scholarship was all the rage for penetrating the world of Islam to assess and expound it in highly intelligent terms.

I realized, however, that the study of religion involved the transfer of methods of analysis developed in one tradition and carried to others. It is hard to imagine how else it could be. But this meant that religious study was embedded in critical assumptions that were by no means necessarily nonpartisan. I stumbled on this discovery while examining Watt's seminal two-volume biography of the prophet, *Muhammad at Mecca* and *Muhammad at Medina,* where Watt applied, unannounced, a neo-Marxist interpretation of the founding of Islam. Richard Bell's pioneer work on redaction criticism of the Qur'an followed closely the critical historical inquiry that changed our understanding of the New Testament. Historical criticism treats the Bible as a historical document, written by men living under particular conditions and affected by specific historical experiences and social customs.

To get at the meaning of Scripture, historical criticism deems it necessary to peel away the layers of construction built up over time, and to separate the different strands of social and political interests — what scholars call the etiology — that motivated the writers and influenced their literary style. With this kind of meticulous examination of the authorship of the text, scholars can zero in on the subject of human agency and agents as they are shaped by historical forces and personal biases and experiences. With great erudition and industry, and with sharpened tools of deconstruction, scholars went about laying bare the joints and sinews of Christianity, thereby providing an elegant model for the study of other religions. This mode of study represents the triumph of liberal Christianity in the academy and in the church. That impressive liberal achievement blazed the trail for corresponding changes in systematic theology and church history, and it seemed destined to sweep the field of religious studies.

One of the most prominent representatives of the liberal humanistic hypothesis has been John Hick, who was my head of department at Birmingham, and whose encouragement and friendship went above and beyond the call of duty. In equal measure incisive and cordial, charitable and unsparing, Hick's intellectual journey — say, from his book *Christianity at the Centre* to *God and the Universe of Faiths* and *The Myth of God Incarnate* — was something like an exodus from heartland Christian teachings to a multicultural world of religious equality. His was an exodus shared with many other Westerners.

Yet even today it is clear that this naturalist methodology is unquestionably ill-fitted to explicate Islam. For that approach, Islam would have to be structured as identical to Christianity. Its scripture, like that of Christianity, would have to be a translation and interpretation of Muhammad's teaching and significance. That way the religion would become amenable to the same tools of inquiry and construction. But is that really valid? Does the Muslim idea of *asbab al-nuzul,* "the circumstances of revelation," mean the same thing as multiple authorship of the text that involves historical motivation in composition and reception of the text? Can divine agency in Islam be subject to historical contingency, so that personal and material motivation in scripture determines questions of truth?[1] The difference here with Christianity, it seemed to me, could not be more stark.

This difference between the two religions cannot be ignored or dismissed. While historical scholarship of the liberal strain prides itself on openness to other religions, which ought to include Islam, the naturalist

---

1. See the report, Alexander Stille, "Radical New Views of Islam and the Origins of the Koran," *New York Times,* March 2, 2002. Also W. Montgomery Watt, *Bell's Introduction to the Qur'an* (Edinburgh: Edinburgh University Press, 1977). This title is an update of Richard Bell, *Introduction to the Qur'an* (Edinburgh, 1958).

understanding of religion and the critical approach to scripture as human construction are a handicap with respect to understanding Islam. Claims of impartiality based on historical criticism would be vulnerable to the charge of intolerance if scholars refuse to budge with respect to Islam; yet if they yield, they would compromise their own high standards. It is hard to push aside this dilemma.

All this made me realize the limitations of critical historical scholarship not only for understanding other cultures, but also for understanding the workings of God. If Islam's truth claims have been immune to the acids of Enlightenment skepticism, I wondered what it was about Christianity that allowed it to be penetrated so effectively. After all, many theologians saw in critical historical scholarship a welcome rout of supernaturalism. They rushed to announce the dawn of a new age of religious progress in which human solidarity would trump all claims of religious uniqueness.

I found the clue to Christianity's vulnerability in the assumption of critics that the religion existed only to improve our lives here, not to bear witness to the sovereign God as Revealer and Judge. They dismissed any claim of God's involvement in the creation of scripture as cover for human-interest issues without supernatural merit, regardless of how much (or little) proof they had for this claim. Since science and technology are proven engines of human progress, they believed we should let a sentimental Christianity yield the right of way to history's juggernaut. To everything there is a season.

Muslims may understand this way of thinking as being analogous to the doctrine of abrogation, whereby a hitherto-accepted injunction is set aside by a later injunction that improves on the situation the earlier injunction addressed. In this case, since Christian truth claims are distilled from humanistic values, they may be rescinded because of human advances that historical progress has accomplished through rational means. But this seems like the same sort of reductionism I first confronted when skeptics searched my religious conversion for political motivation. In any case, Muslims would object that this procedure uses claims of contingency to nullify claims of revealed truth. It is hard to disagree with Muslims on this point without conceding that humanistic values have the authority to upstage God in our lives. Many Christians tend to evade this challenge by saying that the values of human progress belong squarely with the intrinsic message of Christianity. But that argument is inconsistent with any idea of religion as theistic faith. The fruits of Christian teaching are not the roots of religious truth claims. It would be like saying that shoes are the reason why we have feet, or an umbrella the reason why it rains.

I first encountered this sort of criticism as part of my catechism instruction, and it left me with the distinct impression that we are using the critical method to make the idea of God accountable to reason in order to make it safe to believe. I wondered whether in this we are putting the cart before the horse. Wouldn't the right order be to make critical reasoning accountable to the idea of God in order to qualify our critical powers by moral criteria?

In conversations with fellow students, I noticed how many of them were blithely sanguine about the prospects of an imminent Islamic capitulation. Their take on the situation smacked of professional chutzpah as well as cultural hubris. Just give it time, was the general feeling. It was not clear, though, if Islam was asking for time, and from whom. All that mattered, it seemed, was that we on our side were prepared to be patient. But one suspects that patience is a euphemism for the West's intellectual intransigence, which masks the irony of wanting Muslims to budge so they can meet the West on grounds from which the West is unwilling itself to budge.

The elegant way in which much of this discussion politely omits any reference to God has not beguiled most Muslims, who wonder if an agnostic agenda is driving the debate. Does it matter to the West that scripture is God's revealed word, which cannot be surrendered to any claim of objective, enlightened progress? In this discourse, "revelation" is shorthand for divine primacy and ultimacy. Without that, religion becomes little more than a word game.

In Christianity, critical religious thought produced multiple side effects of heresies and sectarian ideas. It emboldened Tertullian, a third-century Christian author, to lament that the injection of philosophy had produced a mottled Christianity of Stoic, Platonic, and dialectic parts. A few exiled Muslim mavericks may take the bait of such philosophical enticements, but that does not add up to a trend. The work of E. G. Browne,

R. A. Nicholson, Bernard Lewis, and E. I. J. Rosenthal suggests that there may well be a breakout on the perimeters in places like Turkey, Iran, Pakistan (before the split with Bangladesh), and maybe Indonesia. Nevertheless, on present evidence, the West in its unyielding rational skepticism is unlikely to find its mirror image in Islam on the same scale and with the same effect.

On this point I benefited enormously from a memorable meeting with Kenneth Cragg, an Anglican theologian who was one of the foremost proponents of Muslim-Christian dialogue. With his characteristic warmth and humanity, he received me most cordially when I visited him at Cambridge University. On a stroll through the gardens that famously adorn Cambridge, Cragg explained the crucial importance of a theological engagement with the truth claims of Islam, insisting that Christian faithfulness is at stake. He expressed himself on that point in two seminal works: his classic study *The Call of the Minaret* (1956), centered on Islam's Five Pillars of the faith, with a corresponding five-part theological reflection as a response; and *Sandals at the Mosque* (1959), a book that urges Christians to enter the Muslim mind and spirit with the reverence and attentiveness symbolized by taking one's shoes off. It is his skill in exploring the interiority of religious life in Islam that has justly established Cragg as a giant in the annals of twentieth-century Western-Islamic apologetics. He has never minimized or overlooked differences between the faiths, but with unflagging commitment and faithfulness he has devoted his long and distinguished life to promoting interfaith trust and understanding between Muslims and Christians at the meeting points that are common to the two religions.

Given the dim prospects I saw for applying current paradigms to understanding Islam, I determined to look in other directions for a way forward in interfaith relations. I thought we could assess the impact of scripture on communities of believers without impugning believers as self-deceived absent critical historical scrutiny. The history of such impact on personal lives and on societies is no less important than the history of the text. After all, both approaches ultimately address the text, one as subject for critical study and the other as a rule of life. Who is to say that it matters in one sphere more than it does in the other sphere? I grew up in a community where Islam extended and deepened its grip by having the idea of an inviolate Qur'an placed right at the center of people's lives, where its influence bore little relationship to knowledge of its holy language. It was simply the idea that the Qur'an contained revealed truths that have merit in themselves, and not by reason of our understanding, that gave the Book its power. It was to defend scripture as such that my Qur'an school teacher objected to Sufi groups that arrived in town to stage public chants of litanies. The teacher was afraid such practices would shift the focus to our feelings and away from the word of God. For us in the West to appreciate this, we need different critical tools to assess the impact of scripture on believers.

I have a great appetite for books, but I also have a tendency to compare what I read in books with what actually happens in life. In books by Westerners, I read that Muslims would inevitably come to re-examine the truth claims of their faith as modern education took hold in the Muslim world. But I saw something quite different when I looked around. What seems to me so striking about the Muslim world since 1973, the year of the fateful Yom Kippur War between Israel on one side and Syria and Egypt on the other, has been the extent to which the modernizing Western-educated middle class has been largely eviscerated by the forces of religious awakening, rather than religion being drained by the forces of secularization. Even before the 1979 Iranian Islamic Revolution that toppled a secularizing Shah, there was a whiff in the air that the middle-class center could not hold, as the writings of 'Ali Shariati (d. 1977), with their appeal to a disenchanted intelligentsia, made clear. "I have come to create a struggle in their intellects," he wrote, insisting that "What comes into existence after doubt, anxiety and agitation has value." Hounded by the agents of the Shah of Iran, he was allegedly pursued to London, where he was murdered. He was buried in Damascus. In Turkey, too, the secular establishment has had to turn frequently to the army to hold at bay pent-up religious forces. In Egypt, Algeria, Lebanon, Gaza, the West Bank, and elsewhere, the forces of new religious resurgence have challenged any complacency about the inevitability of secular ascendancy. An astonishing variety of movements of Islamic reform and renewal covers the entire political spectrum, from the right to the left, making it difficult to say that modernity is incompatible with the Muslim religious outlook. On a visit to Riyadh's impressive science museum in Saudi Arabia, I was struck by the theme of the harmony of science and the Qur'an, of reason and revelation (Q 30:24). Clearly, the prophets of secularization were wrong.

The lesson I took from this was that Islam constitutes a radical intellectual challenge to the West, not by virtue of any overt offensive in particular, but by virtue of the West's own blind spot on religion. If and when the challenge became overt, a naïve West might think a muscular military response, modulated with economic inducement, would be all it would take to dispose of the problem, showing how the religious blind spot can induce obsessive behavior as an avoidance strategy. In the Sunday school class I taught in Schenectady, for instance, I explained to those bright young kids who were trying to understand Islam through American eyes that Islam was a religion, but that it was also a state, that Islam was very much a this-worldly religion. Islam applies rules of personal obedience and appearance as well as rules of government, banking and finance, international relations, sanitation, art and architecture, music, and so on. Islam does not turn its back on the world.

I started to feel that I was hitting my head against a brick wall regarding Western approaches to Islam, but I began to realize that it is not easy for the academy to give up on the hard-earned use of critical inquiry. There was little in the experience of my eager and curious fellow students to use as analogy in its stead. They thought of communism as a comparable comprehensive ideology, until I reminded them that Islam is not simply an ideology — it is a monotheist faith as well. They didn't know what to do with that.

This should not have been surprising at the time, given how preoccupied students in the 1960s were with the politics of the Cold War and with the parallel decolonization movement. It was a combination that proved potent for contemporary academic discourse. I was unusual in being attracted neither to the Cold War nor to decolonization, which left me without a popular cause of my own. In spite of the efforts of my professors, I was unconvinced by scientific socialism's instrumental view of society; I found it too rough and ready a view of human relationship. The formula of *who* dominates *whom* as the truth of social reality struck me as somewhat willful. Dialectics means conflict, and conflict begets the preordained enemy. Theories we fabricate create the enemies we want — sometimes even if they are enemies we don't need. After all, not every encounter ought to be a contest about pushing others lower down the food chain. My childhood had already taught me plenty about that. There are worse ways than the world of sibling rivalry for learning about how to handle conflict without leaving it to commissars.

Stimulating perhaps as a corrective to the gullible, the Marxist critique of religion nevertheless offered me little help in understanding Islam or in engaging it in any satisfactory way. For any sweeping theory of explanation such as Marxism to pass over a major tradition like Islam suggests a serious flaw. It strengthened my resolve to look at reality untrammeled by dogmatism. However elegant, if theory would not get me to the right place, I would have to find another way to get there. The issues were too personal and too important simply to abandon them.

CHAPTER 9

Boomerang

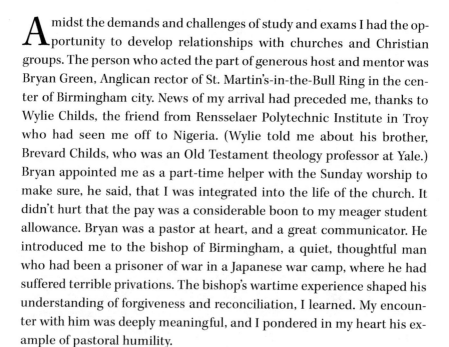

Amidst the demands and challenges of study and exams I had the opportunity to develop relationships with churches and Christian groups. The person who acted the part of generous host and mentor was Bryan Green, Anglican rector of St. Martin's-in-the-Bull Ring in the center of Birmingham city. News of my arrival had preceded me, thanks to Wylie Childs, the friend from Rensselaer Polytechnic Institute in Troy who had seen me off to Nigeria. (Wylie told me about his brother, Brevard Childs, who was an Old Testament theology professor at Yale.) Bryan appointed me as a part-time helper with the Sunday worship to make sure, he said, that I was integrated into the life of the church. It didn't hurt that the pay was a considerable boon to my meager student allowance. Bryan was a pastor at heart, and a great communicator. He introduced me to the bishop of Birmingham, a quiet, thoughtful man who had been a prisoner of war in a Japanese war camp, where he had suffered terrible privations. The bishop's wartime experience shaped his understanding of forgiveness and reconciliation, I learned. My encounter with him was deeply meaningful, and I pondered in my heart his example of pastoral humility.

A lively, bouncy man, Bryan turned St. Martin's into a hive of activity, drawing his pastoral team of curates and deacons into urban mission and the work of the Church Missionary Society abroad. One of his curates turned down the prospect of rapid promotion in the hierarchy to go up to a near-derelict church in the coalfields of Wakefield because he found the challenge appealing. He relished the thought of reviving a dying parish. St. Martin's supported an Australian Anglican missionary in Nigeria whom I had met in my time there. There were weekly meetings of young adults at church and in homes. The simple, unaffected kindness of members of the young adult group, as well as the ease with which they seemed to slip into their religious profession without any prickly self-consciousness, made a deep impression on me. It was simply enjoyable company, where no one was being analyzed or evaluated by anyone else. Nor was there any interest in criticizing or unloading on others. One of the young adults was a schoolteacher who lived in Bourneville with her husband and their new baby. Quick-witted and humorous, she was the soul of friendliness. The young people were attracted to Bryan's style of leadership, with the trust and support he showed for the initiatives of others. The church published a parish magazine that included articles of reflection as well as news and information on events and anniversaries.

Bryan was a familiar name in evangelical circles on both sides of the Atlantic, which was how Wylie got to know him. Bryan invited me to an interview in the pulpit one Sunday after he heard about my religious background. When we got to the part about growing up in a polygamous household, Bryan paused and said he thought the congregation would like to hear more about that. You could hear a rustle rise like a wave in the pews as people bestirred themselves, sat up, and took notice. I explained how Father thought he was the center of life, but how in reality his wives crowded him out most of the time. He was left to nurse the illusion of masculine pre-eminence while the women enjoyed the substance of influence in the domestic sphere. In polygamy, I said, the man led too busy a life of commuting among his several women to be able to accumulate power on his own terms. "Men of England," Bryan interrupted with a smile, "wake up and take note!"

Bryan wanted me to stress the rarity of Muslim conversions. He thought church was so taken for granted in England that people might not appreciate how difficult it was for others in predominantly Muslim societies. In response I gave an example of a Muslim student who was attracted to Christianity enough to want to learn about it. Since he could not find anyone to instruct him, and since there was an interdiction on

Christian literature in the school, the boy hid a stolen Bible under his mattress so he could read it secretly at night. Bryan said he thought that kind of stealing God would readily forgive, to much laughter from the congregation. Didn't I think that was the case? I replied that I thought that was true, but that I didn't know if it followed that one also could — or should — tuck away one's faith from prying eyes. Jesus defied the grave by appearing in the open. It is difficult, I explained, to steal your mother's perfume and to hide it at the same time. In that vein, it is hard to see how under normal circumstances a stolen faith is viable. "Plenty to think about there," Bryan observed, and I picked up the cue to wrap things up. Bryan was appreciative of Islam, and I detected not the slightest negativity in him on that or on other fronts. His pastoral energy sought more positive outlets.

Our next assignment was a road trip to Farnham in Surrey for a weekend mission. A supreme organizer, Bryan had well-laid plans ahead of time, with neighboring parishes saturated with publicity and announcements, and a handpicked team of experienced parsons lined up for the purpose. The target was young people, and that required adequate follow-up sessions through the weekend. Host families were also notified that the two of us needed accommodation.

On the road trip from Birmingham to Farnham, Bryan and I had a hair-raising narrow escape. We left Birmingham in the late afternoon to avoid heavy rush-hour traffic. As evening fell I noticed that Bryan was fading a bit, and sure enough, before long the car veered off the road and ploughed into the dirt. Bryan had fallen asleep at the wheel, but he jerked awake and grabbed control of the steering just in time to keep the car from going deep into the dirt and somersaulting. The seat belts saved us from tumbling out of the car, and thus from any injury. It all happened so quickly, within the twinkling of an eye. There was only time for hair-trigger reaction.

We never talked again about the incident. It was as if it disappeared from our minds almost as quickly as it happened — evidence, perhaps, of psychological defense. The only thing I heard Bryan say to someone in Farnham after we got there was that I appeared calm and collected through the drama. I am still not sure how many people ever knew just how close we came to death. Bryan and I had numerous subsequent meetings after that experience, and yet we never discussed it even once. Still, we bonded, as if living out the truth of the saying that beaten clay makes sturdy bricks.

Bryan asked me if I had ever thought about becoming an Anglican. I gave him a little history of my experience with the Methodists and the Catholics. "Oh, well," he responded, "we would have no difficulty receiving you into the church, though I must warn you that the Anglican church can be so boring you couldn't swallow a cat if you wanted to. The soporific drone of mechanical recitation of the liturgy can be as dull as dishwater." Yet in spite of his breezy assurance, when at my suggestion he consulted the relevant authorities responsible for my oversight, they were adamant in their opposition to the idea, saying the Methodists would not countenance such sheep-stealing by the Church of England. It was the first time I had any indication that the Methodists cared two farthings about my affiliation with them. True to his nature, Bryan said it didn't matter in the least, and that I would continue to serve in his church for as long as he remained there. I could not tell if the rest of his clergy colleagues shared his ecumenical openness on that front, but no one raised an objection, to my great relief. Bryan introduced me to the Scaddings, who were members of the parish and who became my English host family. Lillian Scadding was a wonderful friend — she would be surprised to know that her gift of cutlery as a wedding present still adorns our dining table.

One of the officials opposed to my joining the Anglican church was Tom Beetham, the warden of my college. An ecumenical elder statesman with a distinguished missionary career in Ghana, Tom was a Cambridge-trained mathematician who went on to study theology as a second career. Remarkably, Tom had had a hand in my conversion story, though I didn't know it until he told me. He was at the time responsible for the Africa Department of the Methodist Missionary Society (MMS) in London when he received reports about me. He said the question he had to resolve was how the church could best use my background and academic aptitude; he didn't feel that parish life was suitable for me. Instead, he felt that work in interfaith dialogue with Muslims was a more natural fit for me. So here I was in England several years later, studying Islam in a college where the man who had been an anonymous arbiter of my conversion was now my warden.

This was a significant piece of new information, because his decision had affected me in a very personal way. But I felt Tom didn't know how that decision was received and implemented on the ground, and I was certain he would be disappointed if he knew the details. So here I was, landing on his doorstep as the boomerang he launched from his London office. I refrained from bringing up the subject in deference to Tom's collegial obligations. In any event, by now I had no doubt that Tom was right about the pastoral vocation for me; it would have been a strain for me to work in an environment based on Christian appeasement of Islam. Tom would be dismayed, however, if he knew how much pestering I needed in order to cajole the church into agreeing to baptize me. Yet even I had little inkling how close that pestering was to stiffening the back of the church until years later, when I visited Mission House in London in Tom's company. By that time Tom had long retired from the MMS, but he thought we should pay a courtesy call on one of his colleagues, Grant Johnson. It was a fiasco. Johnson made it clear we were getting in his way, showing he had little time for us. My next encounter with Johnson was worse: he suggested that perhaps the Catholics could find some use for me. It felt like *déjà vu.* Tom was tightlipped in embarrassment, and to spare him further discomfort I avoided the subject. At least Mission House could not take back the baptism it allowed the church to grant me, I mused to myself with mixed gratitude.

During my time in Birmingham Tom was going through a period of deep personal sadness. Elaine, his wife of many decades, was gravely ill and had been given a terminal prognosis. Tom tended to her needs while also administering the college. He spoke to me about the challenge of being pulled between office and home, and said he was grateful to his colleagues for the college assignment that enabled him to be close to home during this time. His calm, steady hand was a real asset for students, who were at the time deep into theological experimentation and in the process questioning authority and tradition. Tom observed to me once that it was interesting to see students embarking on new styles of liturgy and student government without knowing that those new styles had been in vogue a generation earlier. From that perspective student revolution was remarkably old-fashioned: the rhetoric of change was, as it turned out, a conservative sleight of hand.

In his book *Christianity and the New Africa* (1967), Tom undertook a characteristically pithy and magisterial assessment of Christian fortunes in post-independent Africa. He was one of the first to point out that in his lifetime the religion had finally taken permanent root as a continent-wide phenomenon, not by virtue of political establishment but by reason of the indomitable faith of mothers and rural dwellers. Tom was convinced that African Christianity did not need white hegemony to preserve it. He was, accordingly, critical of mission agencies for their slowness to transfer power into African hands. He commented to me about how, with regard to placing missionaries under the control of the local church leadership, Methodist practice was much closer to Catholic practice than to the policies of other Protestant missions.

Tom's perspective on Christianity in Africa was shaped largely by his personal experience of contemporary reports of the huge charismatic movement of the prophet William Wadé Harris of the Ivory Coast. Eventually banned and banished by the French colonial authorities, Harris had an inexplicably durable impact on largely illiterate populations of the Ivory Coast and western Ghana even though he was active for only a brief period between 1917 and 1918. Tom told me how he volunteered for missionary service to Africa after he heard an appeal at a meeting in London for missionaries to help shepherd the vast numbers of Harrist converts who were at the time without any instruction or church. When in 1924 the first Methodist missionary, William Platt, arrived in the Ivory Coast, he was able to scoop up some fifty thousand souls that Harris had converted; with those he was able to constitute the backbone of the Methodist church there. The Catholics also benefited from the Harrist resurgence: in 1917 there were about eight thousand members on the Catholic rolls, but by 1922 there were more than twenty thousand. A Catholic missionary eyewitness conceded that what Harris "did none of us would have been able to do," and that Harris had done in three months what the church was unable to do in twenty years.

After he signed up for missionary service Tom arrived in Ghana to witness the remarkable effects of the Harrist movement. Tom didn't need any persuading about the truth and effectiveness of African leadership, and that African point of view became the guiding philosophy of his work. He didn't feel that Christianity was exempt from the logic of nationalism; in fact, he felt Christianity had a large hand in nurturing the national spirit. If missionaries failed to realize that fact, Tom reasoned, Christianity would survive in African hands without missionary acknowledgment. Missionary investment in Christianity should for that reason be an investment in structures of national development by cultivation of an educated and an ethically-attuned African leadership in church and society. Tom was instrumental in helping to convene an international conference in Salisbury, later Harare, in what was then Southern Rhodesia, from December 29, 1962, to January 10, 1963, on the subject of "Christian Education in Africa," the title of the report published by Oxford University Press (1963). At that time serving as Africa Secretary of the Conference of British Missionary Societies, Tom made a plenary presentation at the conference, whose wide-ranging themes kept a narrow focus on the needs and requirements of the new Africa. Unless unforeseen complications stood in the way, the report urged that the teaching of Latin and Greek in schools give way to the teaching of mother tongues as well as classical Arabic. The goal would be to bridge the gap between Black Africa and the Mediterranean world to the north. The report noted that missions bore the lion's share of the burden of education in Britain's colonies, showing the scale of the missionary role in creating the building blocks of modern Africa.

Even today, anyone reading *Christianity and the New Africa* will be struck by the quality of its judgment, by the rising African spirit that animates the book, and by the sense of measured, careful observation that carries the story along. Tom was too unsparing and too astringent a person to indulge in self-serving missionary hagiography. Yet even where his experience of human foibles led him not to skim over the temptations of power and wealth that Africans would face, he never lost his grip of the role of faith in the emerging societies of Africa. Men and women of character are the backbone of a nation, Tom felt, and nation building cannot happen without them. The recent explosion of Christianity in Africa Tom never lived to see, yet it is uncanny how well he anticipated the impending surge. Tom foresaw the time when Christianity would become a compelling factor in any reckoning with Africa's future.

Along with the Anglican bishops, Ambrose Reeves and Trevor Huddleston, among others, Tom called on the British Foreign Office to end white minority rule in Rhodesia. He reported to me how Lord Home, then Conservative Foreign Secretary, was slow in appreciating the urgency of a reversal of Britain's policy in Rhodesia, which adopted the widely condemned policy of Unilateral Declaration of Independence (UDI) from Britain in 1965 when Harold Wilson was Labor Prime Minister. In a joint letter to the London *Times,* Tom joined those criticizing Britain's refusal to use force to push out Ian Smith, the Rhodesian leader. In private conversations Tom said Britain was merely postponing the inevitable reality of African political ascendancy in Rhodesia, and that the cost of the foot-dragging would come to dog Britain eventually. Of course, he could never have suspected the irony of a liberated Rhodesia as Zimbabwe coming to dog the people, too.

At the University of Birmingham, for convenience, I was enrolled in the theology department while I studied Arabic and Islam under John Taylor in the Selly Oak Colleges. John was a wonderful, empathetic teacher, with a gentleness that allowed him to approach the subject with unyielding rigor. I divided my time between there and the Centre of West African Studies, where I took courses in African History, including Islam in Africa. John Fage headed the Centre, with John Ralph Willis as the newly appointed lecturer in African Islam. Along with Roland Oliver, Fage was a pioneer of African history and a co-founder with Oliver of *The Journal of African History,* still the leading journal in the field. John Hick headed the theology department in the Faculty of Arts and Sciences.

As a friend, mentor, and supporter, Hick was much the greater influence on me compared to Fage. Hick invited me on weekend sightseeing trips with his family, including a trip to Coventry Cathedral, which at that time still bore marks of German bombing in November 1940 during World War II. The huge tapestry of the resurrected Christ that adorned the narthex was a symbol, we were told, of the church's rise from the ashes; it was commissioned for the purpose when the church was reconsecrated in 1962. Hick has since moved much further to the left of Christian orthodoxy, but at that stage he was still exploring with sparkling brilliance the whole issue of the challenge of pluralism for claims of Christian uniqueness. Many readers will be familiar with the controversy Hick has generated with his attack on the finality of Christ, but fewer will know of Hick's personal generosity with students, who admired his warm humanity and genuine openness. At his invitation I joined him for lunch as his guest at the university faculty club quite often, even though I was a lowly student. Interested to hear that I found a hospitable church at St. Martin's-in-the-Bull-Ring, Hick accompanied me there one Sunday, where I introduced him to Bryan. He followed my work in Islamics with encouragement and unwavering interest even though I was studying under someone else. My experience of his integrity as a scholar and as a person leaves me in his eternal debt, and I count myself fortunate to have known so fine a specimen of human kindness. I did not merit his friendship.

The question that had me tussling was probably very far from Hick's concerns: why the religious core of Islam seemed much more stable than the religious core of Christianity. Ever the quintessential controversialist, Hick was moving to the position that Christian orthodoxy was at bottom a miscellany of disputed questions, a view that hauls religion straight into the spin zone. For my part, I wanted to know what brought Christianity to that fate, not whether and how that fate befits Christianity. It's an important distinction, especially from my point of view as a student of classical Islam.

If theology could not help me resolve the question, perhaps history could — not conventional history as the study of power and power relations, but intellectual history as the study of ideas and their impact on movements of social change. I did not know it at the time, but I found out later that the question had been amply discussed in studies by a pantheon of American scholars, including Perry Miller at Harvard, though I never encountered them in my college courses. Also, the question had not yet preoccupied me at that stage.

Having successfully put behind me the demands and requirements of degree work, and before my impending trip to Lebanon to continue my studies in Islam and Arabic, I turned my attention to the mission of Christianity, or what remained of Christianity, in the West. My focus was to try to *understand* what had happened rather than to decry or to applaud it, the aim being to understand the contrast with Islam's public role in Muslim societies. It was in that spirit that I delved into R. H. Tawney's *Religion and the Rise of Capitalism,* an old classic. I decided on a solo trip to set out for the Isle of Skye on Scotland's northwest coast. The book was my return passage to Christianity's role in the rise of the modern West. In work for my degree, as well as in other readings, I saw undeniable evidence of the impact of the modern West on the Muslim world, and realized that it sparked an inconclusive but vehement controversy on the religious front, which expressed itself in Muslim opposition to the Western missionary movement. I was not at this point looking to defend Western missions, but simply to uncover their complex relations with other aspects of the West's overseas expansion.

What makes the controversy particularly vexing is that in the main colonial administrations sided with Muslims to shield their societies from missionary influence. In the Muslim world Christianity was stumped by Western imperialism more than by any other force, with the accompanying Western-inspired modernization furnishing the Muslim world with tools with which to launch and to maintain an anti-Christian cultural-resistance strategy. In a curt response to demands by Palestinian Christians that the British give them the same consideration they gave the Muslims, Winston Churchill objected, saying, "it is no good pretending that you are more closely united to the Christians than to the Jews. That is not so. A wider gulf separates us from you than separates you from the Jew."

I soon learned that colonial officers in Nigeria had also been in open opposition to the idea of a Christianized Africa, and for that reason had sided with Muslim leaders who denounced mission work. A senior administrator said it was colonialism's responsibility to design and transfer into Muslim hands the prestige of a modern state. The official in question saw no role for Christianity in that new order. Christianity in any form, the official insisted, is "synonymous with idleness, impudence, inefficiency, and with all that is meanest in a native or in any other polity." Sir Hugh Clifford, the governor of Nigeria, concurred with that criticism.

Given this set colonial antipathy toward Christianity, and a corresponding support for Muslim institutions, it is indeed not surprising that colonial rule bolstered the fortunes of Islam. The facts on the ground bear this out. In few places under colonial rule did Islam decline, either in numbers or in influence. Quite the contrary: Muslim numbers were higher, and Islam's territorial gains greater, at the end of colonial rule than at the beginning. The bits of territory administrators hacked away from populations adjacent to Muslim centers they gladly turned over to Muslims, including the emirates that were foisted on populations active in anti-Islamic resistance. That was how the administrators defied historical reality to drag the plateau region of Nigeria and secular Fulbe states of Senegambia into the Muslim sphere, stoking the embers of future tension and conflict.

It was the other way around for Christianity. The end of colonial rule removed obstacles in the path of Christian conversion, allowing the religion to commence the indigenous resurgence that was to distinguish it in its post-Western phase. Colonial rule inserted the Western world into Christianity's missionary endeavor more as a costly, complicating irritant than as an advantage. In its overseas expansion, Europe was skeptical about the political merits of the Christian religion. Colonial rule required Christianity to be useful in order to co-opt it; otherwise it would be suppressed. Christianity could not be allowed to use its Western reputation to compromise colonialism's legitimacy as a Western mandate. Being European, missionaries would give the appearance that Christianity was a European religion, a false idea detrimental to colonial rule by offending local sensibility while emboldening converts to claim equality with Europeans. Accordingly, Muslims and colonial administrators closed ranks to fight missions, leaving missions to wage a battle on two fronts: on the home front against imperial opposition, and abroad against indigenous hostility. This realization forced me to look into the sources of the split between Europe and its Christian heritage.

The most important lesson I learned from Tawney was that the new economic organization of Europe was by the "invisible hand" of religion, specifically by the moral stringency that Puritan forms of the religion bred. That moral stringency set such a high premium on religious attachment that only few people could achieve it. Real religion was denied to the majority, who, thus freed from religious constraints, invested them-selves unhindered in worldly pursuits on the basis of self-interest. The paradox, says Tawney, is that the over-cultivated zeal of the elect spilled over into the search for worldly blessings as proof of divine favor. In that way the protection of religion from worldly taint brought about a conver-gence between the Puritan and the entrepreneur, between the saint and the humanist. The Puritan was not opposed to the world, only to the misuse of the world. In fact, the Puritan found worldly success worthy enough to be a divine blessing. In one move, Puritan religion pushed God into the background to promote worldly success, while in the next move it let God in by making worldly success unimpeachable proof of divine approval.

Thanks to this helpful assessment, I began to see that in the final analysis the world, rather than God, became the arbiter of what passes muster. The fruits of earthly success became the proof and vindication of divine favor. Nothing vindicated the saints better than the material fruits of their labor. The Puritan defies his Catholic nemesis by looking to the fruits of toil and labor: *laborare est orare.* Sin remains for both, but for the Puritan its nature and cure are not absolution and sacrament, but conviction and willpower. Grace abounds by personal industry, not by mediation and devotion. As one Puritan divine put it, "The standing pool is prone to putrefaction: and it were better to beat down the body and to keep it in subjection by a laborious calling, than through luxury to be-come a cast-away."

The next step was to account for power without resort to religious underwriting, and that step was identical to the Puritan argument of the entrepreneur unconstrained by religious discipline. Power also needed to be unconstrained by religious rules, and judged only by how it safe-guards the free conscience. That reduced the role of government to the minimum standard of preserving society and punishing wrongdoing. At any rate, government had to vacate the religious sphere to protect free-dom of conscience in the same way that it needed to vacate the sphere of economic enterprise to let risk-taking be rewarded. For the Puritan, free enterprise and freedom of religion are conjoined twins. When govern-ment works to a similar end, it can be judged to have carried out God's purpose. Otherwise government hinders God's purpose when it fetters the free conscience. Herein lies the paradox of why government that is free of religion is government that must also be held accountable to the provision of God for the anointed conscience. The free market is the side-effect of the free entrepreneur, and, by the same token, government is the side-effect of the citizens' collective will. If government is free *of* religion as a revealed blueprint, it is not free *from* religion as the individual's inviolate conscience. Freedom of religion is the seedbed of free enterprise, wherein lies the idea of the individual as the root and branch of society, morality, politics, and law. At the same time, this idea hatched nonconformist separatism as one of its consequences. Religion as personal faith distills into enterprise as personal industry and risk-taking, allowing industriousness to yield fruit as requisite compensation of consecrated labor. Government, by the same logic, is God's instrument for securing and promoting society, and for that reason worthy of the allegiance of saint and sinner alike.

What I find interesting in all of this is not so much the connection of religion and enterprise as the fact that such a connection in Islam produced scarcely any nonconformist sectarianism. Thanks to Weber, we are inclined to view economic enterprise in Islam as feudal in character, forgetting that the religion originated in "a city of high finance," as one authority describes Mecca. Trade was the very lifeblood of Islam, and venture capital existed to drive the economic engine. Keeping shop prospered in the shadow of the mosque, and vice versa. Judgment Day is but traffic in balancing gain and reward against loss and punishment. Faith, in this context, is a kind of risk management: on the positive side, it spurs the pursuit of worldly success; on the negative side, it constrains the impulse of schismatic splintering. Rising or falling is not a question of chopping logic to impose doctrinal rectitude; it is a question of succeeding or failing in achieving material reward. In popular sentiment, what people worship is less who God is — which is why speculative theology is so scarce in Islam — than the appeal of worldly prosperity. Unlike the case in Christianity, Islam's religious polarity of the Creator and the created order does not require sectarian splits to fuel it; it abides simultaneously in scriptural rules of enjoinment as in those of prohibition, in what religion should be as well as in what religion should not be. The unifying, anti-schismatic power of Islam lies in the reinforcing interplay of the double commandment of what God requires as Creator, on the one hand, and on the other, what he forbids in the creature. It is expressed in the Qur'anic formula *amar bi-ma'rúf wa nahy 'an al-munkar* ("to bid to what is approved and to forbid what is disapproved"). The church, on the other hand, undertook that as authority equally to fasten and to loosen.

I had to figure out the implications of these ideas for my career. I thought about the possibility of working with the churches involved in interfaith dialogue, but I didn't know if interfaith dialogue was at all viable in the way churches were used — and not used — to thinking about the subject. Often, interfaith dialogue became too quickly academic and defensive, with disclaimers about Christian intentions not being for the conversion of Muslims. That in turn provoked a reaction among evangelical Christians, who stressed mission to Islam as a corrective to academic evasion. Because these Christians suspected scholarly interest to be a ruse for surrendering Christian truth claims, they mobilized a populist rejection of dialogue. In a different vein, I often heard Christian leaders argue that inter-religious dialogue was not credible unless the churches resolved the scandal of disunity among themselves, which sounded like making interfaith relations a casualty of Christian disunity. The issue divided the churches, so it diverted much valuable energy and resources from work in the field. Hence the uncertainty of my role.

Still, I felt that disagreement among the churches evaded a pressing question about interfaith encounter as the next logical stage in the evolution of cultural consciousness of the modern West. Clearly the West had successfully and profitably tamed Christianity, but was that a convincing template for the interfaith challenge? When in 1968 I set out for Beirut for further studies in Arabic, I was eager to learn and profit from the experience of the ancient religious communities there about how to coexist and engage one another. I had important lessons to learn.

CHAPTER 10

Clipped Cedars

The journey to Beirut took an unusually roundabout route, thanks to the brutal realities of low-budget travel. I was several weeks late arriving because of a dock strike in Venice, from where I was due to embark. It was the cheapest way for a student to travel: by rail from Birmingham, with the Channel crossing to negotiate, before arriving in Venice to board a Mediterranean passenger ship bound for Beirut via Alexandria. I had visited Venice before, and then as now I was struck by how the waterways cut the city into a hundred island blocks on the sea, with the waves splashing against the pathways and glistening in the light as the canals framed the city in its picturesque charm. The traffic noise and frenetic pace that dog modern city life are absent in Venice, where the water lanes reduce transport and communication to the silent punting of painted gondolas.

Meanwhile I took in as much of the art and sights as I could wish, only to run out of walking options as well as the token meal vouchers I was given while the strike lasted. At first sun-girt Venice, ocean's child and queen, as Shelley put it, stirred warm memories of my island childhood, only to dissolve them in the urban milieu of a bustling tourist destination. You get about at the pace of the gondolas plying their winding rotation on the canals. I spent many idle mornings in Piazza San Marco until I was reduced to counting the grey pigeons in my head before tucking into banks of pasta and tomato salad. Vivaldi had never sounded more mellifluous than when on a stroll on the Lido. I visited churches and found them largely empty, except for elderly Venetians saying the rosary and making votive offerings. The younger generation seemed to keep their distance from religion, while the old people who went to church cared not a farthing for things theological. Indeed, Venice's religious imagination has been consummated long ago in music, art, paintings, and architecture, and now bids us stand and watch, and "lean and loaf at our ease," to paraphrase Walt Whitman. The Scottish landscape, echoing with the sounds of imaginary bagpipe music, could not have seemed more different or far away from Venice. In time the strike ended, and we finally weighed anchor and steamed out of the harbor.

What has come to be called the Six Day War of June 5-10, 1967, had taken a terrible toll on Beirut by the time I arrived there in the summer of 1968. Lebanon could not escape the forces unleashed by the debacle of the Six Day War, and the evidence of it was visible in the growing number of Palestinian refugees who were creating a severe strain on Lebanon's social and political fabric. The leader of a militant Palestinian faction, George Habash, persuaded Yasser Arafat that a new anti-Israeli struggle was urgently needed as a replacement for Gamal Abdel Nasser's defeated Arab nationalism. For that Jordan must first be taken over to thwart what Habash called "reactionary Arab regimes" that are willing to do the bidding of Israel and the United States. The calculation that made Israel and Jordan equal targets of Palestinian fury would soon engulf Lebanon, rocking the delicate balance among the various religious groups in the country. The fine-tuned mechanism of representation in parliament and in the leadership structure, in which long-established religious communities shared power, was suddenly jolted out of its axis. While still reeling from that, Lebanon saw its problems exacerbated by the strains on its southern border with Israel, where Palestinian camps in high ferment were multiplying.

Lebanon's kaleidoscope of religious clans includes Christian Maronites, dominant in government since independence; Muslim Sunnis, who prospered in business and shared political power; the Druze, who hold a faith incorporating aspects of Islam and Gnosticism; and Muslim Shiites, for whom Lebanon offered a secure base. The politics of cantonal harmony these groups practiced in effect collided with the politics of armed resistance of refugee Palestinians, and it threw Lebanon into violent swings of fortune. It also brought Lebanon closer to Syria's sphere of influence. Lebanon had separated from Syria to preserve its diversity; now that diversity might be the reason for Syria to intervene in its affairs. The political horse trading that was the standard métier of the country's leaders now threatened to choke them with the explosive potential of unstable Palestinian grievances. The quota system of power-sharing and the residential separation of East and West Beirut could not bear the strain of new transient refugees and their demands of regaining their occupied Palestinian homeland.

At the time people spoke proudly — and with some justification — of Lebanon as the Switzerland of the Middle East, vaunting Lebanon's Levantine reputation as a center of business, finance, the entrepreneurial spirit as well as the corresponding cantonization. That reputation seemed well and truly sealed by Lebanon successfully managing to slip the dragnet of the Arab nationalism Egypt's President Nasser deployed with the creation in 1958 of the short-lived United Arab Republic. My friends there were convinced that Lebanon was exempt from the troubles of its neighbors, and that, even if there were obstacles and occasional breakdowns, the basic institutions of civil harmony remained sound.

The modern history of Lebanon is a palette of leftover components of Ottoman imperial rule, the legacy of the League of Nations French mandate that administered the country after 1920, and pragmatic elements of the modern secular Arab awakening as represented, among others, by the American University of Beirut. Ottoman rule rewarded loyalty with legitimacy; the French mandate offered a buffer against total Islamic assimilation; Arab modernism provided strong cultural foundations. A thriving middle class emerged to reap huge benefits from the resulting social stability. The French had provided the institutional framework when they separated a religiously polyphonic Lebanon from a mainly Muslim Syria, guiding it somewhat uncertainly to independence in November 1941.

As it was, full independence came in stages. The French transferred full powers to Lebanon in 1944, with the final withdrawal of French troops occurring in 1946. Simmering tensions between different Muslim factions, however, erupted into civil war in 1958. Kamal Jumblat and Saeb Salam as faction leaders engaged in an insurrection against the government of President Camille Chamoun, a Maronite, who favored close ties with the West. To save his government, Chamoun turned to President Eisenhower who sent in U.S. troops in July to restore the government's authority.

I was intrigued by how pre–civil war Lebanon came to ration religious privileges without turning religion sectarian. The reasons are easy enough to find. Lebanon's special status as a multicultural, multireligious communal democratic system made it an oddity in the region. In terms of its pluralist heritage Lebanon is too important to be given up to the rival interests poised to tear it apart, and yet too small a country to be able to resist outside influences. Its most effective weapon was to make others believe that its survival was in their interest, too. Sadly the country could not command such deference. In the aftermath of the bloody civil war and after the Americans left, the ancient Christian communities embarked on a mass exodus, leaving a shrinking portion of their co-religionists to tend the flickering flame of survival and hope in their ancestral land. It was crucial to its survival that this remnant preserved its religious heritage.

I was impressed by the role of religion in Lebanese public life as an astute recognition of an interesting fact. The alternative of a French-style secular state would have been extremely damaging to the country, inflaming sectarian factionalism and political fragmentation. As it was, the clan factions that erupted into violence from time to time were a reminder that clans were important political players in the country. This fact was acknowledged by the system of communal politics that allowed a robust entrepreneurial culture to develop, with banking, finance, trade, and insurance enjoying a solid reputation. Religion was present in Lebanese life without stifling or inhibiting it, so that in that sense Lebanon can perhaps be said to be the gift of religion and also the curse.

Yet this arrangement had an ironic side: the Lebanese establishment restricted religious expression to approved representatives. Communal stakes in the spoils of office turned religion into a calculus in the proportional distribution of the goods of public entitlement. Religious groups acceded to their portion of public goods on the basis of the weight the groups carried in society. This system recognized Maronite and Orthodox Christians without turning Christianity contentious. Muslims, for their part, commanded a considerable political asset in this situation by virtue of the fact that they could boast of a centuries-long tradition of imperial power in the region. Christians did not have such an advantage, nor did they have strong allies elsewhere. The burden and indictment of being a Christian Arab is that in spite of the faith's ancient Arab roots, there is little sympathy for the cause in the West or elsewhere. The West's domestication of Christianity severed its Middle Eastern roots completely.

Given all these factors, the idea of Lebanon is not much more than a political convenience in which governance is a function of inter-clan compromise and consensus. The notion of an ideological state and its proliferating command structures is all but impossible to achieve. In Lebanon communities precede the state as the means and end of territorial integrity, and to that extent Lebanon is an important functional variation on the theory of political sovereignty. Social tolerance as a function of the religious status quo fits well into the politics of shared power; in the end, each group knows that it will occupy its allotted seat at the table of power. The house of politics is a multi-cameral structure, with the whole less than the sum of its parts. Communities made the religious wager for a group stake in government, and that excluded the idea of religion as a matter of private conscience and individual liberty. It is not the way the West has come to understand religion, but in Lebanon it is the only way.

At the time the Lebanese seemed rather sanguine about this state of affairs, even though its novelty struck me as something that deserved careful exposition to promote understanding and appreciation of it — if not to deter Lebanon's enemies, at least to encourage its friends. It would be a great pity if secular scruples stood in the way of admiration for the country's unique religious experiment. At a conference I attended in 1972 in the exhilarating mountain setting of Broumana, national religious leaders spoke with swagger about Lebanon as an exemplary model of interfaith harmony and tolerance. It should serve as a beacon of hope for the rest of the world, the leaders declared. It was all too easy to imagine hearing in all that effusive output a not-so-subtle reference to Lebanon's designated place in scripture: the Lord planted the cedars of Lebanon full of sap to give shade to those who please him (Ps. 104:16; Ezek. 31:3-5). Yet a hint of approaching upheaval seemed to hang over the national glow, for barely three years later the adversary clipped the cedars and plunged Lebanon into the civil war that uprooted ancient confidence and shook the nation to its very foundations. What went wrong so suddenly?

Some three years before the Broumana conference, a consortium of Protestant church and mission groups approached me about conducting a series of public lectures in a setting near the American University of Beirut. In the months of preparation for the lectures I met regularly with church leaders to shape the lectures and publicize the events. At one meeting someone expressed a measure of nervousness about the delicate nature of what we were proposing to do. The last time someone had given a public lecture on Christian-Muslim relations, he was deported as a religious nuisance. Was I running that risk, too?

Because of the politics of religious partition, the establishment would not countenance a public reckoning with religious claims, especially if it implied that conversion was an option. It was a reminder that religion can be deemed useful without regard to truth claims. This does not mean that religion is just a political commodity, but that we can draw on its social capital without attending to its truth claims. So religion carries political weight, and politics uses religion as reinforcement. But that is the sticking point. Religion as public expedience may foster forbearance as an asset of civil harmony, but that cannot be the entire rationale for being religious. To require religion to be useful risks converting it into currency for a clientele eager to use it as such, so that being religious is politically expedient, while being expedient pays communal dividend. For some two hundred years Protestant missions in the Middle East came upon this communitarian view of religion with mounting incomprehension and frustration, much to the corresponding befuddlement of Arab Christians and others. Lebanon evolved as a modern society with religion central to its national purpose. I wondered whether the modern West could learn a lesson here as it confronts its own interfaith challenge.

Regardless of the mounting tensions, the lectures went ahead, with fruitful exploration of the political limits of religions. In the end there was no deportation — in fact, there was general appreciation on all sides for the attempt at interfaith understanding. We had underestimated public interest in a friendly conversation about matters of mutual interest and concern. As a Muslim scholar once put it, Muslims wish to dialogue, but they don't know how, while Christians know how to dialogue, but they don't wish to. It may be an overstatement, yet the observation contains a grain of truth. There is a great deal in Islamic religious sources to underwrite a strong program of engagement in interfaith dialogue; the Qur'an devotes considerable space to Jewish and Christian subjects. At the same time there is a great deal in Christian traditions that hinders such engagement, such as fragmentation, the conservative-liberal cleavage, nationalism, and secularism. The colonial legacy and the nationalist response pose an impediment to both sides. In this sphere Muslims and Christians stand in mutual need of each other. To the suspicious mind, however, dialogue is a covert assault on vital truth claims.

Yet rather than give up the attempt at dialogue altogether, I felt we should insist on it, precisely for the reason that in the absence of dialogue suspicions would linger and impede mutual appreciation. Yet before long it became clear that the intricate arrangement Lebanon had created for the purpose of domesticating religion to make it politically useful left people little room to appreciate religion's capacity for expanding horizons beyond those only of communal or personal self-preservation. As a commodity, religion can serve the cause of expedience, undoubtedly, but also, in a less salutary way, it can become inflated sectarian currency for inter-communal strife and enmity, as would be demonstrated all too well in the country's civil war.

The Lebanese civil war affected me in personal ways more strongly than I was prepared for: I had bad dreams about the bloodshed and felt generally deeply anguished on account of it. That surprised me greatly, and I can only put it to the fact that children of my generation in the Gambia had Lebanese neighbors and friends. A Lebanese man married a distant relative on my mother's side. We grew up with Lebanese children, and when I was going to school I was befriended by the Bou-Jowdi family who followed my progress even after I came to America to study. The Mahdi, Milky, Diab, and the Musa families were well established Gambian families in their own right. These and other families straddled the Jewish, Muslim, and Christian lines, and through them Lebanon planted itself in our consciousness and feelings.

Pre–civil war Beirut was mesmerizing in its Mediterranean flair and cosmopolitan style. My roommate was a delightful Palestinian fellow student, and beside him I made deep friendships with Iraqi, Iranian, Syrian, Egyptian, and Armenian fellow students. I was enrolled both at the AUB and at the Near East School of Theology (NEST), which gave me a wide circle of acquaintances and friends. I hit it off with the women who constituted the NEST kitchen staff, so meal times, memorable in any case for gourmet dishes of falafel, kibbeh, hummus, and tabouleh, were also fond social occasions of conversation and laughter. The Arabs are a generous, passionate, and loyal people with a gift for family and friendship; it was a privilege to get to experience that. And it was an important setting in which to pursue my studies in Arabic and Islam.

It was my good fortune to meet people across the great spectrum of Lebanon's social life. Michel, a French Marxist scholar, was professor of economics at the Jesuit St. Joseph University in Ashrafiyeh. He was a fellow passenger on the voyage from Venice. He and his wife, Brigitte, extended a standing invitation for a weekly lunch in their home during that year in Beirut, a boon even in the best of times, let alone for someone on student ration. Michel eventually returned to France to take a chair at Grenoble when, regretably, we lost touch with each other. Huda, a member of the Armenian Orthodox Church, was a fellow student at NEST who opened her flat for a student Bible study group to meet there regularly. It afforded a unique opportunity of community experience in an informal setting. Cheerful, generous-hearted, and willing, Huda was appreciated by all her fellow students. I was especially grateful for the opportunity to experience something of the mystery of Armenian Orthodox worship, as well as learning about the trials and tribulations of the Armenian people.

George Torro was a delightful fellow student — from Aleppo, if memory serves me right. With a mischievous sense of humor and a zest for life, George had been a flight attendant with Middle East Airlines before he embarked on theological studies. He was as entertaining as he was fun to be with, sharing with us the gossip and tales he had gathered on his travels. Milad was an Egyptian student from whom I learned much about the Coptic outlook, inwardly serene though outwardly buffeted. Yousef was a mature theology student from Baghdad who worried incessantly about the family he left behind, particularly with the political state of affairs in the country. Bannipal was an Iranian theology student with a passion for movies, of which Beirut had an endless supply. He would fill the corridor with the lyrics of recently released movies — *Oliver!* was a favorite. The women students loved Dean Martin and Frank Sinatra as well as the Beatles, and everyone loved Umm Kulthum, the Egyptian pop icon still at the height of her popularity, whose ivory voice was the perfect pitch of Arabic eloquence and diction.

Elham, a friend from AUB, was the very personification of the rising generation of Arab women's advancement. She introduced me to the university's tennis courts and to Beit ed-Din, the palace of Lebanon's emir during Ottoman rule. Founded by Emir Bechir II Chehab, the palace took thirty years to build and has remained a showcase of nineteenth-century Oriental architecture. With its strikingly beautiful arcades and brilliantly colored mosaic floors, Beit ed-Din was being promoted at the time as a rising tourist attraction. In its heyday Lamartine, the French poet, once stayed there. Bright, lively, and cheerful, Elham eventually immigrated to the U.S., where she married and founded a successful international consultancy business concerned with improving the lives of women in the Middle East. It was her way of dealing with the anguish of her much-misunderstood people.

Beirut was on the international lecture circuit. Several visiting speakers passed through in my time, among them Iris Murdoch at the local British Council and, at the NEST, Rabbi Elmer Berger, executive vice-president of the American Council for Judaism, whose criticism of Israeli policies made him a thorn in the side of Jewish groups and endeared him

to Arab audiences. He gave a seminar based on his famous University of
Leiden lecture called *Prophecy, Zionism, and the State of Israel,* which was
published with a foreword by Arnold J. Toynbee. I learned later that
Rabbi Berger was founder of a school of thought in the U.S. that created a
devoted following among liberal Jews but also attracted its share of criticism in many Jewish circles. In his Leiden lecture, however, Berger was
arguing for the rescue, as he understood it, of the age-long Jewish escha-
tological tradition from the rough-and-tumble politics of Zionism. His
eloquent passion for Judaism's sovereign ethical law evoked the spirit of
classical prophecy of such figures as Jeremiah, Isaiah, and Amos. Rabbi
Berger was impressive in the way he carried his learning with unaffected
humility and humor. His work is important in showing the biblical foundations of church-state relations and their modern significance — "the
prophets were not parochial," Berger observed. And his acute, pithy remarks would be no less trenchant on the issue of Shari'ah as public law.
As Toynbee noted in his foreword, there is a glimpse in Rabbi Berger of
the truth of scripture that Israel may yet instruct the nations in righteousness. The impression was that the friends Berger won for Israel he
did by persuading them to exchange enmity and violence for reason and
dialogue. Yet it is all too easy in a polarized world for axe-grinding to
make short shrift of Berger's subtlety and nuance, precisely the appeal of
his discourse of reasoned persuasion.

The brisk book trade in Beirut created a book-lover's paradise, with
old classics in Islamic studies available in affordable printings. That may
be taken as a sign that Beirut was as good a place as any from which to
assess the prospects of a rapprochement with the Muslim world. If Beirut was the best place for intercultural understanding, it would serve us
to come there and learn. But if Beirut was an object lesson of the
hardnosed limits of intercultural tolerance, we should regroup and look
for another way.

The sense I got in Beirut, from Lebanese and expatriate alike, was that
the West is deeply resented, not because the West is bad, but because the
West is untrustworthy. Arab friends, many of them admiring of the West,

nevertheless felt that the West would never give Arabs the benefit of the doubt, let alone sympathy. Western missionaries who had successfully assimilated into Arab culture and been rewarded with genuine Arab friendship felt this cultural burden more acutely than most other Westerners. A close English missionary friend who had spent most of his working life in the Arab world and enjoyed the privilege of Arab friendship felt the weight of the cultural distrust of the West very deeply, not because he regarded himself as entitled in any sense to the trust of Arab friends, but because the distrust stood in the way of mutual affirmation. With humility and gratitude to the Arabs he had forsaken his homeland to make his home in the Middle East, and yet an invisible barrier kept him at arm's length. A guileless man, he never flagged in his effort of trying to bridge that barrier.

For diametrically opposite reasons, Christian and Muslim Arab friends alike shared a certain wariness of the West. Christian Arabs felt that associating with Western Christians made them twice victims: it emphasized their status as outsiders vis-à-vis both the Arab world and the West. They keenly felt the attitude Churchill expressed about the gap with Arab Christianity. For their part, Muslim Arabs resented the West for its imperial power, before which they felt powerless and humiliated. In the conflict with Israel, the West repulsed every attempt by Arabs to overcome this humiliation and reassert Arab pride, leaving the Arabs with rankling resentment. Muslims saw evidence of Western encroachment and its insidious influence in Muslim societies. According to this view, the weakness of the Muslim world is the result of a nefarious plot by the West to encircle the Muslim world and to emasculate Islam, regarded as the only force left in the world able to challenge the West's dominance.

To paraphrase a Palestinian Muslim scholar, Islam attracts the fear and hostility of the West because Islam has shown that it can compete well with the West with respect to the West's imperial and global ambitions. What the Arab world does not have is the dubious power of the West to entice, to tempt, to bamboozle, and to corrupt Arab youth with the fruits of Western decadence. A book of Muslim testimonials published in the 1970s, for instance, plays with the provocative thought that the long-suffering Muslims will be more than amply rewarded when in time the West is finally brought to its knees by its own excesses. Look at what happened to the Mongols after they had consumed themselves with ravaging the Muslim world, the authors write. The Mongols fell on their knees and prostrated before the God of Islam, and it is just possible a similar fate awaits the West, may it please God, the book concludes.

Yet for all this distrust and contempt, the larger story of Arab attitudes toward the West is a complicated one, a sort of love-hate relationship that swings with ebbs and flows in the political tide. Whatever the eventual outcome of this intercultural encounter, many observers at the time were convinced that it was important to deal with each challenge one at a time rather than to attempt a sweeping realignment of relations. According to these advocates of *Realpolitik,* it would be a mistake to raise hopes of a strategic advance in relations between Christians and Muslims. Realism requires the acknowledgment of difference while welcoming concrete opportunities of mutual understanding, building trust by taking on one task at a time. Relations here should be based on relations among people, not on the truth claims of the traditions that happen to share a common world.

It is hard to quibble with that down-to-earth view of dialogue, with its logic as lucid as it is engaging. Yet Beirut taught me about its limitations and risks, too. Simply confining religion to the user-friendly world of what is needed and expedient risks allowing suspicions and stereotypes rooted in truth claims to accumulate and to fester unseen. In that subterranean world, what is left unsaid will come to haunt and to trip protagonists on both sides when relations are threatened. As noted, Arab Christians paid a heavy price for this expedient use of religion: it was expedient for the West to discount these Arab Christians as a liability in the West's dealings with the wider Arab world. Put on the defensive, Arab Christians projected themselves as Arabs, not as Arab Christians anymore. Their ambivalence about being Christian is a price they willingly paid to recover and embrace their Arabness with its accepted Islamic connotation. Perhaps one of the most prominent figures of this ambivalence is Edward Said, whose lyrical defense of Islam in his widely acclaimed book *Orientalism* was buoyed by a correspondingly incriminating view of the Christian West — in spite of his own Arab Christian heritage. On any balanced view, this is a partial, if not a partisan approach, one that, perhaps, the West deserves for ideological reasons. However, as a prognosis of the future, or even of self-scrutiny, it is fainthearted.

Many of those who are dissatisfied with the personal aspect of intercultural encounter or with the particular Lebanese brand of communitarian politics find the alternative of dialogue as the encounter of civilizations more attractive. It should be remembered, however, that many Lebanese in education and business spoke eagerly of Beirut as the meeting ground of civilizations, where a flourishing culture of encounter and admixture took place. Yet Beirut became the setting for a tragic anticlimax of dashed hopes and failed expectations. The civilizational approach can elevate the terrain of encounter, persuading people not to give in to pervasive antipathy, but it can also risk becoming the self-serving platitude of the elites. Beirut at least was engaged with religion as affecting real issues in real time, not with religion as merely an academic exercise.

I listened with great interest to what J. Spencer Trimingham, the British scholar of Islam and of Arab Christianity, and at that time a member of the History Department at AUB, had to say about Islam and the West. Married to a Palestinian, Trimingham had no illusions about the truculent nature of the issues dogging intercultural relations. On the contrary, he was a living expression of the tension: he had devoted his whole professional and personal career to fostering understanding of the Arab world among his fellow Westerners, only to find in the last years of his life rejection by those he had regarded as friends and colleagues. The hardball world of politics did not suit him, which was partly why I found his work attractive.

Of the two books Trimingham was writing at the time, only the one on *The Sufi Orders in Islam* has survived and has continued to be reprinted. The other one, *Two Worlds Are Ours: Time and Eternity,* has not. The clue for that may be found in the subtitle, where Trimingham speaks of repossessing "the Christian Gospel freed from the tyranny of the Old Testament reference." Heated controversy met *Two Worlds Are Ours* when it was at long last published, and in the end that controversy consumed it. Critics attacked it in turn as Marcionite and anti-Semitic, with the latter charge packing the knockout punch. The book was seen as a pro-Palestinian sellout. Shy and reclusive by nature, Trimingham was the least confrontational of people, and the reaction floored him.

Scrupulous to a fault, Trimingham shunned public spectacle, and, instead, sought shelter in research, scholarship, and meticulous documentation. Free of clutter, his study and desk were among the tidiest I had seen among scholars anywhere. Friendships were important to Trimingham, and he was in equal measure surprised and hurt by his friends' reaction to *Two Worlds Are Ours*. Yet nothing mattered more to him than that the Arabs should receive a fair hearing in the West. He was puzzled that friends, taking offense at the speck in his work, should see it as more significant than the beam of justice to which Arabs were entitled but denied. Furthermore, Trimingham's interest in Arab Christianity contributed to the controversy: he brought to the surface the unwillingness of the West to acknowledge the legitimacy of Arab Christianity even when pointed out by one of the West's own Christian scholars. The very fact of his Christian profession provoked Thomas Hodgkin, a lapsed Quaker, to criticize his work in spite of the fact that both of them were strong supporters of the Arab cause.

Trimingham, who was a pioneer of the study of Islam in Africa, defined the interfaith challenge as a question of whether in time Christianity can do full justice to the genuine values of Islam, with a similar challenge for Islam with respect to the values of Christianity. Trimingham said the challenge calls for a truer humility in the Christian than that involved, say, in conquest, and for the Muslim, in *jihad*. Trimingham cautioned against snatching at adventitious elements in the two religions to create the illusion of solidarity. Truth need not be agreeable or convenient to be valid.

Although I never asked him, I was curious about what Trimingham thought about the place of religion in Lebanese life. I suspect that his evangelical scruples would have made him unhappy with the cantonal status quo in which truth claims were subordinate to political entitlement. He would have preferred for religion to be divested of interest politics. As he wrote elsewhere, the transcendent figure of Christ remains the point of departure for Christian action and reflection and becomes the specter of what anticipates Christ in society. The church, Trimingham pleads, must not become a clan holdout, but must be sacramentally present in the world, "answering each cry of the human heart [and] offering recreative possibilities," for which there can be no substitute. He thought the Muslim *dhikr* was totally different, valid as an emotional exercise designed to achieve ecstatic union with the Self-existent, but not as transforming sacrament. On this initial reading, national communities as they have been constituted in Lebanon seem a hindrance to Trimingham's conception of Christian witness as an expression of individual faith commitment. Given his expertise in African Islam, Trimingham could have shed light on the role of religion as personal faith, a role different from that of religion as customary practice and "the law of nations," as a classical Muslim jurist put it. At any rate, as I said, I never did engage him directly on the question.

On the matter of the ambivalent attitude of colonial governments to missions, Trimingham's Sudan experience was relevant. In a study on the subject, Trimingham notes that regulations adopted in 1933 excluded missions from any part of the Sudan recognized by the government as Muslim. Furthermore, in Christian schools established elsewhere, Muslim children were forbidden from receiving Christian instruction without authorization by their parents. Lord Cromer came within a whisker of banning the distribution of Bibles when he forbade publicity promoting their sale. The government published regulations concerning conversion, taking due care to ensure Muslim involvement in the decision-making process. It amounted to an officially sanctioned restriction on conversion from Islam. The publicity alone exposed the convert to public opprobrium, and the elaborate procedure of verification discouraged all but the most persistent and foolhardy. Given that Muslim leaders were inclined to regard the colonial administration itself as invalid on account of its infidel status, administrative ordinances touching on religion carried little weight unless they reflected Muslim demands. At the outbreak of the First World War, the Governor-General summed up the policy of patronage of Islam in an address to the *'ulama*. He said the government had facilitated the pilgrimage to Mecca, subsidized and assisted the men of religion, built and encouraged the construction of new mosques, modernized Islamic law, and trained Muslim magistrates to preside over Islamic courts.[1]

Disheartened by the poor prospects of a Western breakthrough in this state of affairs, Canon W. H. T Gairdner, a senior missionary, pointed out that colonial rule remained an offense to the Muslim conscience regardless of appeasement and other forms of blandishment. For all its restriction of missions, colonial rule continued to be perceived by Muslims as an objectionable instrument of Christianity. In the Muslim mind, secularism and Christianity both suffer from the inseparable liability of infidel guilt. This is at the root of Christianity's credibility crisis in Muslim eyes, making the religion a double target of colonial suppression and Muslim opposition. Sudan was among the clearest examples of that fact.

Lord Cromer was not himself immune to the taint of infidel stigma. When on behalf of the administration he donated £30 to the sheikh of the Omdurman mosque, the sheikh declined to acknowledge the gift. When asked why, he replied with scorn, "Do you think I would say 'thank you' to a *káfir?*" The sheikh was apparently unmoved by the threat to bring his remark to Lord Cromer's ear. Trimingham says that missionaries are not justified in blaming colonial administrations for the failure of Christianity to make gains among Muslims. He puts that to Islam's intrinsic resistance and to the foreignness of Christianity. Trimingham could have added that Islam's natural political proclivity enabled it to secure the collaboration of colonial rule, whatever the complex nature of that alliance, while, without that political favor, Christianity came under a cloud. The differential outcome of colonial rule was that Islam prospered while Christianity faltered. Christianity was quarantined.

It is worth pondering how, in its encounter with the modern West, Islam's political gains have helped or hurt the cause of a Christian reconciliation with Islam. What Trimingham calls the foreignness of Christianity may be more about the foreignness of a privatized Christianity over against Islam's political orientation than about missions as foreign sponsorship. The emphasis on the will and conscience of the sovereign individual in Christianity removed it from political life, at least as an organizing principle. In

---

1. J. Spencer Trimingham, *The Christian Approach to Islam in the Sudan* (London: Oxford University Press, 1948), 29-30; 35-36; 26.

the Muslim code, however, the sovereign individual is a misnomer. Perhaps in the unforeseeable future Muslims may forgo territoriality and its politics willingly and embrace privatization on moral and ethical grounds; it would show how faith can thrive without being armed at the same time. Should such a change of heart ever take place, it would break the intercultural deadlock, and open the way for deep, genuine exchange.

Reflecting on these and other issues concerning Islam and the West, I found myself rehearsing the views of earlier writers, with a measure of personal foreboding at daunting challenges ahead. Taking stock of relations with Islam through the Crusades, Ramón Lull challenged the church to embrace a different path. "It is my belief, O Christ! That the conquest of the Holy Land should be attempted in no other way than as Thou and Thy apostles undertook to accomplish it — by love and prayer, by the shedding of tears and blood." That sentiment echoes Francis of Assisi, who went to Egypt in a friendly gesture of meeting with the sultan. For his part, Hendrik Kraemer, the Dutch Protestant theologian, argued that sustained engagement with Islam should not be driven by the motive of spiritual conquest or success but by the urge toward faithful and grateful witness to God. Such witness needs to be carried out by taking due account of Muslim understanding of *din* and *ummah,* of the religious sphere and faith in the social order.

What all this amounts to is the recognition of the need for a religious truce with Islam without that foreclosing on the need and value of joint action. As Pascal said, if we were to do nothing but for certainty, we would do nothing for religion, for it is not certain. Another way to phrase this is to say that if we cannot be religious until we are fit to use religion well, we would make religion an excuse for not being religious.

❀   ❀   ❀

On a brief stopover on his trip to India, Tom Beetham visited me in Beirut to find out how I was doing. We ended up one early evening on a sidewalk café on Hamra Street, where I rehearsed with him my experience of life and my hopes for the future. We ranged over a wide terrain, including the Israeli-Palestinian conflict. Tom agreed that the issue was likely to bedevil relations with the Muslim world, and with the Arab world in particular, but he also noted that it was an issue that was rather remote from the concerns of the churches in Africa. Tom encouraged me to continue with advanced studies in Islam after a period of internship working with the churches. He knew Spencer Trimingham from an earlier period and was pleased that I had linked up with him at the university. By nature observant and perceptive, Tom felt that the politics of Palestine and the challenge of interfaith dialogue required different skills and motivations, and that I should be careful not to confuse the two.

I filled out my experiences with a road trip to Syria, first to Damascus and then to Aleppo. In the drive north from Damascus through Homs, I saw evidence of what used to be known as the Fertile Crescent now wilting under the heavy hand of a socialist command economy: collectivization had reduced all that rich arable land to a dust bowl. The high rise buildings in Aleppo where the government housed the workers were similarly in a dilapidated state of repairs. The Ba'ath Party had sown seeds of ideological control and reaped a harvest of idle incompetence with the economy in shambles. To mitigate this state of affairs, the government proceeded to uncap a gush of anti-Western vitriol to redirect responsibility for failed policies, letting the people starve on inflated resentment of a remote, impregnable enemy. I had just discovered in Beirut *The Development of the Monist View of History* (1895) by Georgy Valentinovich Plekhanov (1856-1918), writing under his pseudonym as N. Beltov, whom Lenin praised for his role in helping "to educate a whole generation of Russian Marxists." Plekhanov is a must-read for any "intelligent, real Communist," Lenin said, because Plekhanov's work "is the best in world Marxist literature." Those high-minded words were fresh in my thoughts when I embarked on my trip to Syria, then in the pro-Soviet camp. The reality on the ground, however, belied the elegant theories of scientific socialist sophistication. The students I encountered in Damascus, for instance, might bristle with state propaganda but, out of reach of surveillance, they swaggered in secret with Arab pride and Islamic achievement. For all the heated calumny their critics heaped on them, the Ummayads created in Damascus the structures and organs of the first Arab empire, with Spain representing that achievement in the Western sphere. Drawing freely on Byzantine models of state and society, the Ummayads showed the value of intercultural encounter, and bequeathed to their successors no less an obligation. Damascus still shimmered with reminders of its past glory.

The Syria trip turned out to be the thematic conclusion of my Middle East experience, though that was not how I had planned it at the beginning. In Syria the Arab cause wore the care-worn face of a disenchanted nationalism, of socialism lavishly subsidized with near-empty promises, and of regional interests inhibited by a common, pervasive sense of confusion. Yet it was a face that was also etched with memories of a proud history and a rich cultural heritage, of a goodwill shared with all humanity. All the glittering rhetoric of political grandstanding could not dim the hope of a better life, and with it the primordial urge of a people to control their own destiny. One wonders why the Ba'athist leaders persisted with trying to force square pegs into round holes, particularly when so much dead wood went into the ideological design of those pegs.

With this perspective I could reflect on the fact that the modernist project, at least in Lebanon, did not seem destined to bring about the rout of religion. In spite of Ba'athist secularism nearby, religion was still standing. However bedraggled and worn down, religion had survived its bruising encounter with a variety of adversaries, including dogmatic nationalism. The survival of ancient religious communities in the Middle East was impressive testimony to this fact, and, in spite of looming threats, reason for not giving in to despair. It calls to mind a well-known Qur'anic verse to the effect that what we consider ours in worldly things is ephemeral, whereas the things of God are imperishable (*má 'indakum yanfadu wa má 'inda-lláh báqin,* 16:98). After all, the human heart, Augustine reminds us, is made for God.

CHAPTER 11

Beyond Jihad

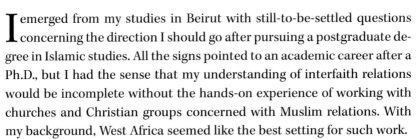

I emerged from my studies in Beirut with still-to-be-settled questions concerning the direction I should go after pursuing a postgraduate degree in Islamic studies. All the signs pointed to an academic career after a Ph.D., but I had the sense that my understanding of interfaith relations would be incomplete without the hands-on experience of working with churches and Christian groups concerned with Muslim relations. With my background, West Africa seemed like the best setting for such work.

Accordingly, I signed up for a period of service with the Islam in Africa Project (IAP), subsequently known as the Program in Christian-Muslim Relations in Africa (Procmura), then headed by John Crossley, a senior English Methodist missionary. Supported by a European Liaison Committee, the IAP was headquartered in Nigeria, where it served the Protestant churches of Africa. It ran study courses for pastors both in Nigeria and across Africa, introducing church leaders to the study of Islam and to a Christian theology of dialogue and mutual engagement.

In the course of that work the IAP produced booklets and tracts on Islam that attracted strong interest from Muslims who appreciated the careful and thoughtful way Christians were trying to understand Islam. Indeed, many Muslims felt let down because the tone and approach of the IAP was so conciliatory. The Muslims wanted vigorous debate, while the Christians seemed to be tiptoeing around the differences between the two faiths. It was intriguing that the gentle Christian approach aroused the suspicion of Muslims — it looked to Muslims as if Christians were seeking to smuggle their controversial doctrines under the innocuous cover of dialogue. Muslims were eager to flesh out the issues. Muslims may not naturally know how to engage in dialogue, but they certainly know what dialogue should *not* be: an exercise in airy politeness.

Yet Christians were often ill-equipped for the deep-level theological engagement Muslims were looking for. On a visit with John Crossley to a village not far from Ibadan, almost in the same breath in which he responded to our greeting, an elderly Muslim leader launched with gusto into a discussion of the incarnation, saying it flew in the face of common sense. He brushed aside all gestures of politeness with his brimming smile, stood his ground, and challenged us to answer him. Grounded in the Hellenic heritage, the discourse of Christian theology is ill-suited to the bush tracks and footpaths of Muslim Africa, and many Christians are simply out of their element when faced with the challenge of explaining it to inquiring Muslims. The naturalist objection of the old man to the incarnation was fundamentally an objection to the three-person language of the creed, and that language translates badly in African languages, particularly because translation is not a matter of translating words but of translating ideas. That kind of fundamental translation of Christianity's Hellenic intellectual freight has scarcely gotten underway anywhere in Africa or in the Muslim world, leaving sincere Muslim queries unaddressed.

Not surprisingly, there was widespread resistance in the churches to engagement with Muslims for fear of exposing Christian inadequacies and weaknesses. The churches welcomed other forms of engagement, especially engagement with action programs and community projects. But Muslims did not see such practical acts of collaboration as a reason for hanging back from truth claims. For Muslims truth is not something you can deduce from its indirect expression in actions. Rather, truth is truth by virtue of having its source in God the Exalted. Muslims are inclined to view Christian action programs as tantamount to Christian retreat from religion, their weak point. They do not understand that for Christians social action is a legitimate outflow of the injunctions of Jesus, an engagement that is grounded in the regard for human beings as made in the image of God. It is instructive to recognize that what looks like retreat from one standpoint is actually a form of faith commitment from another standpoint. Only by action and reflection together can such misunderstandings be faced and overcome.

I came to another surprising realization in work with Muslims. Islam is basically a non-sacerdotal religion; there is no ordained priesthood, no sacramental ritual, no confession or absolution, and no consecrated office. By contrast, Christianity has a sacramental theology based on the incarnation and the atonement, an ordained priesthood, and an office of consecrated deacons and leaders. Yet so many times I witnessed Christians ignoring this theology and instead pitching Christianity as a religion of biblical proof-texts — whose ambiguity Muslims are quick to point out. How can a religion of the incarnation be so book-bound? I wondered. Christians do not go through life with a placard of proof-texts and footnotes slung round their necks, because that would get in the way of getting on with life. Yet Christians seemed to talk as if an index of proof-texts is indispensable to getting on with Muslims. You would think that an incarnate faith would require humble explanation and personal corroboration, not reliance on verbal inerrancy — which for Muslims is precisely the prerogative of the Qur'an anyway. If Jesus Christ is as the apostles taught, the bodies of believers ought to be where their mouths are.

Clearly it is a difficult balance to achieve: Christians must engage with Muslims in terms they understand, but they must also witness in the way they live out the meaning of their faith. Eminent Christian figures have long taught the value of "presence" as silent honor and witness in the Muslim world, and one can never underestimate the power and value of that approach. Yet however genuine and eloquent as a symbol of sacrificial sharing, "presence" offers little defense against resistance, misunderstanding, and suspicion. So there is a lot to be said also for being straightforward and plain spoken, for not concealing your hand, though that also means not thrusting it in the face of others. The open hand offered in respect and friendship is "presence" with a difference, and that difference in terms of mutual openness Muslims will often appreciate even where they do not agree. The cross is God's power, but it does not compel or threaten.

Perhaps Muslims and Christians are divided more by what they have in common than by their differences. They quarrel as sibling rivals; their common roots in the tradition of the prophets separate them. They compete about which side honors Jesus more, differing even about the Jesus they have in common. They fight about whose view of religion is better. For their part, Christians evaluate Muhammad by the vocation of prophecy known to them from the Old Testament, not by the Qur'anic scripture that Muslims regard as impeccable and definitive. The common bond of scripture and prophecy becomes the ground of both recognition and contention between the two sides. That is why, even if laudable in itself, the search for common ground cannot in itself preclude or avert a collision. As we know only too well, family feuds are usually the most bitter of feuds. After all, you do not fight with a perfect stranger. This is why in the academy feuds can be particularly truculent: academics think they know what their colleagues do much better than the colleagues themselves, and vice versa. In the end, without openness and forbearance, proximity and familiarity can be deadly assets of conflict in religion as much as in other areas of life.

Leaving the interreligious world behind me, with Crossley's blessing, I arrived in London in the early spring of 1971 to enroll in the Ph.D. program in the School of Oriental and African Studies in the University of London. My academic supervisor, Humphrey J. Fisher, was a Quaker by religious profession. Thoughtful, attentive, and conscientious, Fisher and his wife, Helga, were hospitable to students, hosting many a dinner in their home just outside London. We became good friends in the course of my studies. Richard Gray also was on the faculty, and I got to know and to appreciate him as a mentor and a friend. Roland Oliver, who was the head of the history department, presided over the weekly postgraduate seminar where, before the whole faculty, students presented their prospectuses for discussion. Even with their supervisors at their side for support and encouragement, students found the experience daunting. The seminar had the atmosphere of a rigorous examination because, although it was never put in such stark terms, how students performed there might well determine their fate about continuing in the Ph.D. program. Attendance was more or less mandatory. I found the seminar a very good experience for learning the ropes and for helping me when my turn came to present.

As I plunged deeper into graduate studies I remembered the gauntlet Trimingham threw down about how Muslims and Christians should be vigilant about representing the values of the religion of the other without the expedient solidarity based on adventitious elements from each other's tradition. Trimingham persuaded me to pursue postgraduate studies in a field other than that of jihad studies, the vogue at the time. I knew from firsthand experience that Islam endures in society not because it is installed by fire and sword, but because of its moral appeal. The everydayness of Islam is a function of its grip on the imagination of Muslims, and I wanted to study that notion using Muslim and non-Muslim sources, even though at the outset I had little idea how to go about it. All I knew was that I had to apply the same critical tools that scholars of jihad were applying, in their case with the considerable advantage of newly discovered manuscripts and archival sources. There is no other way to pass scholarly muster.

For that reason I went to Paris to work in the colonial archives, at that time presided over by two formidable French women about whom other postgraduate students had forewarned me. I approached with suitable deference — only to be disarmed by their friendly and helpful demeanor. They even overlooked my halting French as they helped me hunt down documents in files not always logically labeled or accessioned.

Archival research belongs as a matter of course with historical study, but in my case there was an added incentive. Jihad studies set a very high bar for what should pass the stringent tests of scholarly merit by insisting that a high standard of Islam was the prerequisite to political reform, with the suggestion that Islamic learning was a necessary incubation of jihad and its catalyst. The jihad thesis contends that learned Muslim scholars relied on the inkpot to define corruption and to point to the battlefield and to the political court for remedy. I did not disagree with that argument in the specific instances being considered, but I wanted to challenge it as a generalization and to show that the process of Islamization has also succeeded by more pacific means. I was concerned that jihad studies should not lead to ignorance of pacific forms of Islam and their role in the renewal and strengthening of Muslim religious life.

But this left me with a challenge: the influence of pacific Islamization has often manifested itself in subjective ways, while jihad has objective achievements to study. With a centuries-long track record, jihad has led to the creation of Islamic states and the establishment of structures of society, law, and education. In standard accounts, the warrior and the trader have claimed primary credit for the spread and transmission of Islamic institutions and ideas, even though warfare and economic activity constitute only one aspect of the diffusion of Islam in society. The argument that Muslims spread Islam by the sword, and maintained it by political power and economic leverage, overworks the thesis that the religion owes its success to military and economic subjugation. Historians of pre-colonial Africa, for example, discovered in the medieval Islamic states evidence of African political sophistication long before the era of European control, a discovery that provided the intellectual center of gravity for new scholarship. Yet, valuable as that political approach is, it tended, nevertheless, to minimize the traditions of scholarship that sustained local religious practice.

On the other hand, both historians and social scientists have tended to apply the condescending term "folk Islam" to pacific Islam, on the grounds that it falls well short of the higher and less tolerant forms of Islam practiced by learned Muslims. Here they have used the language and framework of the jihadists themselves, who clearly have an axe to grind and are open about it. Their prejudice, however, has little foundation in objective reality. My central challenge was to show that knowledge derived from the inkpot did not always spill out into battle lines, but instead achieved for Muslim society renewal by the gentler, kinder arts of tolerance and persuasion. It was becoming clear that in order to prove my thesis, I would need to master the archives, but I would also need to head out into the field.

My first stop was to visit H. F. C. Smith at the Ahmadu Bello University in Zaria, where he was the new head of the history department. He was one of an influential group of scholars who sounded the call for attention to be paid to Islamic political institutions. Smith called the great Islamic reform movements of the eighteenth and nineteenth centuries "a neglected theme," and his work provided the focus of scholarly research and writing. From his university post, he kept close watch over the Kaduna government archives.

Even before he finished greeting me, Smith launched into an inquisition of my bona fides and asked what passport I carried. I had not realized how prickly a man he was. An English convert to Islam, he adopted the name Abdullahi and imposed rigid rules on his deferential flock of postgraduate students, all Muslim Nigerians. The cut-to-order dissertations he directed were striking for their predictability. I read a few of them and found it hard to distinguish among them because of the echo effect I experienced in them. A strong hand was evident in their production, which ill served these otherwise highly intelligent researchers. With my introductions from John Hunwick and Thomas Hodgkin, Smith relented and gave me guarded welcome as I informed myself of the state of new historical scholarship over which he presided.

But it was clear that the scholarly path I was committed to following was quite different from what Smith and even Hodgkin had in mind. For me the question was whether we could find evidence of a tolerant, pacific tradition with an independent status and proven impact on society. Insofar as it tried to unyoke Islam from the fiery chariot of the warrior, Sir Thomas Arnold's pioneering study *The Preaching of Islam* pointed in a positive direction. Armed with that book, and with the assistance of Momodou Jabi, the son of a leading cleric, I set out to follow that preaching trail.

What I found was a community of clerics that had maintained a little-known and yet centuries-old tradition of religious moderation against the prevailing forces of jihad. I had stumbled into the Suwarian pacifist tradition, named after its charismatic thirteenth-century founder, al-Hajj Salim Suwaré, who remains a revered figure to this day. Long overshadowed by the achievement and reputation of ruling elites, the pacific clerics used historical modesty to their advantage by cultivating thriving centers of learning, teaching, and travel safe from political intrusion. This Suwarian clerical tradition justified its pacific principles by outliving its political rivals.

In field investigations I was able to establish definitively the existence of pacific clerical communities in medieval West Africa. The clerics resisted attempts by proponents of radical politics to co-opt them. In bad times as in good, they exhibited meritorious forbearance and tolerance, and coupled that with prudent withdrawal and dispersion when their pacific path was impeded. They were wayfarers, so their example and influence spread, and with that their range and appeal. Now there was a tradition of pacifist moderation for ordinary Muslim West Africans to reckon with.

I got to know the descendants of these clerics well in the course of visiting their clerical settlements. I rummaged through their libraries and family chronicles to try to piece together for the first time a comprehensive history of their unusual though still orthodox form of Islam. It was impressive to see how with deft and dogged perseverance they upheld their staunch commitment to peace and to political neutrality.

Historical reconstruction of a little-known subject was a serious challenge, but, thanks to the scholarly habits of the clerics, I was able to build on their accounts from archival and library sources. I thought it would be useful to share my findings with other students of African Islam in two articles: "Field work among the Jakhanke of Senegambia," published in *Presence Africaine: Revue Culturelle du Monde Noir* in 1975, and "The Origins of Clericalism in West African Islam" in the *Journal of African History* the following year. A companion article investigated clerical involvement in slavery and was published as "Slavery, Islam and the Jakhanke People of West Africa," published in *Africa,* the journal of the International African Institute, in 1976. I followed these articles up with the first book-length study of the subject, *The Jakhanke Muslim Clerics: A Religious and Historical Study of Islam in Senegambia* in 1979.

At the end of my research I was in no doubt that this living religious tradition had deep roots in history. The sources document the jihad and colonial controversies that did not spare the clerics; the sources also document the expansion and durability of the tradition. One has to wonder why jihadists allowed clerical pacifism at all, and how pacific clerics related to their jihad opponents. In spite of setbacks, the tradition emerged from its trials strengthened, and, despite cycles of advance and retreat, its endurance has been maintained by chains *(asánid)* of transmission. These *asánid* are social registers of the production of knowledge and values, and are critical for understanding the self-replenishing character of the centers. They show how learning is deployed to promote peaceful renewal as an alternative to jihad.

Anyone coming upon this pacifist community of clerics will be struck by the fact that it represents a striking exception to Islam's reputation as a religion of the sword. In my inquiries about this I received an unwavering answer. Shaykh Faruqi Jakhabi, a respected leader of an old established community in Jarra-Sutukung, Gambia, said to me, "Think of the great harm jihad has done to Muslims, and think, for good measure, of the grave *fitnah,* civil war, in which Muslims shed fellow Muslim blood as the community splintered into rival factions as Sunnis and Shi'is. That is why we believe that a pacific, non-jihad Islam is in keeping with the intention of God and with the true, noble aspirations of the Prophet Muhammad." "Jihad," he stressed, "is not a positive teaching of religion; it is a negative injunction that is circumstantial in nature." To my unspoken incredulity he responded by pointing to the test of time: "We have seven hundred years to show for our faith in this peaceful understanding of religion." His eloquence was matched only by his sincerity.

The professional clerics compete with jihadists for the conscience of Muslim society by making commitment a corollary of tolerance, or, better, by making tolerance a commitment of faith. They draw a distinction between the peaceful Islamization of society on the one hand, which relies on assets and initiatives of civil society, and compulsory Islamization of the state based on Sharí'ah penal enforcement on the other. They feel the challenge of the Islamization of society can be met by peaceful means of instruction and persuasion without the political coercion required by the Islamization of the state, which violates the moral nature of faith.

Over a period of at least seven hundred years these clerics have cultivated Islam as a religion of peace and moderation, and under colonial rule, when they came face to face with demands of political collaboration, they resisted or retreated peacefully. As vicars of the spiritual life, they reject the political office for themselves but not for others. While pledging their loyalty to their political masters, they refuse to surrender their conscience — a position they have adopted toward jihad leaders as well. A saying in their tradition humorously describes their determination to offer both pacifism and political compliance: "If the king asks us to build him a castle, we shall build him a castle. If he asks us to take up arms and go to war, we shall build him a castle. We are entirely at his disposal."

By education, scholarship, itinerancy, and other religious activities the clerics have pursued the path of the Islamization of society as opposed to that of the Islamization of the state. A clerical republic rather than a theocracy is the object of their endeavor. In his *Mi'ráj al-Su'úd*, Ahmad Baba (d. 1603) described the role of these African clerics in maintaining a high level of religious life in his native Timbuktu. Mahmúd Ka'tí also described in his book, *Ta'ríkh al-Fattásh*, the clerical impact in Timbuktu in a similar way, saying the city maintained a policy of excluding the king of Songhay from entering it except once a year when during Ramadan he came as a pilgrim. The king was restricted to observing set rituals that disregarded the prerogatives of royal office. He ministered to indigent Qur'an school children and begged for their prayers.

Ka'tí is a key source on the pacifist clerics of my description, and his discussion of the founding clerical settlement on the Bafing River called Diakhaba makes it sound similar to religious centers I visited in my own time. The *Ta'ríkh al-Fattásh* says that Diakhaba ("Ja'ba") remained an impregnable clerical stronghold, so that even those who were guilty of acts of hostility against the king could claim inviolable sanctuary within its borders. It continues: "they gave it the epithet, 'the city of God' — *yaqál lahu balad Alláh*."[1] The phrase "city of God" enshrines a crucial confessional stance: the repudiation of religion as a state construct, and of the state as a religious construct.

As if by predisposition, the *Ta'ríkh al-Fattásh* stresses the importance of the cleric vis-à-vis the political magistrate. After many attempts to assert his authority over Timbuktu, the Askiya Muhammad Turé, king of Songhay, visited the city in person and summoned the *qádí*, Mahmúd b. 'Umar, to an audience. In the ensuing discussion the *askiya* demanded

---

1. Mahmúd al-Ka'ti, *Ta'ríkh al-Fattásh*, trans. and ed. M. Delafosse and O. Houdas (Paris: Librairie d'Amerique et d'Orient, Adrien-Maisonneuve, 1964), text p. 179, trans. p. 314.

to know why the *qádí* resisted his orders and turned away his message-bearers. After a flurry of short questions and answers, the *qádí* threw down the gauntlet:

> Have you forgotten, or are you feigning ignorance, how one day you came to my house and, crawling up to me, you took me by the feet and held on to my garments and said, "I have come so that you may place yourself in safety between me and the fire of damnation. Help me and hold me by the hand lest I stumble into hell fire. I entrust myself in safe-keeping to you." It is for this reason that I have chased away your message-bearers and resisted your commands.[2]

It is by all standards an extraordinary reprimand, and yet the king, equally remarkably, left the gauntlet where the *qádí* placed it, pleading abjectly,

> By God, it is true that I have forgotten this, but you have now reminded me and you are absolutely right. By God, you deserve great reward for you have saved me from harm. May God exalt your rank and make you my security against the fire. What I have done has provoked the wrath of the All-Powerful, but I beg His forgiveness and turn in penitence to Him. In spite of what I have done I still invoke your protection and attach myself to you. Confirm me in this position under you and God will confirm you (and through you) defend me.[3]

It is certainly possible that the chronicler may in this passage be attempting to paint an exaggeratedly pious image of the *askiya,* but if so he is employing a strategy that shows his royal patron being upstaged by a subordinate official. Unless the story, or a version of it, is true and familiar, fabricating it would be flaunting the seditious idea that insubordination is immune to royal reprisal. It is credible in the context of the separa-

---

2. *Ta'ríkh al-Fattásh,* text pp. 60-61, trans. pp. 116-17.
3. *Ta'ríkh al-Fattásh,* text p. 61, trans. p. 117.

tion of religion from political authority, and also shows, furthermore, the esteem in which religion is held by Africans, king and commoner alike.

The chronicles report many incidents concerning political rulers who tried in numerous ways to render religion politically serviceable. A well-known example is the king of Songhay, Askiya Da'wúd (reigned 1549-82 C.E.), who, as his royal prerogative, appointed the *qádí* of Timbuktu. The official, the revered scholar Muhammad Baghayogho, refused the appointment. The city's leading jurists interceded with him on the king's behalf, but even that failed. Baghayogho agreed to be *qádí* only after the king threatened to offer the job to an ignoramus. The standoff lasted over a year.[4] In another incident, the king was said to have felt slighted when the prestigious Sankore mosque was being built, because he had not been informed. He found out only when the project was nearing completion. Undeterred, he sent a generous donation[5] — which was not turned down, but was used for repairs to an adjoining cemetery rather than for the mosque itself. The king could not have missed the pointed symbolism: his contribution should be a goodwill offering toward the repose of faithful souls rather than a bid for the favor of the faith community. The clerics were determined to show that religion was too important for the state to ignore or to co-opt.

Any assessment of this evidence must conclude that it represents an impressive moral achievement. It shows the penetrating clarity of Muslim views about the limits and hazards of the political co-opting of religion. The fact that it occurred so early in the history of Muslim practice proves that faithful Muslims were led to that position by the resources of their religion.

Some perspective is in order here, of course. The distinction we are drawing between the two kinds of Islamization was never institutionalized at state level as a matter of strict constitutional separation. Still,

---

4. 'Abd al-Rahmán al-Sa'dí, *Ta'ríkh al-Súdán*, trans. and ed. O. Houdas (Paris: Librairie d'Amerique et d'Orient, Adrien-Maisonneuve, 1964), 176. See also John Hunwick, ed. and trans., *Timbuktu and the Songhay Empire* (Leiden: E. J. Brill, 1999), 164.

5. In one account, the donation was received by the *qádí* without prejudice. Subsequently the *askiya* sent some building materials, 4,000 pieces altogether, which were used to complete construction work on the mosque. Hunwick, *Timbuktu and the Songhay Empire*, 154.

there is no doubt that for the clerics, religion was not an imperial office. There is great significance in the fact that the distinction was maintained as a matter of principle rather than because of political patronage.

It would be yielding to too much Jeffersonian bias to imply that Timbuktu was about the separation of church and state. The idea of "church" as institutionalized religion maintained by a hierarchy of ordained officials subsisting on a regular salary is virtually non-existent among Sunni Muslims, at least until the colonial powers and, eventually, a secularized Turkey, created a class of salaried clergy. (Shi'i Islam, by contrast, does maintain a clerical hierarchy.) At any rate, Timbuktu was not a diocesan province in the European sense. Yet for all that, the city did represent a unique and an original tradition of maintaining a nuanced distinction between the spiritual and temporal spheres. All this evidence points to the veracity of the case pacifist clerics have made about a viable tradition of moderation and principle. It did a lot over many centuries to inhibit the spread of radical ideas among West African Muslims, if not to complicate the standard caricature of a monolithic Islam.

The policy of indirect rule adopted by the British in their colonies provided room for clerical pacifism to thrive, but the French and Portuguese policies of direct central intervention posed a major challenge to the clerics. It strained the tradition seriously when the French demanded clerical participation in the colonial system with appointment to political office, which the clerics rejected. As paid agents of the French, the clerics would be required to take up arms against Alfa Yahya, the king of Labé in Guinea, whom the French were pursuing at the time. The administrators took the clerics' refusal to collaborate as proof positive of their nefarious subterfuge with the insurgents. A French platoon mounted an invasion of the main clerical center, rounding up its leaders at dawn and taking them away at gunpoint. The prisoners were sentenced to summary banishment and imprisonment with hard labor.

Responding in the idiom proper to the earned reputation of the tradition, the leading cleric (whose sons I interviewed) composed a brief historical memoir and forwarded it to his captors, explaining in dispassionate language why he and his clerical forebears followed the path of pacifism and moderation. It was not, he insisted, an expedient conceit recently dredged up to mystify the French about the clerics' intentions and motives. Rather, they were choosing fidelity to history and respect for their heritage. He and his fellow clerics, he emphasized, could not forsake that heritage in an expedient and cowardly bid to win the favor of the French. It would be tantamount to renouncing their raison d'être, and he did not believe colonial rule would handicap itself by confiscating the heritage of pacifist moderation that had served society so well across the centuries.

In the end, exile and incarceration were the price the clerics paid for their pacifist reputation. The incident marked a low point in clerical fortunes, but not the end. The clerics used dispersion as a safety valve: they withdrew and regrouped after disaster and beyond danger. In the meantime, for consolation, they said history would be their witness and vindication. They were right.

I could still sense the edgy discomfort of the two heirs of the leading cleric in the French controversy when I spoke with them, by which time they had moved from Guinea to Senegal, due largely to the aggressive secular policies of President Sekou Toure's Marxist-nationalist government. The sons had lost nothing of the vigor of their pacifist commitment, including their faith in its future. They considered themselves authentic orthodox exemplars, remiss in nothing touching the five pillars of the faith, the *aqa'id,* the principles of belief, and the ethical injunctions of scripture. Their version of committed Islam was peaceful, resilient, tolerant, and hopeful. As wise and weathered practitioners of the art of gentle persuasion, these clerics would have no truck with the radicals whose vision of Islam has nothing in it of trust in God, compassion, or respect for conscience. It is not for nothing that these clerics have been worn to the deep hue of *sabr,* patience, by the tanning of trial and tribulation.[6] Their wager for moderation has never been more credible.

Pacifist moderation was tested both by the secular motivation of colonial control and by the fundamentalist motivation of jihadism, and in

---

6. Lamin Sanneh, *The Jakhanke Muslim Clerics: A Religious and Historical Study of Islam in Senegambia,* rev. ed. (Lanham, Md.: University Press of America, 1989).

both cases the tradition survived. Thanks to its historical depth and professional integrity, pacifist teaching had a clear impact on the clerics who persisted against the odds, and its appeal to democratization movements and social advancement suggests the contemporary relevance of that teaching. The picture of peaceful clerical centers rising from the dust kicked up by wars of religion and colonial invasion represents a real achievement. Instead of giving in to counsels of despair and forsaking their vow of moderation, the clerics weighed in on the side of faith and modesty. As of this writing, efforts are being mounted in Mali at long last to construct a memorial mosque to honor the legacy of al-Hajj Salim Suwaré. His mandate and that of his clerical successors can aptly be expressed in the words of the Qur'an: "And walk not in the earth haughtily" (*surah* 17:39), but rather, "The servants of the All-merciful are those who walk in the earth modestly . . . and who bear not false witness" (*surah* 25: 64, 72).

For many years I was able to reflect on the significance of pacific clericalism for Islam's mission, and on what lessons Christians may draw from it. The unusual nature of this type of Muslim mission makes it hard for Christians to know about, let alone to know what to do with. But the clerics' commitment to faith not buttressed by coercion and political manipulation should be relevant as well as instructive. It shifts the evangelistic focus from issues of political leverage to matters of conscience, which lie beyond the sphere of state jurisdiction. On that moral plane, Christians and Muslims have a shared heritage: faith belongs exclusively to the sphere of divine sovereignty, and the earthly magistrate has no power to give or to withhold it.

Part III

⚜   ⚜   ⚜

Even the sparrow finds a home,

and the swallow a nest for herself,

where she may lay her young,

at thy altars, O LORD of hosts,

my King and my God.

Blessed are those who dwell in thy house,

ever singing thy praise!

PSALM 84:3-4

CHAPTER 12

Native Tongue

In the course of processing the sources and writing my thesis I found myself thinking in increasingly certain terms about a lifelong companion. I had already been married briefly in 1968, shortly after I finished at Union College. That marriage lasted three months, by which time, at Tom Beetham's direction, we sought professional advice to see if the marriage could be saved. It became clear to everyone that it could not.

In 1973 I married Sandra. We met in 1972 in the course of preparations for the Manding Conference at the School of Oriental and African Studies at the University of London. We were both postgraduate students, she in African languages, and I in African Islamic history. It had taken that many years to return to the subject, and my busy travel schedule did not help. I had been engaged to another woman, Karen, whom I met on the return voyage from Lebanon in 1969; she was finishing medical school in her native Austria, and I was in mid-plans about a future career. The distance between us, and my unsettled circumstances, proved too great a strain, and when we met again in 1971 the long break proved too big a hurdle to overcome. We agreed to break off the engagement. I was in the early stages of my research, and had no idea where I would find employment afterwards. That uncertainty was the last straw for ending the relationship. It required closing that chapter in my life and moving on, which turned out to be especially difficult in one way: I learned after the fact that a child was involved. It is one of my regrets that this chapter has remained unresolved for so long even though I tried, without any success, to find a meaningful way to build a relationship.

I was having a difficult time financially as well. I was living on a modest student bursary — great for limiting my options, but terrible for peace of mind. One of my brothers needed help as well, and I scraped and scrimped to provide what help I could. But Sandra was unruffled by my precarious financial situation, and we decided that after my studies I would seek employment in Africa, even it be a temporary position. We would take it one step at a time until prospects improved. I did not know what the source of her confidence was, but I was encouraged and strengthened by it.

In a personal session with the English Methodist minister chosen to officiate at our wedding, I was asked if we were thinking of having children. The question floored me. I looked puzzled, indicating I didn't know what lay behind the question. "Oh, considering that you will be a mixed racial couple, have you given any thought to the disadvantages your children would suffer? Would it be fair to saddle them with that burden? What would be the Christian thing to do?"

Stunned, I turned the question around. Given what the minister knew about the social challenges he listed, would he let the wedding proceed with him as officiating minister? He split his answer, saying he would do as I wished.

I do not remember reporting this to Sandra, but given her South African background, there would have been no need to. She was active in anti-apartheid politics in her native country, and would have responded with her experience of racial injustice. But I did wonder whether it would have surprised her to know that the issue was much closer to us in London than she realized.

The matter followed us when a few months later we arrived for a weekend dialogue conference at an Anglican theological college in Mirfield, England, that had a reputation for Anglo-Catholic orthodoxy. The conference organizers saw fit to book us into separate rooms even though we registered as a married couple. With reluctance, they changed the booking upon my insistence. Happily, we did not have to carry out our threat to leave.

❋　　❋　　❋

We set our sights on my finishing my degree and thereafter returning to Africa to serve with the churches in fostering relations with Muslims. Upon completion of my postgraduate studies I was commissioned in 1974 by the British Council of Churches to undertake a comprehensive survey of Muslim immigrants in Britain. Accompanied by Sandra, I visited mosques and Muslim centers across the country, beginning in Surrey and ending in Scotland. I wrote a report with recommendations for the churches to assume responsibility in interfaith and intercultural relations with Muslims. The basis of my reasoning was that the Muslim presence was not likely to sidestep religious issues, as scholars of secularization were inclined to believe. My opinion was vindicated soon after by the staging in 1976 of the Festival of Islam in Britain, a huge multimedia event that helped spread interest in Islam in the country. The churches merely watched from the sidelines.

In the meantime I went on to serve in several faculty positions in universities in Africa and Britain, and that academic path turned out to be a lifelong career. I spent a year conducting research and teaching as a research scholar at Fourah Bay College in Freetown, Sierra Leone, using the opportunity to investigate the history of Christian-Muslim relations in the country. Sandra taught at the Freetown Secondary School for Girls. The political mood in the country turned somber after President Siaka Stevens executed a leading political opponent by public hanging. We began to think we should move, and so in 1975, I accepted an appointment as lecturer at the University of Ghana, Legon.

It was while living in Ghana that we became the happy parents of Kelefa, who was born in England in 1976. Sandra had gone there for the birth of Kelefa. I joined K and Sandra a few weeks afterward, and we spent the summer together living in a flat in Selly Oak, Birmingham. It was a new and fascinating experience in the first few months of his life to watch K develop into an energetic, gurgling little infant. We flew back to Ghana with K lying on his stomach on the floor at his mother's feet in between feedings. He seemed to travel well in that position.

Back in Ghana, where both Sandra and I resumed our teaching duties at the university, we hired a maid, Veronica, to look after K, who had begun crawling and exploring his surroundings. Crawling and flying insects absorbed him for endless hours. On weekends he and I would drive to the university farm a few miles away, where he enjoyed seeing the cattle, pigs, sheep, and goats. I cultivated a vegetable garden on a small patch of ground near the house and was successful in getting a good harvest of yams. K watched the whole process from his stroller. Living near the international airport, I thought to cover the odds by taking K to see planes land and take off — not exactly a scientific way to introduce a child to the allure of aeronautics, but you never know.

We made great friends at the university, and through them we got to know and love Ghana; it became our spiritual home. Our neighbor and my department colleague, Fr. Patrick Ryan, S.J., remained a lifelong family friend. But Ghana was going through a turbulent time. The military government of General Acheampong pursued repressive policies that wrecked the economy, and at one point in 1977 it caused widespread agitation. To quell the unrest, Acheampong imposed a military and police clampdown. The university was targeted, and tanks rolled into campus to round up and arrest students and faculty considered troublemakers.

The disruption interrupted academic life, and it raised the question of how reasonable it was to expect resumption of normal life in the near future. In this uncertain environment we decided, sadly, to leave Ghana. For where, we were not sure. In the meantime we took a trip to Mali to introduce K to Kangaba, the birthplace, according to legend, of ancient Mali, and thus an important source of early Mandinka history. For lineage reasons I thought it was important to take K there, the difficulties of the trip notwithstanding. As it happened, K contracted malaria in the process but, happily, stabilized and bounced back in a few days.

The next place in order of importance for the lineage was Kaabou in Guinea-Bissau, but that would have to wait for another opportunity. Kaabou was where K's ancestral namesake made a last-ditch stand to resist the jihad army that was bent on the forcible conversion of the people. As leader of the heroic resistance, Kelefa Sanneh went down in defeat, but not in dishonor, as his fame sparked the creative genius of the griots who composed songs honoring his name. The myth of Kelefa Sanneh virtually took over *kora* music, and practitioners of the instrument are required to master the Kelefa song in order to be deemed accomplished in the art. Knowing little of this background, K, as it happened, would go on to specialize in music criticism, including writing about *kora* music. He relinquished his childhood training as a classical violinist to do so. The fantasies of parents for their children can have unforeseen effects.

But I am getting ahead of the story. We had little idea of what we would do after returning to England in the summer of 1978, when K was two years old. We had the summer months to regroup and to think about the future. As he trotted along after me on an afternoon stroll, I remember saying to K that we should look inside an empty church — empty churches were becoming all too familiar. He asked me what people did in the church, and I said they came there to pray. He looked up at me quizzically, groping for the meaning of what I said. I thought and asked him quickly, "Would you like us to pray?" He snuggled up close as we knelt down in a short prayer, asking God to look after us and all the children and their parents. Then we bounded out of the church and continued with our stroll, with K being very purposeful and attentive to everything that crossed our path. He seemed to pause in his mind every time I answered a question of his.

Even at that age K was never a bystander. He threw himself into everything in which he was involved. He would not be left out of anything, even dishwashing, so Sandra would set him up with a blue plastic apron, soap and water, and a "classic gag" (plastic bag) that he washed and rinsed several times for the fun of it. Before long he was soaking wet as he chased after the soap bubbles and slapped them to watch them burst and disappear before his eyes. It amused him no end. He was full of anticipation as we mopped the floor after him; he wanted to have a turn at that, too. Nothing frustrated him as much as being thwarted in his expectation of joining in what was happening around him.

The summer in Birmingham was boon time for the family, and we all welcomed the chance to visit shopping malls and duck ponds in Bourneville. The weather held so we could take advantage of the outdoors, including visits to zoos. Sandra and I were no longer rushing off to the office, and so we all spent time together as we accompanied K on his discovery of new things of interest to him. I was also able to meet friends and colleagues to discuss developments in Islamic studies and in interfaith dialogue.

About six weeks into our stay I received word that there were a couple of academic job openings that might be of interest: one at the University of Bristol, and the other at the University of Aberdeen, Scotland. Following interviews at Aberdeen I decided to accept their offer. We moved there in September 1978, renting the house of Harold Turner, a New Zealander and a pioneering scholar of the study of African Independent Churches. He had only recently retired.

Given our tropical background in Ghana, we were apprehensive about the Aberdeen weather and what toll the winter might take on us. We were told that the climate was a mild winter — that normally lasted twelve months of the year. Called the Granite City, Aberdeen is an old medieval town with a reputation for higher education and the professions: theology, law, engineering, and medicine, among others. Aberdonians have a reputation cast in legend for regarding cleanliness as next to godliness. Well-tended rose gardens abounded in the city, which is also famous for its public park system. The road to Balmoral Castle, the queen's private Scottish highland vacation home, runs from the city, and the route is lined with well-tended roses. Sticklers for neatness, neighbors were not slow to ask you to remove dandelions on your patch of ground. The original university site was in Old Aberdeen, the medieval quarter, while Marshall College was at the downtown campus.

In the autumn of 1978 we purchased a flat on Rosebery Street and moved in immediately, working quickly to furnish it before the onset of winter. The following May we had a new addition to the family with the arrival of Sia. I was summoned from the department to be there to witness her birth, with the nurse urging me to get on my skates fast. I arrived just in the nick of time to welcome Sia into the world. K had all along been prepared for his baby sister to join the family. We all hunkered down as the demands and rhythms of a new baby in a new house in a new place kicked in.

We had a few months before winter, which in Aberdeen starts fairly early. By the end of August there is enough chill in the air to make you brace yourself for the cold weather. Autumn is really only a brief interlude of a few weeks, and then winter sets in. The winter of 1979, however, was unusually difficult. Called the winter of discontent, it was marked by a nationwide miners' strike that spilled over into other areas.

We had not yet replaced the old coal-fired furnace in our house, and in the winter of 1979 this proved to be a mistake: we still needed the coal that was now being withheld by the strike. I showed up on picket lines, not to demonstrate, but to beg to buy sacks of coal to heat our cold flat. I bought bottles of liquor to win my way into the hearts of the strikers, explaining that I had a new baby in the house and no other source of heating. "We just moved to Aberdeen recently from Africa," I'd explain. They understood. "You are not the guy we are against. It's the people down south [in England] we are against," they would assure me before pulling up a sack of coal to load into my car. They got to know me in time, with the intervals between my visits showing a pattern of demand that justified the conclusion that the coal was all for my personal use. I had acquired the habit of foraging for domestic supplies in Ghana, bounding from one "logistics" shop to another to collect food rations that the government issued during the shortages, and that habit kicked in in northern Scotland as I turned hunter-gatherer of the precious coal. It evoked memories of my father bringing home sacks of produce with a swagger and a spring in his step.

Andrew Walls, a devoted Methodist layman and my colleague at the university, arranged to have the Methodist church "plan" me into the circuit preaching schedule that had me speaking on Sundays in fishing villages north and northwest of Aberdeen, such as Banff, Buckie, Peterhead, Portessie, and Portnockie. In the process I learned a great deal about the challenging life of a fisherman. I would arrive on a wintry Sunday to learn of a tragedy at sea the week before when a fishing boat was lost, taking down with it a grandfather, a father, and a son recently married, all in one fell swoop. The gift of a parcel of dressed fish as remuneration for my labors had associations for me of the sacrifice involved in bringing fish to shore. Speaking the word of God in this setting demanded being available in a direct and simple fashion. It was instructive to see how religion influenced the lives of these fishing families who had such a vital connection to the demands of earning a living. For all its academic appeal, theological disputation was unimaginable in a place like that. It was at any rate clear to me that my academic appointment brought with it a wider opportunity and responsibility, and I was glad of that.

Back at the university, I plunged into the world of books and ideas. Before I had a chance to settle down, however, I was drawn into the exigencies created by faculty sabbatical leaves, and the gaps they left in the curriculum. Accordingly, I was prevailed upon to fill the breach by including in my teaching responsibilities courses in African Christianity. My reflex reaction against going outside my academic specialty was overcome when a London publisher sent me a book manuscript to review on the subject. The work, intended as a textbook for schools and colleges in Africa, frankly shocked me by its poor quality as much as it alarmed me by the prospects of setting such thin fare before impressionable young minds. Accordingly, I relented and consented to teach African Christianity. Little did I imagine it was going to be the watershed of my career that it proved to be.

While in the middle of combing the field, lining up the requisite texts and consulting authorities in the field, I found myself stumped by a nagging problem in the sources for which I was totally unprepared: the apparent facility with which Western missions downloaded the text of scripture into the vernacular idiom, adopting in the process the local concept of God. We are taught that pagan gods seep with all that is scandalous and unredeemable about polytheist religions — what some deftly refer to as non-axial religions — and yet here were missionaries, who ought to know better, embracing them with equanimity. Gales swept through my mind and left me speechless. It stumped me that, in spite of its relative disadvantage as an undocumented language without any literary works to its credit, the mother tongue should attract the interest and devotion of missionaries who made it the language of scripture — something Muslim agents would never dream of doing.

The thought sat like an undigested lump in my throat. I, like so many others, had been trained to think of Christian missions as Western cultural imposition only. But here was a hint of the religion's vernacular bias over against its metropolitan motivation. None of my colleagues and students seemed to find this in any way disconcerting, so I wondered whether my mind was playing a trick on me. Had I assembled too inadequate a sample of sources, consulted too few specialists? Surely, given the fact that missions were about transporting an official European Christianity, they would not so readily give up their advantage by conceding strategic ground to the vernacular, would they? Who else gave the vernacular such high regard? I was dumbfounded.

The more I read, the more deeply I seemed to sink into the vernacular footprints of missionary agents, and the more restless I became with conventional views. Historians of Christianity had left footprints too deep for my haphazardly assembled reading list to obliterate by way of a newfangled vernacular translation theory, I mused in moments of acute doubt and uncertainty. Surely the tempered judgment of historians had to prevail over my fledgling instincts.

Fortunately and significantly, instinct defied caution, and a beginner's energy shoved aside the set habits of old practice. Angels fear to tread on the ground that now seemed absolutely irresistible to the beginner: *Christianity is a form of indigenous empowerment by virtue of vernacular translation,* it was becoming clear to me. Ethnic self-preservation, it turns out, has a champion in missionary translation projects.

With professional caution, I tested the waters with a paper on the subject at the next meeting at Oxford of the British Association for the History of Religion. The essay offered a thesis on religious domestication in Africa, with Islam and Christianity as case studies. I argued that a radically different conclusion confronted us in Islam, with the sacred Arabic protecting it from vernacular takeover; such a takeover, on the other hand, was the pith and marrow of cross-cultural Christian evangelization. Colleagues seemed in equal measure mildly surprised and interested at the same time, but the idea did not raise much of a fuss. A revised version of the paper was subsequently published in an academic journal, where it entered the limbo of documented neglect.

While continuing with my teaching duties in Islamic studies, I pondered the Islamic contrast of the Qur'an as nontranslatable, and how, in spite of that fact, Islam had done so well in its mission. In its Sufi dimension Islam gives the appearance of developing along comparable lines, except for the fact that Sufi practices have dispensed neither with the Qur'an in its original Arabic nor, for that matter, with other canonical obligations. Sufis have a flourishing extra-mural culture of poetry, chants, music, dance, and devotions, but that is not at the expense entirely of the religion's canonical institutions. The language of Sufi piety is profuse and supple, but its grammar is fixed in Islam's religious structure. That is what stamps Sufism in its distinction from, say, Christian mysticism. Sufi ethics are based on Islamic ethics, and recognized as such, as the work of al-Ghazali shows.

While I was wrestling with the significance of my new insight, circumstances around me were changing. British academic life was going through a period of unsettled readjustment from the impact of Margaret Thatcher's austerity measures. The Association of University Teachers (AUT) soon ran out of options to protest the Tory government's actions, which included cutting back on government allocation for universities. American readers need to appreciate that British universities are maintained at public expense, and that there were at the time no privately financed universities as such. The funding mechanism, accordingly, gave the government control of universities, including control of academic salaries and research funds. The University Grants Commission (UGC) was the central institution that oversaw the distribution of budgetary allocations. Under the austerity measures, the UGC went from being at the service of the universities to becoming the government's weapon of control and direction. Eventually Aberdeen was hit, along with the other universities, as departments scrambled to implement cuts forced upon them.

I had a tenured position, and so there was no concern at the time about my position being cut. (Someone told me that I was the only African in a tenured British post. I didn't know if that was true.) In fact, no positions were being cut at Aberdeen, though incentives were being offered for early retirement, and for the deferring of replacements. Yet even for those whose employment was secure, the impact was real. The ad hoc nature of retirements meant that departments suddenly became lopsided, with crucial gaps being left unfilled. The whole principle of central planning to safeguard traditional strengths was in shambles as replacements and new hiring were put on hold indefinitely. The uncertainty depressed academic morale and strained collegial relations. After all, academics are not necessarily paragons of modesty or mutual deference.

Family duties were a welcome distraction from these preoccupations. We often ventured out to enjoy the Scottish scenery with the children. Aberdeen's well-appointed public parks were a delight. In the early spring we set out for the mountains, with K rolling in the fields of heather on windswept afternoons. Rain was always a threat, and so we hoarded sunny days like gold dust; we were careful not to let their opportunities slip through our fingers. With his adventurous spirit, K was cut out for these outdoor escapades. It was only while riding in the car that he objected in no uncertain terms to having the sun in his face. We would compromise with a window shade without forsaking a picnic under the warm skies ahead of us.

Thanks to the discovery of North Sea oil, Aberdeen became an oil city, leading to more connections with Houston, Texas. The city became host to people involved in the oil industry, which had an inflationary impact on property prices but also brought a welcome change of goods on supermarket shelves. One of my students at the university, Audrey Vincent, had been teaching film in Beverly Hills before she and her husband, an oil man from Houston, relocated to Aberdeen. She found religious studies more fascinating than she had ever imagined, she said. She ended taking a degree and receiving ordination in the Scottish Unitarian Church.

Margaret Thatcher, meanwhile, made known her resolve to use those oil resources of the North Sea to put the coal miners out of business. It seemed a high price to pay to settle political scores. Clearly more battles lay ahead.

At the same time that the road ahead in Aberdeen was looking rougher, I was beginning to be made aware of opportunities elsewhere. The first of these opportunities was an invitation to be a visiting faculty member at Harvard. Given the state of affairs prevailing in British universities, and having only recently arrived at Aberdeen, I worried that it would put the department at risk to leave for the U.S. — and my colleagues shared my fears. Harvard's response was to ask me to consider the offer for the following year. I knew such postponement would not improve the situation, and I let Harvard know that. At that point Harvard put the ball in my court: could I say when I would feel able to take up the offer?

That was how in 1981 I arrived at Harvard on a visiting appointment. Our route from London was interrupted by the effects of the air traffic controllers' strike in the United States. In the coal miners' strike two years earlier I figured out a way to beat the odds; this time, however, faced with the challenge of shielding the children, I found myself completely adrift without a strategy. K was all of five, and Sia two, both just barely aware of the drama taking place around us. It took us two full days to get to our destination in Boston, arriving finally at two o'clock in the morning. Conscious of what the labor unions in Britain called "unsocial hours," I refrained from calling my Harvard hosts at that late hour. We checked into the Sheraton Commander Hotel in Cambridge for the night.

The next day we woke up to a warm, sun-drenched morning in Harvard Square. John Carman, the Director of Harvard's Center for the Study of World Religions, where I was appointed, and his colleague Bonny McBride from the Divinity School helped us with our luggage when we checked out of the hotel to move into our new lodgings. In spite of all the wear and tear, the children could not wait to go out and play on the swing in the yard. We had rented out our Aberdeen flat for the year, fully intending to return. It was never to be.

CHAPTER 13

Turning Point

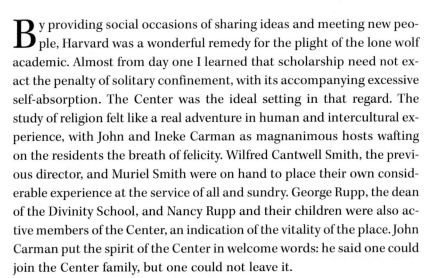

B y providing social occasions of sharing ideas and meeting new people, Harvard was a wonderful remedy for the plight of the lone wolf
academic. Almost from day one I learned that scholarship need not exact the penalty of solitary confinement, with its accompanying excessive
self-absorption. The Center was the ideal setting in that regard. The
study of religion felt like a real adventure in human and intercultural experience, with John and Ineke Carman as magnanimous hosts wafting
on the residents the breath of felicity. Wilfred Cantwell Smith, the previous director, and Muriel Smith were on hand to place their own considerable experience at the service of all and sundry. George Rupp, the dean
of the Divinity School, and Nancy Rupp and their children were also active members of the Center, an indication of the vitality of the place. John
Carman put the spirit of the Center in welcome words: he said one could
join the Center family, but one could not leave it.

As soon as practicable, we enrolled K in the Neighborhood Music
School in Cambridge, where he learned to play the violin. Too young yet
for music lessons, Sia tagged along, flaunting her pretend fiddle. K
threw himself with passion into his lessons, not resting till he had
learned his pieces. The weekends were completely taken up with driving to lessons and performances. With camera in hand, I took loads of
photographs, partly for the family album, and partly to share with
Granny in South Africa.

❋   ❋   ❋

In the time remaining, I got into my stride preparing for the beginning of the academic year. I also shared with colleagues the ideas I had been developing in Aberdeen on mother tongue development in Bible translation. Harvard colleagues were unanimous in their encouragement and support, and that experience changed my hesitancy into firm conviction that I should press forward with my exploration.

Harvard was among the most stimulating of academic environments I had known in my professional life, and it was a tonic to my spirits to meet scholars who were so generous and helpful with advice, comment, and openness to new ideas. Colleagues were happy to allow a fresh exploration of an old subject and to cast new light on materials and sources that we considered too familiar to be challenged, or to challenge us. Instead of feeling threatened or put off by my unusual line of inquiry, colleagues joined in to widen the horizons of inquiry with wise counsel and experience. Aberdeen was the origin and stimulus, but it felt now as if Harvard was the catalyst for the idea that native tongues launched and accompanied the Christian movement through its history.

I noted to my colleagues my surprise that Christianity seems unique in being a missionary religion that is transmitted without the language of the founder of the religion, and, furthermore, how the religion invests itself in all languages except the language of Jesus. It is as if the religion must disown the language of Jesus to be the faith Jesus taught. Christians do not pray, worship, or perform their devotions in the language of Jesus. Written in user-friendly Greek, the Gospels are translated and interpreted versions of the teaching and preaching of Jesus. As C. S. Lewis noted, the New Testament in the original Greek is not a literary language but the international language of the Eastern Mediterranean that had "lost its real beauty and subtlety. In it we see Greek used by people who have no real feeling for Greek words because Greek words are not the words they spoke when they were children. It is a sort of 'basic' Greek; a language without roots in the soil, a utilitarian, commercial and administrative language. . . . The same divine humility which decreed that God should become a baby at a peasant-woman's breast, and later an arrested field-preacher in the hands of the Roman police, decreed also that He should be preached in a vulgar, prosaic and unliterary language."[1] "Isn't that fact significant for the religion and for its worldwide expansion?" I asked colleagues with anticipation. "Yes," they responded, "that is obvious, once you ask the question. Why didn't we think of it before?"

There were plenty of knee-jerk reactions to the idea by critics who regarded Christian mission as willful cultural imperialism and treated the whole question as a long-settled matter. The status quo, however, was unsatisfactory, and the new evidence made it frankly untenable. Going back on this idea now was out of the question. I pressed forward by soliciting the views and advice of colleagues and graduate students across Harvard, and almost without exception they offered confirmation of my initial hunch. I canvassed a wide spectrum of views to test my hypothesis, fully aware that I must take responsibility for it. If one could obtain it, Muslim response to the mother tongue argument of mission would be important, but I was aware that juxtaposing Christian mission with Islam's mission in Africa and elsewhere would challenge too many vested interests. I thought it would be better instead to use a selection of Islamic materials to highlight the promotion of an untranslatable Qur'an and set that against the vernacular case in Christianity without going into detail about Islam's mission, successful as that has been.

I said this not to make an accusation, but simply to state a fact. It is irrefutable that Muslims do not translate the Qur'an for worship, devotion, and witness, and saying that was not saying that Islam did not succeed as a missionary religion, which is patently not the case. It was simply to affirm that, with its untranslatable Qur'an in the original Arabic of Muhammad's preaching, Islam's view of mission and the mother tongue is different from the Christian view. Few things have caused more misunderstanding among scholars than the contrasting attitudes of the two religions to their respective scriptures. On one level the two religions are similar, though on another level Islam is deemed to have the advantage of the newcomer: Islam's religious advantage rests on a supercessionist view of revelation, with the more recent scripture replacing earlier versions as defective or inadequate.

---

1. C. S. Lewis, "Modern Translations of the Bible," in *God in the Dock: Essays on Theology and Ethics* (Grand Rapids: Wm. B. Eerdmans Publishing Co., 1970; reprinted, 1979), 230.

Keen to be seen as consistent and even-handed, scholars barreled their way forward by leveling the field and reducing Christianity and Islam to a uniform proposition: they are identical as religions with a scripture, a prophetic tradition grounded in Abraham, worship of one God, belief in the afterlife, and so on. When it is inflexibly comparative, comparative religion can be that only by disregarding the historical particularity of religion. That approach has the weighty backing of much of the guild of religious historians, and so it is difficult to shift. Yet the price of upholding old orthodoxies here is serious loss of the rich specificity in the study of religion. Categorical generalization minimizes the internal workings of religious practice, with concepts edging out content.

One criticism of the uniqueness of Christian vernacular translation is the view that, broadly defined, translation occurs widely in other spheres in Islam, even if the Qur'an remains in the sacred Arabic. Besides, there are translations of the Qur'an into numerous languages around the world. But scriptural translation in Islam has no canonical status, so that translations cannot substitute for the original Arabic Qur'an. As Muhammad Marmaduke Pickthall says of his own renowned and widely used translation, "The Qur'an cannot be translated." However good and faithful a translation may be, "it can never take the place of the Qur'an in Arabic nor is it meant to do so." Pickthall's translation was authorized and published in 1930 by the government of Hyderabad, and subsequently by others, including Saudi Arabia and Egypt. And yet theological warrant forbids Muslims from adopting translation of the Qur'an in worship, whether at home, in the mosque, or on the pilgrimage. Translation must yield to the original Qur'an, rather than become its displacement.

By a happy coincidence, there were at the time plans afoot to mount a conference at Harvard Divinity School on translation in Buddhism to which I was invited to present a paper on my ruminations on the subject. That paper, which formed the germ of the book I wrote later, was included in a volume published in Tokyo. The editor, a Japanese Buddhist scholar, observed that the implications of Bible translation, as I set them out, were of great interest to scholars of Buddhism. It was affirmation from an unsuspecting quarter, showing how the study of Bible translation can advance understanding of the religious process across cultures. Although predominantly Asiatic in membership and cultural outlook,

Buddhism is a missionary religion, and while translation has been an important mode of the religion's spread in Asia, translation still fills a vastly different role in it.

At its heart, translation is cultural contingency — each linguistic system operates by its own unique set of rules, making a uniform, universal translation impossible. Because languages are different, translation is an exercise in linguistic particularity and style, and, by general consent, such things have an impermanent, ephemeral status in Buddhist thought. For Christianity, on the other hand, translation is the warp and woof of religious identity; linguistic difference is not so much an obstacle to be overcome as a necessary boundary of identity and adaptation. This fact implicates Christianity in the historical process, not just as a vague, speculative notion, but in the detailed and specific sense of vernacular and mother tongue appropriation as an authentic religious process. Christians came upon language not as an obstacle, but as an asset in its own right. It led to systematic, rigorous documentation of the world's languages, without which cultures remain marginal and remote. As a human cultural artifact, language is not just a matter of mundane utility, but, in scripture, of divine significance. Christian vernacular bears a universal message, well expressed in the words of Walt Whitman in his *Song of the Open Road:* "I find letters from God dropt in the street, and everyone is sign'd by God's name." Without the specific, earthy embodiment of language, Christians would not know themselves or their God.

The most tangible expressions of this vernacular impulse are the orthographies, grammars, dictionaries, and other linguistic tools the Western missionary movement created to constitute the most detailed, systematic, and extensive cultural stocktaking of the world's languages ever undertaken. Like any other thing fashioned by human hands, it would be foolish to pretend that all this work was carried out with unvarying brilliance, for there were awful specimens of incompetence and misguided zeal. Nor is it plausible to pretend that the work was inspired by pure, altruistic motives, for there were often crass motives of partisanship and paternalism. Yet even the flaws show the enormous scope and scale of what was achieved. It would be surprising if people of modest or dubious talent did not do some prospecting of their own in so broad and consequential a movement. No good thing is without its contradiction.

❋   ❋   ❋

It is important to bear in mind that I came to this subject reluctantly and incredulously. The issue upsets too many shibboleths; it collides with too many announced positions; it transgresses too many norms of career self-interest; it calls into question too many certainties of the guild; and it flies in the face of too many deeply entrenched canons of decolonization and its nationalist allies for it to be a natural career path for anyone. Furthermore, scholarship in mission crosses the interests of too many established disciplines to be given unchallenged acceptance in the academy. Academic dynamics can be very similar to those of the polygamous household in which I grew up. Departments are like co-wives in the university's paternal embrace, with members of the faculty their consummated offspring, complete with sibling jealousy. Academic collegiality is rife with the prickly hackles of paternal siblings whose jockeying for position all too often trumps being agreeable. Academics are friends by force of circumstance, not by reason entirely of disposition. With rights and prerogatives entrenched in endowment and tenure, faculty members' allegiance is to the maternity of their disciplinary conception, and by extension to the university's conjugal reputation.

Given such dynamics, universities tend to establish multidisciplinary programs only when enticed by outside funding. Without outside funding, the cause of mission studies is likely to languish without departmental legitimacy. With little incentive for collegiality, the academic fence-hopping of interdisciplinary pursuits like mission studies carries high career risks for untenured scholars. By its nature, the study of religion is not the prerogative of any one discipline, and yet religion embraces its departmental status largely on that pretext, and, if necessary, by rejecting religion as a truth-bearing phenomenon. Academic commitment here is deemed a truth superior to that professed by any one religion. This means that academics compete for truth claims of their own, even if they don't say so.

I am grateful to say that Harvard was more open on this matter than was my religion professor at college. I was encouraged by Dean Rupp and by other colleagues to present a preliminary outline of my work to the monthly faculty seminar in the Divinity School. I remember particularly the encouragement of Wilfred Cantwell Smith, well-known for his searing criticism of Christian missions. Wilfred knew that I had no ulterior motives in pursuing the subject, whose appeal, he felt, lay in intellectual possibilities it offered to wrest mission studies from colonial sponsorship and Western paternalism. Wilfred knew of my respect for Islam, and so there was no question that I was trying to set up a favorable comparison for Christianity against Islam. Harvard offered a genuinely supportive environment for honest inquiry in that regard. Typically overworked and overlooked, academics are understandably gratified by such collegial encouragement, and I was no exception.

Eventually my book *Translating the Message: The Missionary Impact on Culture* introduced the subject to the guild and to the general public. It went into some seventeen printings before a second enlarged edition replaced it nearly twenty years later. It argues that Western Christianity is itself the upshot of a series of specific vernacular adaptations and cultural adjustments no different in nature from the vernacular appropriation that was underway in non-Western societies. The difference is that in the post-Western world, the vernacular process is unburdened by conquest or subjugation as a prerequisite of conversion, allowing Christianity's appeal to arise from its truth claims only. Even without its colonial baggage, the Western advantage is not God's prescription for non-Western societies, because the West's success and the Third World's inadequacies do not in themselves dictate the terms of God's favor or God's righteousness. Post-Western Christians have learned well the lesson the West received from the apostles that salvation is God's unfettered gift, not a token of Caesar's favor.

Happily, missionary translation has now become a familiar topic in many academic fields, though, curiously enough, not in academic theology, whose resistance is hard to fathom. Perhaps theology is too much the adopted child of the West to empathize with post-Western developments, so that the idea of God by non-Western names sounds like heretical deviation from hallowed Enlightenment norms. Christian theology is a facet of Europe's nationalization of the idea of God, so that the role of God in human affairs can be denoted by claims of cultural entitlement: rich nations have a corresponding advantageous access to the mind of God, while poor nations *ipso facto* have a poor grasp of the gospel. It explains why Third World theologians fret so much about theology, objecting to its cultural baggage while still being deterred by it.

All this leaves vernacular Christianity with little positive role in the West. Mission fields were once colonial domains, appropriately remote, but now they were to be considered frontiers of authentic Christianity? Many felt that to be nonsensical, and without a shred of credibility. In whatever formulation it occurred, the Christianity of non-Western societies was separated by too great a gulf from the Christianity of the West to amount to much theologically. Post-Western Christians forfeited the empathy of shared religion by virtue of falling short of the West's cultural standards. The unwieldy term "Two-Thirds World" gives the illusion of the West surrendering the quantitative argument without budging necessarily on its qualitative reservations.

In 1965, the Gambia gained independence from Great Britain, as part of a sweeping movement toward independence for many African nations. The end of colonial rule, and of the accompanying global Western ascendancy, was expected to set in motion the demise of Christianity. In place of religion, nationalist ideology prescribed an omnicompetent, omniscient Messianic state: the state can see it all, thanks to its secret police apparatus; can do it all, thanks to its command economy; and can be it all, thanks to the army. History ordained national leaders to be oracles of salvation for their people.

But when my family and I were on holiday in Banjul, it became clear to me that nationalist fervor was dissipating almost as quickly as it had bloomed. I met with many who had welcomed independence, only to grow disenchanted soon afterwards. Jamil, a Lebanese trader who had been enthusiastic about independence, was in a grim mood about what was transpiring. Business was faltering in the unpredictable political environment where rules and regulations were set, only for bribes to punch loopholes in the ordinances. Political independence was looking like a cruel joke. In many places, though certainly not in all, nationalism was an empty promise, and was never viable as a long-range rallying project.

It was on the heels of post-nationalist disenchantment that, catching nearly everyone by surprise, the worldwide Christian awakening arrived to open a new chapter for the church in Africa. I developed my theory of translation to try to explain and elucidate the new religious map of the continent. The awakening was occurring in areas where colonial rule was supposed to have turned people against the religion. Accordingly, populations that the decolonization movement sought to wean from the West in order to capture them for the nationalist cause were flocking to Christianity. In country after country, and across all the major denominations, vast throngs of converts were turning up in the churches, openly and secretly. There seemed to be no satisfactory explanation for it. All the indicators pointed in the opposite direction.

Nevertheless, in the Third World a growing surge has overtaken the churches, which have struggled to make do with makeshift structures and rudimentary catechesis as they try to respond to the pressure of new converts. Painful inadequacies are being revealed in the organizational strength of the churches by the crush of new converts. This is an exact mirror image of the situation in the West, where declining membership numbers, falling baptisms, waning observance, an aging priesthood, and a critically low birthrate show Christianity increasingly being pushed to the margins. Once a Christian stronghold, Europe has been moving rapidly to the unaccustomed position of being on the margins of the coming Christian awakening. It has created a new fault-line between, on the one hand, the contracting Western heartlands in spite of their impressive heritage, and, on the other, the post-Western frontiers that are growing in spite of their meager financial resources. Each needs the other, and yet tensions remain.

I was drawn to this post-Western resurgence as my next professional concern. I described it in my book, *Disciples of All Nations: Pillars of World Christianity* (2008). This was a project that followed logically from studying the effects of Bible translation as well as the debacle of the nationalist cause.

There has been skepticism about whether all these conversions to Christianity are genuine, and whether, furthermore, the numbers are trustworthy. Yet the skepticism confuses what the figures reveal with where the figures come from. The rigorous vetting that goes into the compilation of data, and the systematic review that experienced people on the ground carry out at periodic intervals, allow researchers to scrutinize their results over a period of time spanning decades, and even centuries. The paper trail of this inquiry provides critical documentary evidence of the method and process of data gathering, and takes account of gaps and difficulties encountered. By publishing the figures so gathered, researchers can revise or adjust subsequent figures in light of new evidence and experience. In this way, hearsay or secondhand information can be appraised, its repetitive character noted and, where necessary, discounted. The resulting figures give us a retrospective perspective on growth and expansion, taking due account of natural and man-made disasters, fertility rates, life expectancy, migration, and other social variables.

Beyond issues of reliability, critics have faulted the resurgence for failing to deliver the Third World from its chronic problems of AIDS, corruption, tribal conflict, and general backwardness. For that reason, however otherwise accurate, the numbers are meaningless, for they indicate no movement toward improved sanitation and a higher standard of living. At this point of skepticism one realizes that critics have a much larger target in mind than mere quibbles about numbers, and that is the view that Christianity is valid only when it brings about a higher standard of living. In this view Christianity should be a stepping stone to a better life here and now, or its spread is extension of an illusion. Perhaps we should take the statistics as evidence of social regression, of movement backwards, the critics insist. These critics see progress as an evolutionary vaccine against the parasite of religion, explaining why the parasite migrates and festers in areas of limited progress, infecting those still fixated on their childhood fantasies. In the critics' view the breeding grounds of religion are the shadow lands of progress.

Except by being equally dogmatic, one can provide no satisfactory answer to this sweeping objection except to say that it ignores a crucial dimension of the reality of religion and its roots in the human spirit. Religion has an other-worldly dimension, to be sure, but indubitably also a this-worldly dimension of moral progress and social justice. In their different ways St. Francis of Assisi and John Wesley attacked poverty, but attacked equally the dehumanization of the poor. The witness of Mother Teresa of Calcutta was in part a challenge to the idea of progress without social conscience. In that respect the breeding grounds of religion are the spawning fields of the struggle for justice and dignity. The religious voice is often a critical reality in the otherwise callous world of greed and self-centeredness. Progress cannot outgrow justice.

Critics who are jaded with the religion of their upbringing and are still in the throes of recovery find it hard to be sanguine about the rising fortunes of a religion that has been the source of their disappointment. But the criticism is overreaching in the sense that one may no more blame the early Christians for their faith not preventing the fall of the Roman Empire, or a Christian Europe for not preventing Nazi and Stalinist pogroms, than post-Western Christians for the resurgence not preventing the political and economic collapse of their societies. The stakes cannot suddenly be higher for Third World Christianity than they were for Western Christianity. Accordingly, it is better in all these cases not to treat the gospel as an earthly formula in spite of Christianity's existential implications. After all, Jesus said that his Kingdom is not of this world (John 18:36), and that worship of God is not an economic or political precursor (Luke 4:1-8). If Christianity has any intrinsic merit, we should not be surprised if its appeal persists against disaster and misfortune, if believers do not wilt under fire. Instead of blaming believers for that, we should acknowledge them in humble solidarity. Such moral stamina would not be a deficiency in any of us, for that matter.

At any rate, the statistics point unflinchingly in a new and unanticipated direction, showing a religious landscape in ferment as profound as it has been unpredictable. In 1900, Christianity's center of gravity was emphatically in the North Atlantic, with Europe and North America together accounting for 82 percent of the world's Christians. A hundred years later, the picture had changed dramatically, with the southern hemisphere emerging as the new center of gravity. Today only about 35 percent of the world's Christians live in the North Atlantic region. In spite of that stunning change, surviving mental habits still locate Christianity's intellectual and political center of gravity in Europe and North America. The physical map of Christianity looks very different from the mental map of the religion, and since most people take their cue from their mental picture of the world, it is not surprising that Christianity's intercultural history is still so little understood.

Of course, the most optimum outcome of the worldwide resurgence would be for a polycentric faith to align itself with a corresponding cultural diversity that combines the experience and assets of the historic heartlands in the North Atlantic world with the great dynamism and broad frontier impact of the religion's southern shift. It would mean the cultivation of a multivalent empathy. But as yet we seem a long way from such an optimum outcome, perhaps because the mental constructs of the religion are hard to budge. As of now, Europe seems too haunted by its past religious bogeymen to be stirred by the wind of change blowing in its face.

For all that, the Christian movement continues to surge, and with it the gap with the old heartlands. While in Africa and Asia the old gods are being toppled by the new tide, for instance, in the old strongholds of Europe and North America the new gods of secular materialism have been provoked into staging something of a comeback, with churches turning into cultural and entertainment monuments. From the perspective of the history of Christianity, these two contrasting patterns need not diverge, for the evangelization ferment of the frontier contains forces of renewal that can banish the growing shadows of materialism spreading over Europe and thus open the way for the return of theistic faith there. Instead of bemoaning the slide into neo-paganism and rehashing old theological assurances in response, the West can recapture the initiative it unwittingly surrendered in its costly pact with secularism. For its part, frontier Christianity may avoid the trap of righteous indignation at the West as a colonial bugbear and thus affirm evidence of the religion's undeniable polycentric character.

Once it regains its lost innocence, the West can regroup and deploy its superior assets for intercultural partnership as one element of a moral strategy of global engagement. The fact that the current awakening appears to have overcome the barrier of the decolonization complex suggests that the time is ripe for such an alignment. One hopeful sign is the spillover into the West of the post-Western resurgence. New centers of community life and youth empowerment have been springing to life as a result of the flows of religious communities that are riding the tide of immigration into Europe and North America.

❁ ❁ ❁

But the question remains: if Christianity is taking root off the beaten track, among barely literate populations, what can be the attraction? We should discount several reasons right off the bat. It cannot be because of material motivation, of which there is little to speak of. Nor can it be because of Western paternalism, since hinterland regions are often far behind the line of Western economic advance. Political disaffection in turn is not a convincing argument, either, because political disaffection is typically an urban phenomenon. At the roots of the awakening are that it is vernacular, rural, young, and largely illiterate or semi-literate. But there are exceptions to every rule: the new charismatic groups in Ghana and Kenya, for example, operate largely in English.

One unifying theme in the origins of the awakening was the adoption of the local name of God. The undisputed evidence of the widespread use of the indigenous name of God in post-Western Christianity proves a certain compatibility of the religion with indigenous religious ideas and concepts. Where this compatibility is impaired, the Christian impact is to the same extent diminished. I do not know of documented cases of Christian conversion occurring in societies where the indigenous name of God is unknown. The pattern of de-indigenization of the name of God that is evident in Muslim Africa, such as among the Wolof, Toucouleur, Fulbe, Manding, Hausa, and, to some extent, Bambara, is largely missing in Christian Africa.

This embrace of the local name of God is a vital difference between Christianization and Islamization, and the discrepancy has lessons for the history of religion generally. Without the indigenous anticipations of the religion, the prospects of Christianity taking root are slim. Unless converts are able to call on the name of God in the vernacular, they remain fundamentally at risk of sliding away from the faith.

Vernacular translation, then, is key to cultural retrieval, renewal, and transformation, the secret to intercultural encounter in its positive phase. Without translation and its indigenous currency, cultural symbols in their isolation atrophy and eventually disappear when challenged. In Islam "Allah" is not translatable for the purposes of worship and devotion. Adoption of Islam in a traditional religious society strains reliance on the old deities. It may take several generations, but eventually "Allah" will have no acceptable local rivals or analogues. Surviving traces in the society will likely consist of attributes, such as the great one, the powerful one, the mysterious one, the one who cannot be comprehended, the owner of all things, the master of creation, protector, guide, judge, and leader, and so on. Such attributes were once knowingly predicated of a personal being whose name has now been suppressed, buried as it is under several layers of the Islamization process that the pilgrimage to Mecca seals.

In my own experience I did not realize how Muslim socialization effectively weaned us of any vernacular confidence. There was no grammar or dictionary of the language, and, thanks to Islamization, we never thought that was a shortcoming someone should remedy. At age five, our parents enrolled us in Qur'an school, where we learned the letters of the Arabic alphabet in order to memorize passages of the Qur'an for use in worship and devotion. There were no translations of these passages; their merit lies in correctly reciting them, not in personally understanding what they say. And certainly no one thought to study the vernacular and write a grammar and a dictionary of it. What is not worthy of religion is not worthy of study. Being absorbed in that task did not leave us with surplus energy with which to raise questions about the neglected vernaculars, let alone about what should be done to save them.

That is why it is difficult even now to speculate on how we felt about this situation. It was a non-issue, which is not to say that it didn't have implications for culture and for issues of personal identity. Unconsciously, we learned that authentic personhood was a matter of imitating models of excellence prescribed by the text. Prominent Muslim visitors, therefore, reminded us of whom to look up to as examples. It was the psychology not of projection, but of assimilation into something other than what we were. In a pinch, we consulted the imam, official spokesman of the *ummah,* not a medicine man of the family or lineage. Often, the medicine man was actually a woman diviner, as I discovered when Mother dragged me by the hand under cover of darkness to consult her as the family oracle. Under a veil, the diviner could use the vernacular to her heart's content. She was all too aware that, in contrast, daylight and all its prerogatives belonged to Islam.

Many scholars have argued that in practice Muslims are every bit as syncretistic as local Christians, and that religious mixing is as much a feature of Islamization and conversion as it is of Christian conversion. But can one be Muslim and African equally if that means placing one's mother tongue on the same pedestal as the Arabic Qur'an? Here the answer is no longer so straightforward after all, suggesting that there is an asymmetry involved. The two languages are not equal, at least not if your profession of Islam has any standing, and not unless you are prepared to run yourself ragged hustling between the two options.

What happens to people when they are plunged in the stream of Islamization in which, excluded and forbidden in the prescribed worship, their mother tongue loses all primary religious merit? What kinds of personal outcome accompany this process? What mother-tongue complex, for instance, does it create for converts? What strain does the religion place on surviving sociolinguistic ties and habits? Where does one begin to answer important questions of identity: Who am I? What am I here for? These tough issues are hard to evade or to resolve, especially because any written evidence is likely to be in a language other than that of the disqualified mother tongue. Mother-tongue testimonies normally play second fiddle to Arabic.[2] In their turn, folk customs lack the authority of the Muslim canon. They may be invaluable for showing the latitude hybrid Muslims allow themselves, but in the decisive rites of the faith they cannot compete in the open with the orthodox code. That is why my mother adopted the covert path to avoid an open conflict with Islam. Many an unwary Muslim has come to grief by straying from that covert option.

The argument that Muslims are typically lax in observance, and so are pragmatic rather than inflexible in following the prescriptions of Islam, does not come to grips with the question of parity at all. In his authoritative historical survey, Reuben Levy noted that Islam's rigid code is conducive to simplicity, so that vast numbers of Muslims in Africa and elsewhere submit to the voice of religious authority and eagerly adopt

2. J. Haafkens, *Les Chants Musulmans en Peul* (Leiden: E. J. Brill Publishers, 1983); M. Hiskett, *A History of Hausa Islamic Verse* (London: School of Oriental and African Studies, 1975).

and help to propagate the religion while being lax with respect to the duties defined as "branches" of root belief. Not given to speculation, such converts rely on the profession of faith *(kalimah),* accompanied otherwise by a vague deference to the religion's fixed canon as the only necessary and sufficient condition for their Muslim status. The detailed, punctilious observance of the duties can be overlooked without that getting in the way. Only active denial of God's oneness and of Muhammad's prophethood can render faith null and void. Conduct is a hit-and-miss affair, and so nominal Muslims need not forgo their reputation to be zealous foot-soldiers.[3] The name Muslim is worth more than the sum of the duties attending it.

In this situation, a lax Muslim who knowingly observes folk customs will be careful not to see that as a substitute for Islam, for that would signal that Islam is not his or her professed faith. Islam *qua* Islam is not commensurate with folk customs, especially where these customs require a profession of faith. Local Muslims may try to sugarcoat the contradiction by grasping for *hadith* support to make folk customs palatable, but that is risky: someone more knowledgeable in *hadith* matters may call you to task and leave you begging for indulgence. Against a *hadith* canon, you persist only by incurring condemnation. The real thing cannot be both. Islam is enthroned in the heart and on the lips of the believer, not in the groves of primal innocence. Over several decades I wrote papers dealing with Islam's complex pattern of expansion in Africa, and, thanks to the encouragement of a publisher, these were eventually published as *The Crown and the Turban: Muslims and West African Pluralism* (1997). A companion volume came out at about the same time as *Piety and Power: Muslims and Christians in West Africa* (1996).

The crux of the matter is that, however heartfelt, the sounds and tones of the vernacular can never substitute in Islam for the sounds and tones of the sacred Arabic. I am not saying anything different from what Muslims have long maintained. What seems revolutionary and controversial is the Christian comparison being brought into play, and on this point scholars seem unprepared for the implications. Mental constructs

---

3. Reuben Levy, *The Social Structure of Islam,* 2nd ed. (Cambridge: Cambridge University Press, 1965), 39, 192-93.

are really stubborn, whatever the evidence, and conventional wisdom about Christian cultural imperialism is impregnable to the witness of facts. Scholars who have been too wedded to ideas of missionary imperialism, and whose antagonism appears to precede all else, are unlikely to be swayed by the evidence.

At the Center for the Study of World Religions I was alerted to the fact that many colleagues assumed that Christianity is too Western, its cultural forms too European, to be included under the rubric of a world religion. That intrigued me. Partly to remedy that shortcoming, and partly also to indicate current trends, I adopted the term "World Christianity" to designate the radical change in the religion's main axis. The term is a way of getting at the expansion of Christianity in a diversity of societies and cultures, with the focus on the local and indigenous roots of the post-colonial resurgence.[4]

"Global Christianity" as an alternative designation has also been suggested, and insofar as it is an attempt to break free of a parochial view of Christianity, the term is worth discussing. But in the end I reject it, because it evokes too strong a parallel with globalization as an economic and technological process orchestrated from financial centers in the West. By contrast, World Christianity has such long and diverse roots, so many different independent actors and manifestations, and such a rich plurality of cultural idioms that it is hard to see a consciously synchronized master plan. Besides, the disenchantment with economic globalization, in which resources of local scale are dwarfed by those of global scale, finds no parallel in the indigenous forces driving religious resurgence. A bottom-up approach is more in tune with the facts on the ground than a top-down approach.

The vernacular sources of Christian awakening in a post-colonial, post-nationalist era justify our understanding the phenomenon, in its worldwide scope as well as in its worldwide roots, as a post-Western

4. See Lamin Sanneh, *Whose Religion Is Christianity? The Gospel beyond the West* (Grand Rapids: Wm. B. Eerdmans Publishing Co., 2003).

event. What is different about it is its culturally diverse polycentric character. It is not the diocesan model of Roman vintage, but communities of faith characterized by an inclusiveness of idioms and practices that has little resemblance to the organized and regulated boundaries of the diocesan Western prototype. What we had expected to see in post-Western Christianity turns out to be an anachronism of colonial proportions, a habit that prevents us from appreciating how an ancient faith need not hew to its antiquarian roots to blossom under present conditions.

In its scope, range, and diversity, World Christianity has now opened a field to us that is unimaginably greater and richer than the old rubrics ever allowed. World Christianity overcame obstacles local and foreign to surge with the primal impulse of the gospel; as a source of renewal and hope, the movement should challenge us to overcome our cultural shibboleths and bring us into our true ecumenical inheritance. Christian unity is now a matter of intercultural openness more than it is a question of doctrinal axe-grinding. The way ahead lies in embracing that reality as a worldwide challenge.

In my time there, interest in World Christianity grew at Harvard. Eventually that led to extensive discussions about establishing a chair in World Christianity. Colleagues there recognized the importance of what was afoot in World Christianity, and I have reason to believe that I may have had a small part in helping to bring about that realization. But the effort to establish such a chair at Harvard failed, at least for the moment.

Meanwhile, Yale approached me about assuming their long-established chair in the field. I drove down to New Haven for conversations with faculty and students and also with the president of the university, and I was encouraged by signs of their interest in my coming to Yale. I accepted their offer. It was time for the next leg of my journey to begin.

CHAPTER 14

Homecoming

In New Haven the children proved to be ready for the next step in their young lives. K entered Choate Rosemary Hall, a prep school in Wallingford, Connecticut, while Sia was admitted at Foote School for middle school. Thanks to the possibility of carpooling with other parents, K opted to be a day schooler. We took into our home a paraplegic Muslim boy from West Africa for whom we succeeded in securing a year's scholarship at Choate as a day student. He and K joined the carpool, with K helping to carry his bag of books. Sia was glad to have her brother at home, while all of us continued with the round of weekend music and ballet rehearsals and performances. It was not long before we reached the limits of New Haven's cultural offerings, which made Boston look decidedly enviable. The proximity to New York City, however, compensated for any deficiency. Besides, the children were too absorbed in routine and recreation, and with the thrill of ever-growing new discoveries, to fuss about what they left behind.

We were all glad for new friendships and new opportunities. K finished on a high note at Choate and was admitted at Harvard, where he graduated *summa cum laude* in his major. K had a successful career at the *New York Times* as a pop music critic before becoming cultural critic at the *New Yorker*. Sia went on to St. Paul's School in Concord, New Hampshire, as a boarder. She was eventually admitted to Columbia University, where she graduated *magna cum laude* in Latin and ancient Roman history. She spent three years teaching in Washington Heights in New York City as a volunteer in the Columbia program arranged with the City of New York. She did well enough in her LSAT exam to gain admission to all the law schools she applied to. She chose Yale, where she had a very productive and fulfilling time. Human rights and civil rights have remained her passion, which led her eventually to a career in Alabama with the Equal Justice Initiative that specializes in defending death penalty cases that law firms turn down. It does not pay conventional firms to defend such cases, whose victims are disproportionately poor and black.

The fact that the children were flourishing in their own way settled any doubts we might have had as parents about whether we had been well advised in the move from Harvard. There was only one way to face, and that was the future. In time I settled into my duties at Yale Divinity School, with a concurrent courtesy appointment as professor of history in Yale College. (This instance of double assignment is probably a remnant of the time when professors served the institution for the honor, instead of working for a paycheck.) Sandra also received an appointment as Lector of Zulu in the Yale African Studies Program, and was immediately thrown into classroom duties as she guided students through the rich intricacies of Zulu, including leading Fulbright summer programs in what would be winter in South Africa. She was able to establish partnerships with colleagues at Yale and at other institutions in the U.S. and in South Africa, all of which she found immensely fulfilling.

On the eve of my departure from Harvard I had been mulling the idea of a book about the role of blacks in the antislavery movement, a subject that took me back to my senior essay project at college. I had abandoned the idea of publication as moribund because I was unhappy with the results of my college forays into the field. But when Peg Fulton, the humanities editor at Harvard University Press, approached me about writing a book for her — and gently stayed after me for some seven years, despite my continuing procrastination — I finally halfheartedly sent her a few pages of suggestion to buy myself time to dodge her once more. Promptly came back the answer: Harvard Press would issue me a book contract. That left me without recourse. The resulting book became *Abolitionists Abroad: American Blacks and the Making of Modern West Africa* (1999), and to my utter surprise it was a success, being reviewed in *The New York Re-*

view of Books. It was a long-delayed fruition of the scattered seeds of my college days at Union, and it took Peg and Harvard to make that possible.

The book was an examination of the threefold impact of the eighteenth-century evangelical movement, the antislavery campaign, and the American Revolution on West Africa, which was the source of the Trans-Atlantic slave-trade, and an acknowledgment of the role of blacks in steering the campaign for abolition and emancipation. On both sides of the Atlantic William Wilberforce tends to get all the credit for abolition; I wanted to buck the trend and demonstrate the pivotal role of blacks in their own cause. But I also wanted to illumine the often overlooked issue of West Africa's place in the eighteenth-century Atlantic world. Africans in the New World served a role much greater than that of victims and beneficiaries of philanthropy, important as those things are. The cultural forms New World Africans developed contained elements of inventiveness and stamina that made them well-suited to the new frontiers being opened up in modern Africa. In the politics of reform they served an exemplary role for places well beyond their origin.

The wider issue of the role of victim populations — condescendingly referred to as "people without history" — as agents of change represents a challenge to the established idea that pedigree and privilege are the real game-changers of history. If that were so, chiefs and rulers would not have colluded in the slave trade and fought so valiantly to preserve the status quo. It was the victims and their Western backers who forced them to change their dilatory ways.

A few years into my new assignment I had a chance encounter with a colleague, Fr. Jerry, a Catholic priest. Sharing a corridor, we fell into the habit of exchanging greetings on a more-or-less regular basis, and I think I turned up occasionally at Mass when he celebrated. Fr. Jerry welcomed me, along with several others who were not Catholic, and, as far as I can remember, the question never came up about church affiliation. After all, I had participated at Mass in the Vatican by invitation, and was glad for it. I certainly had not thought about becoming a Catholic, accepting the question of my religious affiliation as long settled.

Yet in retrospect I can see that little was settled in my spiritual life. A number of small impediments kept stumping me along the way, and in themselves they could be brushed off as of no consequence. But over a relatively short span of time their accumulation compelled returning to the subject. I noticed that being a regular church attendee of several years' standing did not save me from being treated as a visitor even by people I helped welcome as newcomers. Being well known by the presiding pastor was no guarantee of presumption of belonging either. The campus Protestant groups affiliated with a denomination I thought I was a part of had difficulty thinking of me as one of them.

Looking in other directions, however, only postponed running into familiar cultural roadblocks. I recall a lecture trip to Kentucky where I presented a sketch of my religious journey to a very appreciative seminary audience of students and faculty. One student there, Cindy, drove me to the airport, and from our casual conversation we developed a family friendship. Eventually, Cindy came up to New Haven and visited one of my classes at Yale, where we had discussed the possibility of a travel seminar to the Gambia to learn about life in a Muslim country. Cindy decided to join the trip even though she was not a Yale student. In the course of that, she met her future husband, who was one of my students.

Once a debutante and since a born-again evangelical, Cindy seemed restless in her religious life. Given her practical bent, she wanted to know not just what books or writings I found helpful and would recommend to her, but how as a professional academic I maintained my devotional life: "How do you keep your batteries charged, Lamin?" Surprised not so much by the question as by my defensiveness to it, I bestirred myself. "Oh," I said with purpose, "here at Yale we teach and study and write about religion, but we don't *do* religion. That's something churches do. Yale employs us as scholars, not as believers." Cindy looked at me quizzically. "But, for you, is that enough? Can that sustain you as a person? Scholarship may be great, but you need fellowship. You have to have a destination to make life's journey worth the effort. So tell me how you charge your battery." Cindy had succumbed to — or resumed — an American occupation with the cause of personal fulfillment framed in a sound bite.

I responded prosaically, saying how teaching, research, writing, tutoring, and mentoring students have their reward of rich fulfillment, and that getting up every morning with that prospect in mind was a great blessing. It was very gratifying to write letters of recommendation for outstanding students with a bright future. With the other part of my mind I acknowledged to myself that even at Yale, teaching and studying and writing *about* religion might not be an adequate or a finally responsible understanding of the vocation of scholarship, and that my being defensive was a telltale sign that something was amiss. Cindy had exposed a sensitive spot. The privilege of scholarship in a great university cries out for commensurate commitment to a mission in life, and that obligation cannot be concealed under the pretext of professional objectivity.

In any honest reckoning I knew that my standing in the academic community was mixed in with many cultural qualifiers. However diligent at teaching and productive in scholarship one might be, there were still uncomfortable reminders even at the Divinity School that without a New England pedigree one was on a cultural watch list. That fact brought down many a great person. I learned that was the case with Liston Pope, who turned up at Yale having come up from the South. He became dean of the Divinity School, only to buckle under the cultural pressure. Yale in my day was a very different place from what it was in Pope's time in the 1940s and 1950s, but, like all venerable institutions, its assumptions of privilege and power still had gravity. As one head of department put it not so subtly, having a voice is not a matter of rules; it's a matter of culture. Scholarship could not make up that cultural deficit. At meetings and on committees one spoke on sufferance. Survival was a matter of letting sleeping egos lie. If I could pass only by sheltering behind a white graduate student, I would do so gladly. At the lunch counter, at the check-in desk at the library, at an academic conference or workshop, the message delivered was subtle but unmistakable: cultural assimilation was out of the question and, short of being branded on the forehead with name and title, standing up was no guarantee of being given a voice. You may earn your turn on the floor, but that might not garner your share of respect.

I recall my introduction to Hans Frei, a theologian at the university. Frei was a legendary figure at Yale, loved and admired alike by students and colleagues, one of whom represented Frei as a man who stood out for his people-friendly approach and his warm personality. "That's what makes him rare," he pointed out. I wondered secretly what the norm was. I needn't have worried about that, thanks to congenial colleagues I found. Still, I couldn't tell Cindy that, and in any case it would have made no difference to her opinion that the academic profession should not be an excuse for accepting a mission in life. In fact, it would strengthen her conviction and leave me with no recourse.

Scholars in my place and position shoulder a special burden of forbearance. Any response to cultural discrimination other than simple denial can justify the charge that being thin-skinned is evidence of cultural immaturity and, therefore, proof of one's illegitimacy. In other words, accepting slights uncomplainingly seems the only way of demonstrating that you are seasoned enough to deserve inclusion and acceptance. If you are sensible, you back down and back off even if you are in the right.

I recall stirring a hornet's nest when I jauntily trotted along to the Yale Co-Op on Broadway in New Haven, saying I had been a member of the Harvard "Coop," as it is known, and now wished to transfer to the Yale equivalent. The young woman challenged my claim to faculty status on the application form, saying I was trying to cheat my way into the bonus membership category. "At Yale we don't have people like you as professors," she muttered offhandedly. I was too confused in the moment to know what to say in response — particularly because she was herself black. She seemed to be *defending* Yale in saying that. But for its irony, such devotion is something money can't buy. Cultural elitism never succeeds so well as when it turns those it targets into its defenders. Elitism gains by the trivial concessions minorities covet for approval.

In another example, a Boston-based African American academic asked matter-of-factly that I scrub his name off the list of applicants for a faculty search in church history in spite of his very respectable credentials. He met my surprise with the observation that the field was never conceived with people like him in mind. In spite of the theory of affirmative action, professional ethics barred me from assuring him sincerely that he did stand a chance, and a good one at that. In a final gambit I urged him not to quit this soon. He was dry-eyed about what he considered the reality of invisible cultural impediments that would not budge, at least not at the time. He would rather allow the impression of black inferiority to persist than to lose the wager of official equality and come away singed. He had had his fingers burned far too many times for that. "By the way," he cracked in a parting shot, "not to pick on anybody, but after 300 years, how many folk like you are there in a place like that?" It was a complicated question, I realized. There may be other concessions like me, he implied, but is that because our color was insurance for affirmative action? Blacks in elite institutions, he offered, are a functional quota: they give discrimination the token specimen by which to defend itself. Did that mean me? He said the Boston environment was no different, to assure me he meant no personal ill will. I wanted to say Harvard taught me otherwise, but I would sound defensive.

"He would not make a congenial colleague," I could imagine someone saying to confirm my Boston friend's distrust of it all. Yet even I caught myself thinking in a momentary flash that my Boston friend was being too thin-skinned, until I reflected on why blacks were so thinly represented in the academic study of religion. I still couldn't help wondering, though, what he thought privately of my consorting amicably with the other side. In my private moments, I shared my friend's bruised feelings, even though it would be unbecoming to tell him that. It happened in the course of that search that a white female colleague spewed racial epithets at me — without response from the other committee members. Indeed, a senior administrator was once quoted in the local newspaper as saying that even Yale should not be expected to be exempt from the prevailing racial prejudice of the larger society, and that theological study did not and should not make a difference. This same administrator said my contacts outside the university showed I was not a team player, as if academics were billeted in platoons and confined to barracks. He did not last long at Yale, but that was for other reasons.

In the meantime, I found necessary sanctuary at the nearby Overseas Ministries Study Center dedicated to hosting international Christian leaders and scholars. In due time Jonathan Bonk, the Mennonite director there who did his doctorate at the University of Aberdeen, became a godsend of a friend and colleague. The fair wind blowing from that quarter expanded and steered my professional course toward more congenial, welcoming shores, including, with Yale's eventual acknowledgment, the launch there of the multivolume series of the Oxford Studies in

World Christianity. Yale Press was unable to follow through after several years of considering the proposal.

Without abandoning my optimism, I realized that the academic arena is mined with cultural disadvantage in spite of its high ideals. Its climate of polite civility is effective at inhibiting those whose difference makes people feel ill at ease. The noble tradition of humane learning from our seventeenth-century forebears has reached us as a meandering river rather than simply as a straight arrow.

❋   ❋   ❋

Talking about racial and cultural difference may seem tangential to Cindy's line of questioning, but it is not irrelevant to it. As an evangelical, Cindy too was an outsider in this setting. Evangelicals have a pronounced allergy to university religion per se, and the New England strain irritates them most of all. They blame it for the decline of faith, morals, family, community, law and order, and the other cherished values, as well as for its highbrow affectation. Evangelicals resent the intellectualism that sets itself above scripture and keeps a condescending distance from the churches, and they pounce like a bull seeing red. It is an interesting development that Harvard and Yale should each and together come to fall so low in the scales of evangelical Protestant esteem when they were once high points of the Puritanism and awakening that swept over early America. Who else should be trusted? evangelicals wonder. Evangelicals are fidgety anyway, and with cause they can become readily combustible. As a cultural outsider myself, I sympathize with their prickly hackles.

Though solicitous of me, Cindy had no doubt on an Ivy League campus that she was stepping on illicit ground, regardless of what I told her, and was interrogating me to see how deep a bargain I had struck with the devil of elitism and in what state that left my confession. I looked odd to her, an African seemingly at ease in a secular university, not homesick for native simplicity yet not giving up on religious obligations. Was I a converted enough Christian intellectual to incline to the distrust of intellect as faith's ally? Something wasn't quite checking out. For my part I was eager to hear Cindy's own view of things, for she reminded me all too well of the Puritan resolve to be "blind in no one's cause, but best sighted in her own."

On her second trip to New Haven, by which time she had married the student she met in my class, she was frankly shaken and unsettled. Over lunch at a popular local restaurant, she broke down in tears about her anxiety that Christian liberalism had mined the religion of her husband. She was worried about how that insidious influence would dog his ministry at a conservative and upscale Protestant church in South Carolina. It was the kind of place where the minister would buy me expensive clothes for looks but balk at welcoming me, liberal theology being beside the point. I didn't tell Cindy that. In my wildest dreams I never imagined a lunchtime public setting for this tearful display over liberal infidelity, and couldn't decide in a timely enough fashion what to say to her or to those at the surrounding tables. I sputtered out fragments of encouragement to help soothe her, assured her that her husband is a good and caring person, and appealed to her strength and conviction as assets of their young lives together. When I turned around all eyes were fixed on us, making the thought of dessert an excruciating exercise in prolonged embarrassment. I could imagine customers thinking all this crying was because of my ill treatment of her. The lunch couldn't end soon enough, and, without waiting for dessert and coffee, I jumped for it. I just hoped no one was looking hard enough to recognize me, and that there were no cameras trained on us. The wrong conclusion would have been entirely too easy to draw, especially for the suspicious.

All this left me restive, glad for a chance to talk about religion but simply worn out by the evangelical-liberal quarrel — and by the cultural assumptions that ride on it. Historical facts of the Christian movement, I discovered, took second place to considerations of cultural advantage. Even the simple and obvious truth that Jesus did not speak English was too easily lost sight of.

My claim is that no one language can substitute for the truth of God, that as children of God we learn and speak the language of faith always imperfectly and provisionally, and that the divine perfection is beyond cultural advantage or disadvantage. But this claim is too often overridden by assumptions of Western preeminence. The view that we are equal before God in the sense of our being equally inadequate vis-à-vis our Maker and Redeemer is inflected by the rules of equality of opportunity to help minorities participate in white middle-class society. Middle-class culture acts as arbiter of values and relationships, with religion considered as one option in the menu of choices. In a written assignment on Islam, one of my students felt uncomfortable discussing the hardships and inconveniences Muslims undergo on the pilgrimage to Mecca, so strange for her was the idea of religion as obligation. She confessed that she found the whole notion of "sitting on the ground, sleeping on mats on dusty roads without adequate toilet facilities, riding on overcrowded buses," and in general forgoing the lounge-style comforts of American life in conflict with much of what she regarded as normal religious life. She was certain it would turn most Americans away from a religion that demands that kind of commitment. The hardships would make people uncertain of the truth of their faith, she concluded.

If I looked at religion this way, I would have to conclude that I have been laboring in a stony meadow. What merit is there in the teachings of the prophets who lived and died centuries before the age of silent plumbing, air-conditioning, automobiles, paved roads, jet travel, and lavish wardrobes? Is their early death proof that the easier life and longevity that we enjoy today would have improved their grasp of the truth and enhanced their closeness to God? Are we better than they are because we happen to be better off? My student suggested Christian tours to the Grand Canyon and the Rockies as clean and pleasant alternatives to the pilgrimage to Mecca. Western Christianity had me befuddled.

Long aware of the widespread nature of such attitudes, I decided on a two-pronged study to see where I would come out on the issue. The first was *Encountering the West: Christianity and the Global Cultural Process* (1993), in which I tried to distinguish between a cultural and a theological reading of Christianity. I concluded that the cultural interpretation has become the dominant intellectual position, with its fortunes rising from accelerating secularization and the demand for personal autonomy.

That conclusion surprised and jostled me, and for help I turned to Lesslie Newbigin, a leading ecumenical theologian who bore deep scars from his bruising contest with liberal Protestantism. Himself something of a lost child of the Enlightenment, Newbigin wavered between reason and faith. On one side, he employed the method of philosophical discourse to disarm reason and to reinstate faith to the preeminent position as arbiter of life and values, while on the other he argued that it is only by faith as the action of a gracious God that we can know ourselves and our place in the world. For Newbigin, faith supersedes reason, though, in a surprising turn, faith is consistent with reason. Gifted with a fluent, lucid pen, Newbigin wrought his dazzling arguments to urge the church not to flinch from contending with science and reason. Two of his books are representative of his thinking: *Foolishness to the Greeks: The Gospel and Western Culture* (1986), and *The Gospel in a Pluralist Society* (1989).

The unresolved tension of Newbigin's ideas left me undecided between resting my confidence in the power of reason, on the one hand, and on the other looking to the divine act in the Jesus of history about whom reason remains skeptical, if not hostile (1 Cor. 1:18-25). As I understood the argument, the believer fights for truth over self-interest; the atheist fights for self-interest over truth; while the liberal is not particular about the order, but will do either to accommodate his or her audience. The subject of attachment for the believer is the target of rejection for the atheist, and the heat of the battle keeps the liberal from taking sides. All this helped shake my resolve and confidence in liberal Christianity, because I had no accepted cultural ties to its audience.

The second prong of my study was an examination of the way students and colleagues thought about these issues. At my request, first at Harvard and then at Yale, students turned in questions that described their criticisms and objections to Christianity and to missions. For more than ten years I collected these materials and, supplemented with similar objections from audiences I addressed throughout the U.S. and elsewhere, I streamlined and edited the questions and sat down to answer them. The result was the book *Whose Religion Is Christianity? The Gospel beyond the West.* The question-and-answer format found an enthusiastic audience among the general public, and the book sold several thousand copies in the first round. It is probably true to say that many readers identified with the questions — largely, I suppose, because the questions were genuine questions, not pro forma queries rigged up to provide a foil for predigested answers — and it piqued the readers' interest how I went about responding to the challenge.

I have not been able to determine if my Yale students read the book, and if so what they made of it. I did come across opinions expressed in their papers that alerted me to the likelihood that they were not familiar with the book's treatment of the issues. There could be other reasons for the omissions. Whatever they were, I was left wondering about what effect I could have on students with a hardened secular worldview. I remembered the remarks of Audrey, my Aberdeen student, about how I could walk with open eyes into the secular wilderness that she felt was the America she had left behind. It is surprising how words spoken on the fly can come to haunt you.

One day Fr. Jerry found me in the corridor, deep in thought about such matters, and he lobbed a simple question: why didn't I "take care of business and enter into communion with Rome"? "Oh," I said, "after all these years of putting me off, Rome couldn't care less." "But it doesn't make sense at all for you to wait any longer to take care of business. I'm certain Rome would be ecstatic. Try them."

Did Fr. Jerry know something I didn't know? Whatever prompted him to say that? I reported the conversation to Sandra, and she shared my incredulity: the Catholic church, she said, would not accept me. More than anyone else, she knew what trouble I had had on that front. In any event, she stayed put as an Anglican.

But Fr. Jerry's question touched a nerve in me. With some trepidation I approached Fr. Robert Beloin, the university Catholic chaplain, about joining the church. He said yes, he would be happy to receive me. At first I thought his prompt and straightforward response was simple politeness. I could not help hearing in Fr. Beloin's response echoes of the ministers back in West Africa. Yet however slim the possibility, the hope of finding acceptance was so powerful that the prospect whipped up waves of keen anticipation in spite of my lingering doubts. I would sit alone in my office for hours mulling over the idea, full of envy of those Catholics who treated their membership of the church as nothing more than an accidental birthright. Yet they had the one pearl for which I would risk drowning. They would not speak of me in the third person once I possessed that.

The goal moved one step closer when the chaplain said it was my choice whether I wished to be received privately or in public at the Easter vigil. Without a moment's hesitation, I chose the public Easter option. I remained on guard, however. Was this going to be a repeat of my Protestant experience? The question showed that my confidence was in shreds, and I was a mere rag of spent optimism. It showed how much I needed revitalizing more than Cindy or Fr. Jerry suspected.

Once I had made the decision, I informed some friends. "Congratulations," said one. "You will wonder what took you so long." The words connected unsuspectingly well with my pilgrimage narrative. Friends said they would be praying. Protestant colleagues, hitherto aloof, were somewhat ambivalent. In any case, the wheels rolled into full motion, and at the next decisive turn Fr. (later Cardinal) Avery Dulles landed prominently into my life. I first met Fr. Dulles at Harvard when he gave some lectures there, and I was struck then by the fact that he also had been a sincere seeker of the truth. I never imagined that one day he would consent to present me before God at the altar. But he did in fact agree to be my sponsor when Fr. Patrick Ryan, a long-standing Jesuit family friend, was unable to do so because of travel commitments. Fr. Dulles traveled to New Haven from Fordham to join us for a family dinner. He and my son had Choate and Harvard in common, so there was plenty of pleasant conversation around the dinner table. We adjourned for the Easter Vigil Mass at the chapel on the university campus, where Fr. Dulles concelebrated with the chaplain. The congregation gave him a warm round of applause.

A rousing, joyous event, the vigil combined aspects of the Easter rite with the culminating power of the church's liturgical calendar. Catholicism is all things to all people, unquestionably, but at worship it is simply superlative. The altar properly overshadows the pulpit, I suppose because the divine self-giving is really the first and last word — and our gratitude the most fitting and acceptable response. Without that, preaching is display and salesmanship. Preaching is for us; worship is only for God. The Roman Catholic church is a worshipping church before it is anything else — and so that it can be anything else. The idea is echoed in the ancient words of the church: *lex orandi, lex credendi, lex vivendi,* which translates as "how we worship reflects what we believe and guides how we will live." No setting was more appropriate for the culmination of my spiritual journey. I had finally come home.

But sadly, this home was not a peaceful place. Consider the delight of Catholic colleagues who rejoiced in my being received in the church because "now you can criticize the church." At the time the church was scarcely visible for the dust of controversy swirling around it about pedophile priests and the official cover-up that left Catholics in open agitation. Huge punitive damages, and the threat of more, bankrupted many parishes, and drained or diminished the coffers of many more. Cardinal Law of Boston became a lightning rod of anger at the time. Inquiries in Ireland into church-run orphanages intimated long-running abuses that the authorities knew about and concealed, thus allowing the abuses to continue. In another case, in July 2004, John Paul II intervened in Austria following a child pornography scandal at the seminary of Sankt Pölten. Eventually Pope Benedict XVI's past as Archbishop of Munich and later at the Vatican would come to dog him as allegations surfaced that he aided and abetted the cover-up of pedophile priests, including some under his jurisdiction. Never one known to be deterred by shyness, Hans Küng, for one, was emboldened to offer a six-point program of a hostile takeover of the papacy. Other malpractices dogged the church, such as the scandal of financial embezzlement at New York City's Covenant House, a charity dedicated to the welfare of street kids. I followed the story of financial malfeasance at Covenant House because I was supporting its work with my widow's mite.

There is a personal side to consider, too. In some respects Catholicism is little different from liberal Protestantism in its attitude to other religions, particularly Islam. Catholic apologists have a pronounced allergy to anything emanating from Rome that is less than appreciative of other religions without regard to the fate of Catholic communities in the affected areas. This hit me forcefully when I decided to visit the Catholic bishop in the Gambia, who as a young priest parried my advances and barred my way to the church, to tell him of my becoming a Catholic. He responded with an energetic defense of why, then or now, the church would never allow any one individual's conversion to jeopardize its good relations with Muslims. He noted the Muslim ban on pigs as polluted, saying it allowed Catholics to corner the market on what, after all, is good food. Muslims want inferiors, and Catholics will eat swine meat for that. As a devout Catholic with a sound Muslim pedigree, I risked the rationale of the church's deference to Islam.

This man of God had little idea how cogently he had defined the stigma of Christians in a Muslim society. He seemed offended at having to return to the subject, and would not offer me a word of welcome, nor did anyone else. Since this was ground I had long ago covered in my pilgrimage, I ignored the oversight, though not the general point the bishop was making. The irony was inescapable: the bishop's unwillingness to acknowledge me was because of his implicit acceptance of Islam's eminent domain. He was wondering whatever possessed the scion of a proud heritage to think of condemning himself with guilt by association. Here he was, suited for battle on Islam's behalf, while gladly turning his back on one of his own.

At any rate, all this is to say that there was plenty to criticize in the church, even though I was unsure why one needed the sacrament of membership to do so. The church was — and is — under public scrutiny, not by ecclesiastical license, but by virtue of what the church proclaims and teaches. I was reluctant to accept the implication of the representation of Catholic colleagues that the church is nothing but a function of the exigencies of its practice, that as an institution it cannot rise higher than the men and women who serve it. In that view, the church reveals — and conceals — better than most the untrustworthiness of men and women. We are told that we need forensic tools to hold the church to account as a condition of our faith in the institution.

I didn't know quite how to respond to all of this until the scandal hit pretty close to me. Shortly after I arrived at Yale, I had a Catholic priest as a student who was based at the time in Hartford. He was bound for a second missionary stint in Sierra Leone, where previously he had served many years. What no one told me — or, as far as I know, anyone else at Yale — was that the priest had been undergoing treatment at a rehab facility in Hartford for pedophile clergy. His actions had led to a $75,000 out-of-court hush settlement that his religious order paid to one of his victims.

With all that baggage, the priest was dispatched from Yale back to war-torn Sierra Leone, where he continued to molest boys enrolled in the Catholic school under his care. Still nursing their wounds of war, and glad to have a second chance, the priest's victims had much to risk should they report the abuse. The ravages of war make for haunting flashbacks, after all; maybe the boys were projecting their wartime trauma on the priest who had come to be a self-sacrificing Good Samaritan. There was simply no chance that the boys would get a hearing, even though the priest's religious order knew the truth about him. Things only changed when stories started surfacing that he plied the boys with palm wine to get them drunk before assaulting them. The story is remarkable for the way the church connived in aiding and abetting the priest's conduct in remote rural Africa, where he was given complete license with the children in spite of instructions from the Hartford treatment center that he could not have unsupervised access to children.

When news of the scandal broke, the religious order responded by quietly withdrawing the priest and having him laicized. There was no apology, let alone restitution to his victims, who became disillusioned with the church. One of these victims declared despairingly, "They shattered my dreams." Sierra Leone suffered a horrendous civil war, but the sexual abuse of boys who thought they were spared and had a chance to rebuild their battered lives, only to be debauched and betrayed by the church that should have been a sanctuary for them, was a tawdry abandonment of trust and faith. It was as if the boys had to endure another round of victimization as penalty for surviving their country's civil war, and for looking to the church for a better life. It would rub salt into their wounds even to insinuate that it is the will of God what happened to them.

Yet, however understandable the deep disappointment is, and however well justified, the shame and anguish would just fester if cynicism and despair were our only recourse. These children ought to be able to feel kinship with him who "hath no form nor comeliness; and when we shall see him, there is no beauty that we should desire him . . . and we hid as it were our faces from him; he was despised and we esteemed him not" (Isa. 53:2-3). An apostolic gesture in the form of a pastoral statement would be a powerful embodiment of the words of the gospel to the effect that "in as much you have done to the least of these, you have done it to me."

Meanwhile, it cannot be lost on anyone that the spirit of charity the church nurtures through the sacraments should, in the present circumstances, be withdrawn from it as the faithful turn in shame and revulsion from wrongful conduct within its ranks. Transparency and accountability became watchwords of dissent where dissent was the voice of the faithful. The fact that moral abuse and ethical lapses respect no boundaries of denomination, or the progressive-conservative distinction, is no grounds for exculpation or for complacency. Still, as in everything else, there must be limits, for the sake of hope. If the prescription of removing the symptoms of the problem strikes at the apostolic structure of faith, it would be worth pondering in what other dark channels the rank symptoms would be discharged once the valve of pastoral authority is breached. Even justifiably disenchanted Catholics know better than to cut their nose to spite their face. That's no way to take care of business, as Fr. Jerry would say.

CHAPTER 15

Rock of Ages

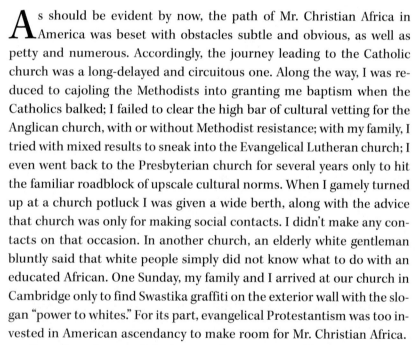

As should be evident by now, the path of Mr. Christian Africa in America was beset with obstacles subtle and obvious, as well as petty and numerous. Accordingly, the journey leading to the Catholic church was a long-delayed and circuitous one. Along the way, I was reduced to cajoling the Methodists into granting me baptism when the Catholics balked; I failed to clear the high bar of cultural vetting for the Anglican church, with or without Methodist resistance; with my family, I tried with mixed results to sneak into the Evangelical Lutheran church; I even went back to the Presbyterian church for several years only to hit the familiar roadblock of upscale cultural norms. When I gamely turned up at a church potluck I was given a wide berth, along with the advice that church was only for making social contacts. I didn't make any contacts on that occasion. In another church, an elderly white gentleman bluntly said that white people simply did not know what to do with an educated African. One Sunday, my family and I arrived at our church in Cambridge only to find Swastika graffiti on the exterior wall with the slogan "power to whites." For its part, evangelical Protestantism was too invested in American ascendancy to make room for Mr. Christian Africa.

I was forced to conclude that mainline Protestant churches had given up on me as unassimilable. I recall my discomfort at a dinner in Boston at the home of a United Methodist minister. As the evening wore on, he and his wife began sniffing out my social and political views. Americans, I reminded myself, are a kind and fair-minded people, but what happened to make liberal Christians so prone to fishing for enemies? My stunted political sense was pounced on as proof that I was a closet reactionary waiting to be outed. That was what gave me a hunch that the Protestant impasse of race and politics was now at a turning point. To banish the shadows of racism by prescribing political correctness is to hold race hostage to political prejudice, and that is something liberal Christianity, in both its Protestant and Catholic versions, is prone to do. It is as if your Jewishness or blackness is just a free-speech issue. I didn't understand how being Jewish or black should compete for votes to be valid, and so I scrambled for an exit strategy from this cultural confinement.

As distilled in the hymns of Charles Wesley, classical Wesleyan piety shares affinity with Catholic practice, as is clear in the church's liturgical celebration, and it suggested a natural transition for me. Wesleyan spirituality helped steer me in the direction of the Catholic church, however meandering the path. With dwindling prospects of acceptance by Protestant churches, and short of being left spiritually adrift on the street, I was nudged against any conscious design to take up again the Catholic path.

And here I gladly acknowledge the friendship of solid Muslim friends, including leading officials in the Arab world, who never wavered in their conviction that faith in God and nothing else should be the center of life. Of course, they wish that I would return to Islam, where, in their view, theistic commitment comes before anything else. They should know my deep and unbounded appreciation for them, even if I am not able to come to where they are.

My children have asked what bound me to Christianity after all I have gone through, and it's hard to know how to answer. A different form of the question has been asked by several Muslim friends, including inquirers who wished to join the church. They demanded to know why I converted, hoping my answer would be encouraging to them. My plea to them not to convert took them by surprise. I told them, "You must be out of your mind to contemplate such a thing." "Then why did you do it?" they pressed. To take my own medicine, I rejoined: "because I was out of my mind." They looked me over, knowing that I had not lost my mind, and yet wondering what had really clinched it for me.

My response to would-be converts was my clumsy way of indicating that I would not wish on anyone the exposure of conversion compounded by the ambivalence of church and Christian groups. "It feels like being left in the lurch," a Muslim friend said as he emerged fresh from a secret reading of John's Gospel. It's an unforgiving choice, he said, whether to take the high risks of conversion or to shut your mind to the truth. He had a miserable time of it, with a feeling of moral paralysis, and he died unfulfilled. Many people have led immensely successful and fulfilled lives without religion, including some much-cherished friends of mine. But, as this friend discovered sadly, not everyone has the talent.

I certainly don't, if that is not clear by now. I could never escape the fact that my power to reflect on myself clamored for acknowledging a purpose above and beyond the present. I could find no peace without the God who preceded me there. And it demanded membership in a faith community. It was not enough to be a thinking Christian and having constantly to invent argumentative reasons for being so. I am not that tough-minded. Besides, religion is like second nature to me.

As for my children, I have never felt licensed to preach at them or to begrudge them their freedom to come to their own mind about things. My responsibility as a parent has been to support them unreservedly and to surround them with the love and care that are innocent of any idea of getting them to do my bidding. In that process, to the extent that I helped them, I became a better parent, and we became a better family. Nothing would please me more than their deciding to embrace the church, but the fact that I would forbear to require that of them demonstrates better than anything the freedom that is at the core of the gospel. The love of God is not ours to bargain with. The nature of love is expressed better in leaving footprints than in wagging one's finger with commands. Examples make better teachers.

In my search for a church home, I looked for basic things: a faith community devoted to worship of God as revealed in Jesus; reverence for the scriptures; apostolic faithfulness; sacramental witness and service; ecumenical openness; freedom from nationalistic ideology; commitment to the family, to peace and justice, and to the common good; theological education that is grounded in tradition and open to the world; and a spirit of charity that forgives, affirms, embraces, and honors without being self-righteous, naïve, or gullible. The call to holiness I understand as the call to self-giving, of giving ourselves to God, and to God's service. Catholicism marshals two thousand years of Christianity's immense and complex intercultural heritage and insights to place them at our disposal for the great adventure of a faith-filled engagement with life. It has often been a force for good in personal as well as in public life. It is a church well equipped to meet the demands of personal faith, as well as the needs of security, justice, and responsibility in organized national communities.

In its current resurgence outside the West, Catholicism is poised to play a major role in the demand for a new design of society based on the dignity of human beings as human beings, not simply as consumers or as subjects of the state. The rising tide of disenchantment with political failure is challenging church leaders to fill the breach with moral force. Mending fences with corrupt and discredited regimes will no longer do.

John Hick's contention that classical Christian teachings have, in one form or another, been in dispute, producing what critics have derided as a mottled Christianity, is probably less true for Catholicism and Eastern Orthodoxy than for mainline Protestantism. Catholicism's doctrinal core is arguably more stable than that of many other variants of Christianity. Even if its directives are contested, the church's magisterium is recognized for what it is. The catechism and the instrument of papal encyclicals together have defined Catholic faith just as that faith is enshrined in the church's liturgical life, with Jesus Christ at its core. Against the cultural fragmentation of modern life, that is a considerable advantage. While in the mood, Catholics may crack wise at this heritage, and from the flanks even nibble away at it, but it's hard to dismiss it as of no value.

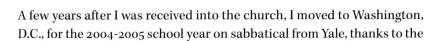

A few years after I was received into the church, I moved to Washington, D.C., for the 2004-2005 school year on sabbatical from Yale, thanks to the award of the Kluge Chair in Countries and Cultures of the South, an award made by the Librarian of Congress, James Billington. In my beautiful office located in the magnificent Jefferson Wing of the library, I studied Shari'ah law and politics in Nigeria, with the resources of the library at my beck and call. It was like a dream come true. The time there afforded me the unique pleasure and privilege of working closely with Prosser Gifford, the Director of Scholarly Programs at the library, as well as meeting new colleagues and friends. A scholar, among other things, of the decolonization process in Africa, Gifford was a most wonderful host and colleague. His genial spirit hovered over the place, and the corridors rang and vibrated with gusts of his hearty laugh every time someone in his office or on the phone cracked a joke. He helped create an environment of genuine scholarly exchange and personal interaction in the library. The friendly atmosphere helped academics at long last to shed their inhibitions, relax, and open up to each other. I took the opportunity of being in Washington to visit old friends and make new ones.

Being on Capitol Hill in Washington brought me out of the ivy-clad academic cloister and gave me an invaluable vantage point on politics and on the policy-making process as such. It became quickly apparent to me that a huge gap exists between the unmatched resources of a dynamic democracy, and policy makers guided by short-term political calculations. I doubt whether there is anywhere else in the world such a high concentration of experts and specialists in as many fields as there are in Washington, D.C., or where the gap is so great between them and the policies of government. I learned, in that sense, that a dynamic democracy can take a huge toll on the purveyors of scientific knowledge and accumulated experience, because what is politically expedient may not be reconcilable with what evidence and experience require. Political mobilization thrives in a parallel universe of its own making, with the effect that the world of facts and evidence is often too tame and innocent for the cutthroat business of winning allies and disarming enemies.

The habits of a dynamic democracy, for that reason, appear to be at odds with the profile and culture of Catholicism, which is how the subject is viewed in much of America. The formula that if you cannot vote you will be oppressed makes the church an oppressive institution implicitly. Yet there is something really jarring about this stereotype, never mind its sunny view of liberal democracy as redeeming truth. The reputation of authoritarianism that has trailed Catholicism everywhere implies that a dictatorship of the papacy is the yoke Catholics must bear to be Christians in America. Quite apart from the inappropriateness of looking upon the church as an elected assembly, I think this view ignores what is plain for all to see, namely, the fact of widespread contestation among Catholics of the whole range of directives from Rome — and even of the term "Roman" as a qualifier of Catholicism. Catholic dissidence is fiercely unsparing of the Roman source of religious teaching, which makes obedience a rare commodity when you find it. I was often dismayed to see the lengths to which Catholic critics went in their defiance of the church. Yet I think a preoccupation with an imperial view of papal authority amounts to a distraction from where the shoes of the successor of Peter really pinch. Pope Benedict XVI once spoke of his great distress at the attacks even of faithful Catholics on his motives for deciding to reinstate a Holocaust-denying bishop when the pope had not been informed of the true facts of the case. One can only imagine his disconsolate sense of abandonment by members of his flock, but the episode illustrated the complicated nature of Catholic obedience in general.

Tocqueville's reflections on Catholicism and democracy in America are worth recalling in current circumstances. He writes that Catholicism has been erroneously regarded as the natural enemy of democracy when in fact, among Christian denominations, Catholicism is one of the most favorable to equality of condition among people. In the Catholic church the religious community comprises only two classes: the priest and the people. The priest alone rises above the rank of his flock, and all below him are equal. In matters of doctrine, the Catholic faith places all human beings on the same level: it subjects the wise and the ignorant, the person of genius and the common crowd, to the details of one and the same creed; it imposes the same observances upon the rich and the needy, the same austerities on the strong and the weak; it listens to no compromise with mortal men and women, but, reducing all the human race to the same standard, it confounds all the distinctions of society at the foot of the same altar, even as they are confounded in the sight of God. If Catholicism is like an absolute monarchy, as some have contended, it means that if the sovereign be removed all the other classes of society are more equal than in republics. Tocqueville notes, by contrast, the paradox of the tendency of Protestantism to make persons independent more than to render them equal.

When we shift our gaze from America to, say, Africa, a similar Catholic paradox meets our eyes. The best way to explain this is to summon the notion of domain as conquest and occupation, which is how Catholicism and its Protestant variants spread in Europe, South America, and elsewhere. Domain contends with the threat of hostile or recalcitrant neighbors, who must be removed or subdued in order for the church to assert its authority and influence. With hostile neighbors on the prowl, the sword was required to earn a measure of security and freedom. The church, accordingly, pitched the gospel on the points of the sword and the throne, and adopted the fruits of conquest to promote and defend the religious vocation. In the vast empty spaces of North America, by contrast, the tasks at hand carried fewer risks and challenges, and so religious officials could afford to relax their vigilance and adopt a more lenient view of things, fortified only by the energy of adventure needed to occupy the breathless vistas before them on the Western frontier. The experience produced the can-do optimism of the New World religious outlook.

Africa fell somewhere between the two models of domain and adventure. Africa's sporadic chieftaincy structures had nothing of the reputation of formidable technical resistance. The monotony of bush tracks, broken only by the haphazard nature of hamlets, and homesteads, and the occasional trading center, suggested little of inexhaustible abundance of reward for enterprise. The unhealthy climate foreclosed the opportunity of settlement after conquest. The exceptions were the elevated parts of the continent that included South Africa, where conquest, commerce, and settlement went hand-in-hand.

Catholicism entered the African world in the sixteenth century armed with the weapons of exploitation and occupation, only to crumble in the course of the eighteenth century from decline and indifference. Not until late in the nineteenth century in East Africa, and the early decades of the twentieth in West Africa, did Catholicism emerge invigorated from its indigenous incubation. With imperious confidence, modern Catholic missions, like their Protestant counterparts, embraced the enlightenment canon to invest in schools, clinics, printing, and other technical infrastructure in spite of the fact that the promise of growth lay elsewhere.

In East Africa, nearly 2,000 missionary priests had poured their hearts and souls into the enlightenment cause even though they had little to show for their toil. It left them with an open contradiction. In 1928 the Apostolic Visitor to East Africa bluntly told the bishops gathered for the occasion in Dar es Salaam, "Where it is impossible for you to carry on both the immediate task of evangelization and your educational work, neglect your churches in order to perfect your schools."[1] Priests consumed themselves in pursuing the path of development and social advancement: building and equipping schools and hospitals; running community errands with the mission car; and attending social occasions where they drank milk and honey beer. Fr. Vincent Donovan, an exasperated missionary, pointed out to his bishop the irony that as of the date of his letter (May 1966) no child who had attended a Catholic school went on to practice the Catholic faith on leaving school, nor was there any indication that existing students intended to do anything different. Frustrated and discouraged, Fr. Donovan told his bishop he saw no point in continuing with business as usual. Failure to plumb the religious depths of indigenous evangelization, he believed, would more than likely condemn the enterprise to failure.

Following his decision to apprise the bishop of his frustration with the enlightenment approach to mission, the priest looked to the untapped potential of the indigenous discovery of Christianity as the future course of Catholicism in Africa. Events elsewhere validated his contention. Catholicism's renaissance took root not at school, in the tool shed, or in mission stations, but among ordinary people who were not yet done with attending to family shrines, consulting local oracles, and memorizing tribal genealogies. These new Catholics, whose parents attended no schools and knew nothing of the world of paved roads, silent

---

1. Vincent Donovan, *Christianity Rediscovered* (Maryknoll: Orbis Books, 1978), 7.

plumbing, electricity, or computers, took their faith in a direction that was in convenient proximity to the old ideas and practices. Finally, the gospel had a credible foothold in indigenous affirmation, shedding in the process its foreign baggage.

At this point the bishops had to deal with a reality far different from the prescribed directives of the rulebooks. They might maintain the appearance of official rectitude, but the bishops were faced with questions of fundamental re-conceptualization, thanks to the indigenous upsurge. A vital connection to the African primal world was made, and the church was there to reap the windfall. It is nothing less than *Christianity Rediscovered*, the title of Fr. Vincent Donovan's memorable testimony of his personal recovery of the message in the Maasai culture. There really was no plausible alternative, as Rome for so long recognized. What took much longer to recognize was that the indigenous discovery of Christianity would have a whiplash effect of pushing Europe to the periphery of the emerging heartlands of the faith. Old habits die hard, and the mental constructs of the church have remained largely immobile in spite of a realignment of Christianity's European landscape.

The Catholic church today finds itself faced with two uneven challenges: retreat and defensiveness in the old European heartlands, and surge and ferment in formerly frontier societies. The resources expended in tending new flocks in frontier regions fade into insignificance when compared to investments in old heartland structures and institutions that have been largely deserted. This imbalance in resource allocation is exacerbated by the inclination to impose on resurgence and renewal the forms and priorities of the rapidly declining European heartlands.

On paper, the intellectual case for those forms and priorities is as impregnable as the Rock of Ages, just as the paper trail is intimidating by reason of sophisticated erudition and sheer bulk. To the objection of many of my Third World Catholic friends, it is difficult to express yourself from any part of the world of Catholicism without doing so in the language and logic bequeathed by Europe. That language has a life of its own in spite of the dwindling ranks of those who once patronized it.

At any rate, a bifurcated Catholicism has insulated the church from consequences of decline in the old heartlands, revealing a church with a remarkable capacity of adaptation that is often ahead of itself even when it is slow to recognize the fact. Monks, monasteries, libraries, cathedrals, and the lumbering machinery of ecclesiastical discipline that shaped the Latin West are virtually missing in the present surge of Catholicism in Africa and elsewhere, without that in any way impeding the expansion. Catholicism has outlived its old forms and gone through a revival as a consequence. Vatican II frames Catholicism's modern profile, true, but in another way post-Western developments also frame Vatican II: wherever its intellectual center is, Catholicism's statistical center of gravity is now in the Southern Hemisphere.

In 1960 Catholics in Africa numbered some 23 million; in 2011 the figure is some 200 million. In Europe, by contrast, a German archbishop observed that he was spending thrice as much time presiding over funerals as he was officiating at baptisms. The current estimated birthrate of 1.4 children per household in Europe means the population cannot replenish itself, which leaves the church locked in a downward spiral of decline. It puts the growth in Africa and elsewhere in a critical light. The mental adjustment needed to assimilate the new reality is in serious arrears, and the lag is mounting with time. Sooner or later the discrepancy is bound to show up on the church's scale of priorities, including perhaps the election of a Third World pope for the first time. I recall a Jordanian businessman from an old Arab Catholic family telling me at a banquet sponsored by King Abdallah in 2007 that his old mother was praying for an African pope. It impressed me that the Catholic impact in Africa was being noticed in the most unlikely of places.

Present and future prospects of the church have changed the equation between the West's claims of cultural superiority and post-Western claims of the religious initiative. I happen to occupy the borderlands between the two, allowing me to contemplate the double advantage to be gained by combining the deposit of the church's impressive if waning heritage in the West with the religious momentum in Africa and beyond. The moral defensiveness that has pinned the West down breaks into a guilt complex about religion as intolerance, and religious decline feeds this complex by taking a toll on religious confidence. Legislation may intervene to strip what is left of religion's credibility, handing the churches the crumb of a not-for-profit shelter for consolation. But even that offers little protection against ideological prejudice.

❁   ❁   ❁

My personal pilgrimage at long last brought me to the door of the mother church in a fashion I least expected. But another surprise awaited: the church turned out to be very different from my pre-Vatican II memory and encounter with it. The institution went through a radical self-examination at Vatican II in a process called *aggiornamento*, Italian for "updating." It was the term Pope John XXIII employed to describe the church's self-renewal and self-readjustment. The irony of the *aggiornamento* is that in Europe it was followed by steep and extended decline of the church, whereas in Asia, Africa and elsewhere, the *aggiornamento* was connected to an uptake in numbers, size, and momentum.

I discussed the matter with a German Jesuit recently, asking what chances he gave Europe to recover its Christian heritage. He couldn't have been grimmer. Yet I think it's important to separate this question from the matter of the church as a force in Europe's cultural identity and intellectual cohesion. For all its scientific and technological achievement, Europe still requires a sense of its moral identity to be a coherent historical force, which is what Pope Benedict XVI tried to say in his 2006 Regensburg speech before it got away from him with his side remark about Islam and violence. Europe would not be Europe without its great Christian symbols and monuments of monasteries, libraries, art, architecture, music, literature, and philanthropy. People may define themselves by emphasizing what they are not, but that is crucial to who they are. It may be considered a defensive form of self-identity.

But defensiveness has ironic side-effects. The sufferings of Christians often are met with silence, or with free-floating statements about human suffering in general, while petitions and campaigns are mobilized on behalf, say, of wildlife in neighborhoods, of Falun Gong in China, or of primates in Congo. In addition, Catholics have succumbed to political inquisition of other Catholics, and in the process Catholic faith drops in importance behind political determination. When people say, as I have heard them say, that being Catholic is not important, they are saying that something else that is not for the time being stated is more important. Whatever that is will always trump Catholicism for such people, and as a result the church becomes segmented into groups of the like-minded. We end up downplaying religion largely on the basis of other commitments that do not always receive the same scrutiny as does the church. It should be clear that I am not arguing that criticism of the faith is out of bounds, but that we should not forget that dogmatism thrives in other parts of our lives. Henri de Lubac's warning is worth recalling here: leaving God out of the equation will only mean falling back on pursuing one another in circles. The church has to be a safeguard against cultural sectarianism.

For me Catholicism became an exit strategy from the confinement of the upscale liberal agnosticism that has long commanded the world of academia. I felt a lively sense of emancipation surrounded by the signs and symbols of the mystery of God in the ungrudging, faithful witness of the church. That fact was the connection to the worldwide community of faith spread within and across national boundaries. It relieved me of the double burden of having to face wearying interrogation by other Christians, and of the defensiveness it begets. I could identify myself with other Catholics without having to work the levers of citizenship, race, language, education, taste, class, sex, or education. My privileged position in an elite university accustomed to thinking of itself as entitled to due deference ceased to determine my religious standing. Being Catholic does not assume anything about my cultural attainment, not even about whether I practice the Catholic faith, scandalous as that may sound.

I can understand why cradle Catholics hug their Catholic identity with the nonchalant attitude of knowing that they belong without the in-convenience of believing. (Contrast this attitude with that of born-again evangelicals, who often parade the fact that they believe without the dis-traction of belonging to a faith community.) I can understand, I say, even though I cannot be that way myself, though I could claim a comparable status as a cradle Muslim. There are avowed Muslims who are also largely non-comprehending and indifferent. I knew them and envied them because I was, regretfully, so unable to be like them. I thought something was amiss with me for being religiously preoccupied when the majority of my peers seemed to be thriving without a care for the world, or for the thought of God. Catholicism attracted me for reasons very different, but also for reasons very consistent: it offered me peace and acceptance without the requirement of self-approval. I did not have to be self-congratulatory and judgmental of others to know that I am a redeemed and forgiven child of God, which is to say, I can believe and belong at the same time and in equal measure. It took a huge load off my back, making believing and belonging symmetrical with personal inclination, not with national or cultural standing.

Catholicism met my need for Christianity with a social, communal face, of faith as the New Israel that draws the peoples of the world in one family of God. Catholicism helps to reorganize issues of equality, justice, cultural clout, political leverage, racial advantage, and material resources from the perspective of truth as a universal reality. In this circumstance, faith supplies the angle that frames life ethically — after all, faith without works is dead (James 2:20). The motivation it produces is best expressed in the words of Diogenes of Athens: "The people of Megara feast as though they were going to die on the morrow; they build as though they were never to die!" Even as a repressed minority, the believers, says an ancient Christian writer, feast at their religious banquet, i.e., the Eucharist, as though they have no care, but live as though they owe the world a debt; they are lavish in their faith, but modest in their habits. They pay dearly for their faith, but give gladly to charity.

The nonbeliever can reject this way of accounting for life and substitute a different calculation, in which lavish habits are unconstrained by any thought of answering to a higher power. In the absence of the idea of God, the nonbeliever may make merry as though there is no tomorrow (Isa. 22:13; 1 Cor. 15:32), even though life will present challenges that mock the idea of merry-making. Self-indulgence may achieve the Epicurean ideal, certainly, though with the ironic twist of inflaming the appetite, much like the candle effacing itself in its own incandescence. When I recall my boyhood friends who went astray in this regard, I feel a sense of deep loss that our commingled laughter and playful pranks, once so animated and so artful, have since been washed out by cruel fate. I prefer to think that a solicitous mystery now holds their end.

I recall an encounter with a New York City rabbi who was at the time visiting Union College. Someone had told him about me, and, wasting no time, he bore down on me: did I not think that it was taking a backward step converting from Islam's monotheism to Christianity's Trinitarian God? While regaining my balance, I responded in the flush of the moment that I thought monotheist religion and Trinitarian religion alike were occupied with God as the greatest mystery, and that the language of One and Three in that context was symbolic and analogical. The Trinity, I noted, made the two-fold claim of the one God and His three-fold reality. The idea is well developed by John Henry Newman: "He is truly Three, if He is truly One; He is truly One, if the idea of Him falls under earthly number. He has a triple Personality, in the sense in which the Infinite can be understood to have Personality at all. If we know anything of Him, — if we may speak of Him in any way, — if we may emerge from Atheism or Pantheism into religious faith, — if we would have any saving hope, any life of truth and holiness within us, — this only do we know, with this only confession, we must begin and end our worship — that the Father is the One God, the Son the One God, and the Holy Ghost the One God."[2]

I never saw the rabbi again, but I never forgot our brief encounter, I guess because I had only recently been baptized and everything was still so fresh for me. I brooded long on the rabbi's sharp question, wondering how he as a professional understood human language about God, who exceeds all our measures. It is really a simple question whether language is only so that we can claim God or, as the rabbi would agree, so that God can claim us. We may recall Anselm here: "O Lord, you are not only that than which nothing greater can be conceived, but you are greater than all that can be conceived." God is than whom is nothing greater. Reason glimpses the truth of God to come upon its own fullest scope: the more of truth reason discovers, the more of its own breadth and depth it attains. That intrinsic connection the Trinity embodies and demonstrates uniquely. Worship becomes the natural and logical next step in the Trinitarian experience of God, for it is in worship that truth can grasp us genuinely, the point at which reason fulfills its own end, who is God.

2. John Henry Newman, "The Theory of Developments in Religious Doctrine," *Fifteen Sermons Preached Before the University of Oxford Between 1826 and 1843* (London: Longmans, Green, and Co., 1900).

Although he was dismissive of the doctrine of the Trinity, Ibn Hazm (d. 1064) of Córdoba, still goes on in his *Ring of the Dove* to defend God's unity as the unity of love, of the lover, and of the beloved, a sentiment that is remarkably faithful to Trinitarian faith. Similarly, even though he is regarded as official guardian of Islam's stringent monotheism, regarding the Trinity as a breach of God's nature, al-Ghazali still evokes the sentiment when he speaks of the worshipper being centered in devotion to God. "The very least," al-Ghazali writes, "that will keep the spirit just gaspingly alive is that the heart shall be present at the moment of *takbir*," i.e., the moment of declaring that God is than whom is nothing greater. The language of faith seeks and thrives by the divine intimacy that prompted it. God is not alone, and at that point our claim of God evokes what conceived and preceded it, namely, the truth of God claiming us.

Reason points to where faith precedes and leads, and that is to the existence of a coherent, purposeful universe as God intended it to be. To know God is not only to know the universe fully; it is also to consent to God knowing us. It's like seeing for the first time, or being turned to face a new direction. Conversion makes us attentive, so that we may not forget God in our self-knowing. It allows the Psalmist to declare with a grateful heart:

> When I look at thy heavens, the work of thy fingers,
> The moon and the stars which thou hast established;
> what is man that thou art mindful of him,
> and the son of man that thou dost care for him?
>
> Psalm 8:3-4

Nothing else makes us more human, makes us more like what God intended us to be. As a sacramental community and as the repository of the liturgical tradition, the church abounds with the gifts of God for our flourishing. Recreational pastime offers much that is congenial to our nature, but the church shines the lamp on the path of salvation, undaunted by setback, and unmoved by fear or favor. In the course of my pedestrian struggles, I came to appreciate that truth is something God does to us before and more than something we do to God, theological caviling notwithstanding. Theory serves and is enriched by sacrament;

that is why in my early life I thought agnosticism was evasive of the existential reality. The traditional Anselmian formula of faith in search of understanding seems a tantalizing way to state what is involved; rather, understanding must seek faith to make inquiry at all purposeful. If you don't believe that what you are searching for is worth the effort, you search in vain, and doing it rigorously makes no difference whatsoever. Giving ourselves freely to God and to one another allows understanding to blossom in all its depth and range.

Reason, it is true, can help convey us to that position, but it cannot duplicate or substitute for the act of self-giving in mutual trust. In that regard, I found that what at the time looked like simple coincidence, or even a string of haphazard occurrences in my life, came in retrospect to form the elements of a demand for a decision to go in one direction rather than in another. The reason it all came together in the way it did became obvious, as did the fact that I had little conscious control of how it happened. What seemed like a chance encounter turned out to be for a purpose. Because I arrived too late, for example, there was no space on an early flight that was cancelled in the end because of unexpected mechanical trouble; I ran into a helpful uncle because I took a wrong turn in the road. All this gave a sense of coherence to life, giving me a credible and compelling sense of direction. The idea echoes Coleridge's observation about the lantern on the stern that shines particularly bright on the waves behind, making retrospect an occasion for thankfulness and for looking ahead. Even the vagaries and vicissitudes of life in the end fail to contradict the reality of a narrative thread by making us believe that life makes personal sense, that we can rely on it, especially where, as Augustine affirms, it tallies with the experience of other people. The thirst that made me scoop a sip here, and a sip there, led to the stream brimming with the water of life; only then did here and there rise to view. The Lord of life had been here and there, too, though I did not always realize it at the time. Finally, in the hallowed sanctuary God led me, and filled my cup of gladness to overflowing. I was glad to be in the house of the Lord (Ps. 122:1).

In his encyclical *Fides et Ratio,* "On the Relationship Between Faith and Reason," John Paul II expresses this idea with all the persuasive force of his pastoral office. "In believing," he affirms, "we entrust ourselves to the knowledge acquired by other people. This suggests an important tension. On the one hand, the knowledge acquired through belief can seem an imperfect form of knowledge, to be perfected gradually through personal accumulation of evidence; on the other hand, belief is often humanly richer than mere evidence, because it involves an interpersonal relationship of faithful self-giving with others. . . . [K]nowledge through belief, grounded as it is on trust between persons, is linked to truth: in the act of believing, men and women entrust themselves to the truth which the other declares to them." He continues: "Human beings are not made to live alone. They are born into a family, and in a family they grow, eventually entering society through [the activities of the family]. From birth, therefore, [human beings] are immersed in traditions which give them not only a language and a cultural formation but also a range of truths in which they believe almost instinctively. . . . This means that the human being — the one who seeks the truth — is also the one who lives by belief."

Gratitude is the natural response here, and for that purpose the church has instituted the Eucharist, where mystery joins faith to embrace and to overtake understanding. That way the divine life touches something universal in all of us, whatever our rational powers or personal condition. This experience is capable of being transcribed and described in numerous and diverse ways, suggesting that Islamic witness to God (than whom is nothing greater) has transcribed and described this perennial truth in its own way. The Qur'an speaks of Jesus as God's mercy, as God's *rahmah,* a claim not so alien to the way St. Paul describes Jesus as God's righteousness (Rom. 3:25), the righteousness of eternal redemptive merit, not the righteousness of finite human wisdom (1 Cor. 1:30; 1 Cor. 3:18ff.). This modifies the strict interpretation of divine transcendence that Muslims invoke against the incarnation. For Muslims, the Christological issue is a nagging theological issue: whether, as Christians contend, it is permissible to speak of God assuming human form and being endowed with human qualities, without that conflicting with the idea of God as transcendent and omnipotent, of God in the elative as *Alláh-u-akbar* ("God than whom is nothing greater"). The church speaks of God assuming human form as the incarnation, a way of transcribing the divine mystery that is explicitly rejected in the Qur'an (*surah* 112) and by Muslim tradition generally, though Muslim Sufis tease the issue to their own advantage. Yet the Muslim objection need not be final or absolute, for that would allow language to determine if God may freely become what is impossible for us to conceive. Letting God be God means that God is free to be what God is. Without the freedom, divine power is curtailed, and therefore voided.

My earliest childhood memories of worship are thronged with scenes of the mosque. To earn supererogatory merit, my grandmother volunteered regularly to sweep the grounds of the mosque just before the dawn prayer, in case any stray dogs passed that way in the night. Thanks to being fast asleep in bed at that early hour, I don't remember ever seeing her set out. But occasionally I caught a glimpse of her returning with broom in hand, her tattered prayer rug under her arm. The dust on her forehead was sign that she had remained to pray after sweeping the mosque, and lingered with friends afterwards. It explained why she was late getting back, allowing me the chance to catch her in the act, so to speak. Otherwise, she never spoke of her good works. This silence belongs with the silence of the mosque, which is broken only by the litany of worship; then, even the intervals of pause vibrate with the humming of the sacred words. Once you stepped inside the mosque — always with the right foot, of course — all conversation ceased abruptly. There was no announcement to that effect; it just happened. Old men and old women would finger the rosary and intone quietly to themselves the prayers of remembrance of the names of God and of the prophet before the worship proper commenced.

When as a child I attended worship, I was riveted by the mosque's clean, sparse atmosphere, the emptiness of the place exuding a palpable sense of transcendent stillness, so evocative of the lively adoration of "silent night, holy night." There are no pictures or images in the mosque, no furniture or furnishings beyond the most basic, so that the human voice, bearing only the words of the holy book, can break forth as it bounces off the blank and bare walls, wrapped only in humble devotion. Prone to wander and to stray, imagination has no images to feed it, and is shackled to the oral performance of the immaculate word. It is not the beauty of holiness, but the awe of the litany, that adorns the mosque. In the world, we shouted with people; in the mosque, we listened to God.

Why were these people, typically beset with clamor and clatter, so quiet and so still now, as if waiting on a holy power? As a child it impressed me greatly that worship reduced adults to bending, kneeling, crouching, and prostrating, with the act of worship setting aside their lofty standing for the moment. As I grew up and started imitating the adults, I came in turn to learn to wait and to be still so I could commune with the holy power, wherever it was. In the end, that waiting and listening habit stuck, even if that holy power remained invisible, intangible, and remote. We learned that religion was not a feast for the eyes or a reward for the senses any more than truth was as a nail for the hammer of reason to knock into place. The path of faith began with the still, small voice unmuted enough to fill the breast with awe and wonder, and rose with the shout of the muezzin's call.

For all that, a pestering curiosity would poke me, demanding to know what was there to believe when I could not see anything or anyone. Yet with all my youthful impetuosity, I never ventured, nor dared to think of venturing, into the mosque unattended, lest I stumble on the holy power and be struck dumb for my recklessness. The ethereal, haunting attributes of God as All-Powerful, All-Knowing, and All-Seeing were drummed into us so insistently that they solidified almost into a physical fact. My picture of God was of a being whose mind was so big and whose ears were so good that I could not do anything or be anywhere without God knowing and seeing me, and whose name was so holy I could not say it without being mindful (Qur'an 59:21-24; 87:2; Ps. 99:3).

My schoolyard friend Jini-jini would not understand, but I felt beset all around. Because I could not escape, I was compelled to face God, at least in my thoughts. "Even before a word is on my tongue, lo, O Lord, thou knowest it altogether" (Ps. 139:4). When I didn't say my prayers or keep the fast, I felt I had broken the law; when I lied, I felt remorse; when I stole something, I felt condemned; when I acted uncharitably, I felt guilty; when I thought ill of someone, I begged God for forgiveness; when I did not give to the beggar, I felt mean; when I swore, I felt fearful of punishment. The All-Powerful God simply crowded out the thought of anything else: only by actively worshipping Him could I abide the terror of

His inexorable vigilance. The fact that I did not evaporate in a vapor of divine retribution I took as a sign that faith had preserved me, that faith had protective sacramental merit. I was thankful. I think all of us as children believed that, and it soothed us in our zone of childhood indiscretion. Because we fell short, we needed religion to cover our backs, and for that reason worship assumed a big role in our lives. In both a positive and a negative way, its shadow fell over childhood imagination that had nothing to do with the conscious will. What we didn't know could hurt us no less than what we knew, and so we needed cover before God — even, and especially, when we were not aware of needing it.

All this left me with a strong feeling that I was never alone, that wherever I was and whatever I was doing, the holy power witnessed it, even though I could not see or touch him. This feeling I shared with others, and their anticipation and acknowledgment strengthened it. It is for this reason that the mystery of the Eucharist, which is at the core of Catholic liturgical life, felt like the logical culmination of my religious upbringing.

To go back to a previous point, I could not at the time understand why the argument of political motivation for religion was such a scandal when I heard it. It makes perfect sense if your background is secular, which, I grant, is likely the case with most people in the West. But how could it apply to worship as I was raised to understand it, or to the other obligations of the religious code? It was more the fear of retribution, and the desire for everlasting reward, that was the driving force of religious practice. Religion is our eternal summons, not simply society's compliment to us.

Of course, Catholicism is emphatically no more immune to the corrosion of secular individualism than Protestantism. It would be naïve to suggest otherwise. The social scientist can claim as much of an authoritative intellectual role as the theologian in expounding the phenomenon of religion in Catholicism as well as in Protestantism, and perhaps in time that will come to be true also for Islam.

Yet even at this stage of Catholicism's advanced assimilation in the secular West, there is a sufficiently recognizable residue of the old teaching of the church as a divine institution, rather than simply as a club or as a registered association, to allow the church to check individualism in its most implacable manifestations. Revelation has not been surrendered to contextualization, nor tradition to globalization. Although it has long stepped back from the concentration on a spirit-spooked, vision-filled world that saturated the Middle Ages, and it has adjusted its outlook on the unity of Christians and on other religions, the Catholic church nevertheless has resisted falling for the idea of truth as a matter of individual opinion or choice, and of the church as a function only of the interests and predilections of those it ministers to. Miracles still happen, but only as exceptions that prove the rule. It remains fascinating that in the age of televangelism and the megachurch movement, the Catholic church has ceded ground to the prosperity gospel preachers who offer wealth, health, success, and instant miracles for cash first and last. Religious indulgences have staged a comeback, apparently, only this time not in the Catholic church. Religion as a market franchise will take on cargo of any and all dimensions — other than that of the crown of thorns.

With the knowledge that the road ahead is not unclaimed, even if still uncharted, the outcome of this account of my life is not much more complicated. Firm trust that God is transforming and renewing creation obliges us not to be weighed down by past difficulties, but to keep our eyes firmly turned to the future. In *Pilgrim's Progress* John Bunyan tracks the faith journey with the aid of characters depicting basic virtues, ideals, and aspirations to drive home the point that we can say "mission accomplished" only with the sense of our reward lying not in our power, and not being without cost. Mr. Valiant-for-Truth, a leading character, reflects challengingly on the imperative of the moral life born of struggle that summons each one and spares no one. It is appropriate for his words to serve as fitting conclusion of one individual's journey in life and in what lies beyond:

> And though with great difficulty I am got hither, yet now I do not repent me of all the trouble I have been at to arrive where I am. My sword, I give to him that shall succeed me in my pilgrimage, and my courage and skill, to him that can get it. My marks and scars I carry with me, to be a witness for me that I have fought his battles who now will be my rewarder.[3]

3. John Bunyan, *Pilgrim's Progress* (New York: Penguin, 1965), 370.

Index and Glossary

277